THE WEEKLY READER
BEGINNING
DICTIONARY

The Weekly Reader Beginning Dictionary is also published
for school and library use as *The Ginn Beginning Dictionary*
by Ginn and Company, a Xerox Company.

THE WEEKLY READER BEGINNING DICTIONARY

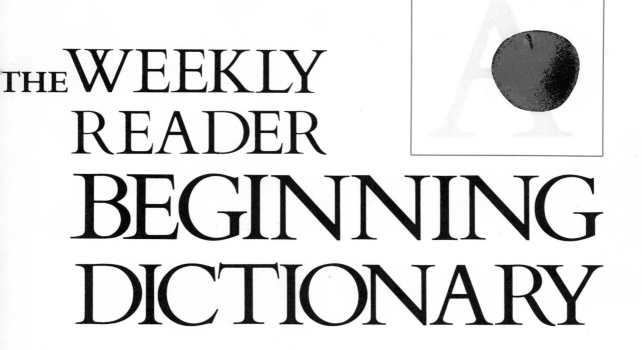

WILLIAM MORRIS

Editor in Chief

XEROX FAMILY EDUCATION SERVICES

MIDDLETOWN, CONNECTICUT

Staff

Editorial Staff

Editor in Chief: William Morris
Executive Editor for Mr. Morris: Mary Morris
Publisher: John E. Schmid
Editorial Director: George H. Wolfson
Managing Editor: Mary Lou Kennedy
Consulting Editor: Thomas Duncan
Assistant Editor: Regina Grant Hersey
Definers: Jo Ashley Bacon, Leo Grant, Ruth Wolfe Harley, Lucille Sette, Pearl Watts
Copyreader: Virginia Frecking
Editorial Assistant: June Goodrich

Design and Production

Book Designer and Art Director: Jos. Trautwein
Artist: Ken Martin
Book Production Manager: William Miller

XEROX FAMILY EDUCATION SERVICES

PUBLISHING, EXECUTIVE, AND EDITORIAL OFFICES:

MIDDLETOWN, CONNECTICUT 06457

XEROX ® IS A TRADEMARK OF XEROX CORPORATION

Printed in the United States of America.

Published simultaneously in Canada

Library of Congress Catalog Card Number: 73-86458

ISBN: 088375-102-X

All words that are believed to be registered trademarks have been entered with initial capitals and labeled "trademark." However, the absence of such a label should not be regarded as affecting the validity or legal status of any trademark.

Introduction

by William Morris

This may be the first dictionary you have ever used. It will not be the last. Dictionaries are among the most helpful and interesting books you can find. This one is so bright and colorful that you will want to read through it, instead of simply looking up a word or two.

Let's look at what a dictionary is and how it can help you. A dictionary is a word book. It is a book you use to find the meanings of words you have never seen before, or words you want to know more about. These may be words that you find in books you read in class or at home. They may be words you find in magazines and newspapers. They may be words you hear or see on radio and television.

There are many kinds of dictionaries. Some are big, heavy, and dull-looking. These "grown-up" dictionaries are not really as dull as they look. But, for now, you will find this dictionary much more interesting and helpful.

It tells about words that you are likely to meet in your day-to-day reading. To be sure that we had the right words, we talked to many of your teachers in all parts of the country. The teachers, in turn, talked with their pupils—young people just like you—to find out for sure what words you wanted to know about.

We found that you were interested in words about animals (including unusual ones like *aardvark, burro,* and *buffalo*) and games (from *king of the hill* to *tick-tack-toe*). You wanted to know more about new words from travels in space (*space sta-*

tion, astronaut, and *lunar landing*). And you wanted words about the food you eat (*hot dogs, hamburgers,* and *hero sandwiches*).

You will find all of these words—together with thousands more—in this book. Many of the words carry with them full-color drawings. These pictures will help you to learn about a particular bird, animal, tree, or flower.

We hope you will learn from these colorful pages that words can be fun. Some of you may remember what Humpty Dumpty said to Alice in *Through the Looking-Glass:* "When I use a word, it means just what I choose it to mean—neither more nor less." And Alice replied: "The question is whether you *can* make words mean so many different things."

Alice was right. We can't make words mean anything we want them to mean. We must learn to use them accurately. That's what this new dictionary will help you to do. And you may find that working with words and playing with words can be a lot of fun.

Aa

aardvark   An animal with large ears and a long nose. The *aardvark* lives in Africa.

aardvark

abacus   A counting tool made as a frame with rows of beads. An *abacus* can help you add and subtract.

ability   Skill in doing things. Jill has the *ability* to shoot marbles well.

able   Having the skill, power, or understanding to do something. Dave is *able* to take good pictures.

aboard   On or in a train, bus, ship, or airplane. Everyone must be *aboard* the bus by ten.

about
1. Having to do with. My book is *about* stars.
2. Nearly; close to. It is *about* six o'clock.
3. Around; here and there. The baby walks *about* in her playpen.

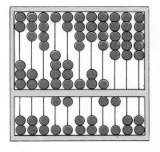

abacus

above
1. In a higher place. The sky is *above* us.
2. More than; better than. The price of the coat was *above* what Mother wanted to pay.

absent   Not present; missing. One child was *absent* from school today.

accident
1. Something not expected that causes loss or injury. Jan was hurt in the car *accident.*
2. A chance happening. Jim found five dollars in the street by *accident.*

ache　A dull, steady pain. I didn't sleep because of the *ache* in my tooth.

ache
ached
aching　To have a dull, steady pain. John's stomach *aches* from all the candy and ice cream he ate.

acorn

acorn　The fruit or seed of the oak tree. A tiny *acorn* can grow into a big oak tree.

acre　A unit of land measurement that is a little smaller than a football field.

acrobat　A person trained to do stunts such as tumbling and balancing. We saw a circus *acrobat* ride a bike along a high wire.

across　1. On the other side of. Bill lives *across* the street from Jane.
2. From one side to the other. The road was 50 feet *across.*

act　1. Something that is done. Opening a door for a person is a kind *act.*
2. One of the parts of a play or a show. I am on stage in all three *acts* of our school play.

act
acted
acting　1. To play the part of. Ted will *act* the king.
2. To behave. Be sure to *act* politely.

action　Movement. We went into *action* and had lunch ready in no time.

activity　Action that takes place; something being done. There is much *activity* at our house on a Saturday morning.

actor
actress　A man who acts a part in a play, movie, or TV show. A woman player in such a show is called an *actress.*

acrobat

add
added
adding

To put together to make more; to increase in amount or size. If you **add** 12 and 12, you get 24. We are building an **addition** to our house.

address

1. The number, street, town, and state where a person lives.
2. A speech or talk. The fire chief will give an **address** on the dangers of fire.

adhesive

Tape with one sticky side, used to keep bandages in place.

admire

To think highly of; to look upon with great liking and respect. I **admire** firemen for their courage.

adobe

Bricks made of clay and straw, dried by the sun. Some people live in **adobe** houses.

adobe house

adult

1. A grownup. Your teacher is an **adult.**
2. A fully grown animal. When the bear cub becomes an **adult,** it will be fierce and strong.

adventure

An exciting experience that may be dangerous. Landing on the moon was a great **adventure.**

advice

What one person may tell another to do about something. My **advice** to you is to eat slowly.

afford
afforded
affording

1. To have money enough to buy something. Glen can **afford** to buy the best kind of bike.
2. To spare; to be able to give up. Can you **afford** the time to stop by my house?

afraid

Frightened; scared. Lisa was **afraid** of the huge dog.

after

1. Behind; to the rear of. You are **after** me in line.
2. Past the hour of. It is **after** nine o'clock.
3. Chasing or in search of. Did you see the cat run **after** the mouse?

afternoon The part of the day from noon till sunset.

afterward
afterwards At a later time. We went to the store and *afterward* went to a movie.

again Another time; once more. Come to see us *again.*

against 1. On or upon. Tim leaned *against* the fence.
2. Opposite to. It is *against* the rules to run on the stairs.

age 1. The number of years old. Scott will be eight years of *age* on his next birthday.
2. A time in history. We live in the space *age.*

ago In the past. This TV show started ten minutes *ago.* The show is about people long *ago.*

agree
agreed
agreeing To think the same; to have the same opinion. Ken and I *agree* on a safe way to get to school.

ah A word showing surprise, joy, fear, or other feeling. *Ah,* our team won the game!

ahead In front; before; leading. Our class is *ahead* of the others in the paper drive.

aid
aided
aiding To give help to. Dad will *aid* us in building a tree house.

aim 1. The pointing or directing of an object at a target. Take careful *aim* and hit the bull's eye.
2. A plan. My *aim* is to read one book a week.

aim
aimed
aiming 1. To point or direct. Cindy *aimed* the ball at home plate.
2. To plan; to try. We *aim* to win the game.

air The atmosphere around us; a mixture of gases that we breathe but can't see.

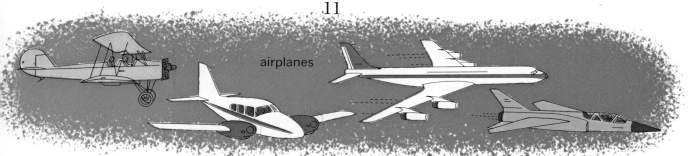

airplanes

air conditioner   Equipment that cleans, cools, or heats air. The *air conditioner* made the theater comfortable.

aircraft   Airplanes, helicopters, gliders, blimps, and other machines that fly in the air.

airfield   A landing place for aircraft; an airport.

airmail   Mail that travels by airplane.

airplane   A vehicle with wings that travels through the air. *Airplanes* fly by means of propellers or jet engines.

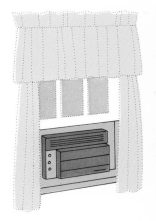

air conditioner

airport   A place where aircraft land and take off. Passengers leave or arrive by plane at an *airport.*

alarm   1. A sudden fear. The noise in the house filled Karen with *alarm.*
2. A sound or other signal that warns of danger. The fire *alarm* saved many lives.

alarm
alarmed
alarming   To frighten or warn. The news about the flood *alarmed* people.

alarm clock   A clock that can be set to buzz or ring at a certain time. My *alarm clock* wakes me up in the morning.

alas   A word showing sadness. *Alas,* we can't play ball because it's raining!

alarm clock

alcohol   A liquid used in medicines, fuels, and some drinks. The nurse used **alcohol** to clean the skin around my cut.

alert   Quick to understand and act; watchful. Kirk was **alert** and stopped the cat from killing the bird.

alike   Much the same; similar. Kim and Dot have sweaters that are **alike.**

alive   Having life; not dead. Some animals must hunt to stay **alive.**

all   1. The whole; everything or everyone. **All** the people wanted to build a new school.
2. Entirely. Jim was **all** alone in the house.

alley   A narrow street between or behind buildings. The **alley** was filled with garbage cans.

alligator   A large reptile having strong jaws, sharp teeth, and a long tail. An **alligator** lives in water and on land.

alligator

allow
allowed
allowing
   To let; to give permission to. My parents **allow** me to choose my own clothes.

allowance   Money, food, clothes, or supplies given to someone at regular times. Mark gets an **allowance** from his parents.

almost   Nearly; not quite. It is **almost** time for recess.

alone   Without anyone; by yourself. Sometimes people need to be **alone** to think.

along   1. Following the path of. We walked **along** the street.
2. With an onward motion. "Come **along**," said Mother.
3. As company; with someone. We are going to the store and you can come **along,** too.

aloud   With the voice. Read *aloud* so others can enjoy the story.

alphabet   The letters of a language arranged in a certain order. Our *alphabet* has twenty-six letters.

already   By this time; before a certain time. Betsy was *already* up by seven o'clock.

also   Too; besides. Mary liked the movie and I liked it *also.*

altar   A kind of table used as a center of religious activity in a church. People came to the *altar* to give thanks to God.

altar

always   1. At all times; every time. Nancy is *always* late.
2. Forever. Some animals will *always* be wild.

am   See **be.**

amaze
amazed
amazing
To cause great surprise; to fill with wonder. The beauty of the mountains will *amaze* you.

ambulance   A vehicle for carrying sick or injured people.

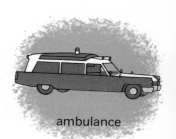

ambulance

American   1. A person born in North America or South America.
2. A citizen of the United States.

among   1. In the middle of. Dave looked *among* the papers to find his homework.
2. With a share for each. Sam divided the candy *among* his friends.

amount   The number that tells how much there is of something; total. A foot of snow is a big *amount* to fall in one night.

amuse
amused
amusing
To give pleasure to; to appear funny to. Playful animals *amuse* people. Puzzles are of great *amusement* to our family.

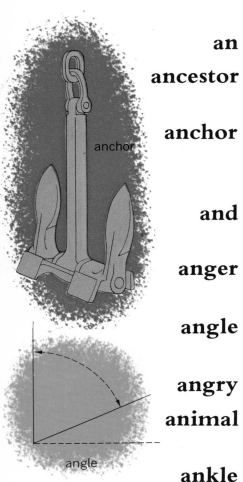

anchor

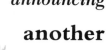

angle

an	One. *An* elephant is a big animal.
ancestor	A family member who lived long ago. An *ancestor* of Teddy's was an early settler.
anchor	A heavy object used to keep a ship in place in the water. An *anchor* is dropped overboard on the end of a strong chain.
and	Together with; added to. Cake *and* ice cream are good to eat.
anger	A feeling of rage or fury. The loss of his watch made Bob feel great *anger.*
angle	A figure formed by two lines going out from the same point.
angry	Having a feeling of rage or fury.
animal	A living thing that is not a plant. Bears, fish, and birds are *animals.*
ankle	The part of the body that connects the foot with the leg. Your boot covers your *ankle.*
announce *announced* *announcing*	To make known; to make a statement about. The mayor will *announce* his plan tonight. The radio *announcer* read the late news.
another	1. One more; an added one. Have *another* cookie! 2. Different. Jim has *another* shirt on today.
answer	1. A reply; what a person says when a question is asked. Linda's *answer* was "No." 2. A solution. What's the *answer* to the riddle?
answer *answered* *answering*	1. To reply to. Please *answer* my question. 2. To do something when a bell rings or some other signal is given. Please *answer* the doorbell!

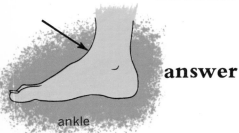

ankle

ant
A crawling insect. An **ant** lives with a group of other **ants,** usually in the ground.

antler
A horn on the head of a deer, moose, or similar animal.

any
1. A part. Jane did not want **any** of the candy.
2. Some. Do you have **any** money?
3. Every. **Any** plant needs water.

anybody
Any person. "Can **anybody** tell me?" asked the teacher.

anyone
Any person. Has **anyone** seen Charles?

anything
Any object. Do you want **anything** at the store?

anyway
In spite of that. It is raining, but we will play **anyway.**

anywhere
In or at any place. Put your coat **anywhere** you like.

antlers

apart
Into pieces or sections. The puppy tore the box **apart.**

apartment
A room or number of rooms for a person or family to live in. Our **apartment** is on the fourth floor of the building.

ape
A large monkey, without a tail, that is able to stand and move on two legs.

ape

appear
appeared
appearing
1. To come into view or sight. Before rain, clouds **appear** in the sky.
2. To seem; to look. Did the actor **appear** to be old? Dad's new beard has changed his **appearance.**

apple
A round fruit that is red, green, or yellow.

apple

apron

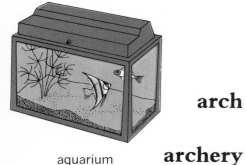

aquarium

approach
approached
approaching

To go near to; to come close to. The rabbit quietly *approached* the vegetable garden.

April

The fourth month of the year.

apron

A piece of clothing worn over the front part of the body to protect other clothes. Bill wears an *apron* when he cooks.

aquarium

1. A glass tank or bowl in which fish, water animals, or water plants are kept.
2. A building where live fish, water animals, or water plants can be seen. Our teacher took us to a museum and an *aquarium.*

arch

The top part of a curved opening such as a doorway. The *arch* held up the roof.

archery

The sport of shooting with a bow and arrow.

are

See **be.**

area

1. A region or section; a territory. Tom's family lives in the northern *area* of the state.
2. The size of a surface. What is the *area* covered by the rug?
3. A space for a special use. Dad parked the car in the parking *area.*

arch

aren't

A short form of "are not." *Aren't* you going to the party?

archery

arithmetic The study of numbers in addition, subtraction, multiplication, and division; mathematics. *Arithmetic* is my favorite subject.

arm 1. The part of the body between the shoulder and the hand. The sleeve of your coat covers your *arm.*
2. Something for or like a person's arm. Janet rested her book on the *arm* of the chair.
3. (Plural) Weapons. The trucks carried guns and other *arms* to the soldiers.

armchair A chair with sides on which you can rest your arms.

armchair

army A large group of soldiers trained for battle.

around 1. On all sides of. Tom walked *around* the block.
2. Near or about. Jim will come home *around* three o'clock.
3. In an opposite direction. Please turn *around.*
4. Here and there. Let's look *around.*

arrange
arranged
arranging
1. To put in order; to make neat. Let's *arrange* the dishes in piles.
2. To plan or prepare. The captain will *arrange* the trip across the ocean. Dad made an *arrangement* to buy a new house.

arrive
arrived
arriving
To reach; to come to a place. The plane will *arrive* at the airport tonight. The *arrival* of the ship caused excitement on the shore.

arrow 1. A thin rod, with a sharp pointed end, that is shot from a bow. Tim shot an *arrow* at the old tin can.
2. A sign used to show a direction. The *arrow* showed the way to the football field.

arrow

arrowhead

arrowhead   The pointed tip on the end of an arrow. Indians made ***arrowheads*** of stone.

art   Paintings, statues, music, poetry, or other beautiful things created by man. The picture was a work of ***art.***

artery   A tube that carries blood from the heart to other parts of the body.

artist   A person who creates paintings, statues, music, dances, or similar beautiful things.

as   1. Equally. Can you sing ***as*** well as Tom?
2. In the same way; in the same manner. Do ***as*** Jim does.
3. While. Sue waved ***as*** the plane took off.
4. Since; because. We must hurry ***as*** we are late.
5. Though. Tired ***as*** Al was, he couldn't sleep.

ash   1. A gray substance that is left after something has been burned. The ***ash*** from Uncle Tony's pipe fell on the floor.
2. A kind of shade tree or the hard wood from that tree. ***Ash*** makes good lumber.

ashamed   Feeling sorry for something bad or foolish that you have done. Ralph was ***ashamed*** after pushing Sally.

ashtray   A dish or container for the ashes from cigarettes, cigars, or pipes.

aside   To one side; away. Dick put some money ***aside*** for his trip.

ask
asked
asking
1. To use a question to learn or find out something. ***Ask*** Mother what time it is.
2. To try to get from; to request someone to give you something. ***Ask*** Betty for more flowers.
3. To invite. Dad ***asked*** Uncle Ed to supper.

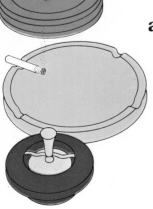

ashtrays

asleep Sleeping. The tired boys are *asleep* now.

asparagus A green plant whose young stems we eat as a vegetable.

aster A flower that looks like a daisy and comes in many colors.

asteroid A small planet that moves in a path around the sun between Mars and Jupiter. There are many *asteroids* between Mars and Jupiter.

astronaut A pilot or traveler on a spacecraft. The *astronaut* landed on the moon.

astronomy
astronomer The science or study of the sun, planets, and other bodies in the heavens. The *astronomer* looked through his telescope at the moon.

asparagus

at A word used to tell:
1. Where. We are *at* home.
2. When. We eat *at* noon.
3. How. He ran *at* a fast rate.
4. In what direction. He threw rocks *at* the tree.

athletics Sports; games; physical contests for which you need qualities like speed and strength. *Athletics* can help make you strong.

aster

atmosphere 1. The air that is all around the earth. Spaceships fly beyond the *atmosphere.*
2. The feeling that is present. There was an *atmosphere* of joy at the party.

atom
atomic The smallest bit into which a material can be divided. The splitting of some *atoms* makes heat and energy. Some submarines are run on *atomic* power.

attach
attached
attaching To fasten or join; to connect. Dad *attached* a new light to my bike.

astronaut

attend
attended
attending

1. To be present at; to go or come to. Lucy will **attend** my party.
2. To pay attention; to take care of. Sal **attends** to the needs of his dog.

attention

1. A careful listening and watching. Please give your **attention** to the teacher.
2. Thoughtful acts; care. Don likes **attention** when he is sick.

attic

The section of a house just below the roof. Mother stores old clothes up in the **attic.**

attract
attracted
attracting

To gain the attention or interest of; to cause to draw near. The big sign **attracts** many shoppers to the store. Magnets have an **attraction** for metal.

August

The eighth month of the year.

aunt

1. The sister of a person's father or mother. Dad's sister is my **Aunt** Ann.
2. The wife of a person's uncle.

author

The writer of a book, poem, story, or play.

auto

A car; an automobile.

automobile

A car; a motor vehicle that has its own power and carries passengers.

autumn

The season between summer and winter.

automobiles

avenue   A wide street. We crossed First *Avenue* at the traffic light.

aviator   A pilot of an airplane. The *aviator* flew the plane to Chicago.

aviator

awake   Not asleep; knowing what is happening. Tom is *awake* and eating breakfast.

award   A prize; an honor. A blue ribbon was the *award* for the winner of the race.

away   1. Absent; gone to another place. The doctor will be *away* for three days.
2. From a place or person. The ship sailed *away* from the shore. Now it is far *away.*

awful   1. Causing wonder or great fear. The hurricane was an *awful* sight.
2. Very bad; not pleasant. The soup tasted *awful.*

awfully   Very. It is *awfully* noisy in the classroom.

awhile   For a time. The postman talked *awhile* with Dad.

ax   A tool with a long handle and a sharp blade, used for chopping wood.

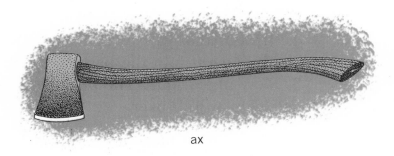

ax

Bb

baby A very young child. The *baby* slept in her crib.

baby sitter A person who takes care of a child while its parents are away.

back 1. The rear part of your body, from the bottom of the neck to the hips. The boy sat on the ground with his *back* against a tree.
2. The rear side or part of anything. We sat in the *back* of the car.

back
backed
backing To move backward or toward the rear. The driver will *back* his truck into the driveway.

baby

backward
backwards 1. With the front in back; with the first part last. The silly boy put his hat on *backward.* Jim counted *backwards* from 20 to 1.
2. Toward the back or rear part. Dad drove the car *backward* into the parking space.
3. Slow in learning. The *backward* puppy could not learn to roll over.

bacon Smoked, salted meat from the back and sides of a hog, usually sliced thin for cooking.

bacon

bad
badly 1. Wicked; not good. Cheating is *bad.*
2. Causing harm. Candy is *bad* for teeth.
3. In poor condition. My uncle has a *bad* back.
4. Serious. The accident was *bad.* The driver was *badly* hurt.

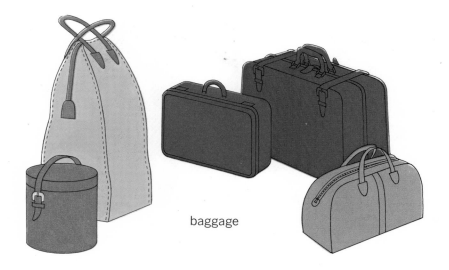

baggage

badminton   A game like tennis in which a light ball with feathers on it is hit with rackets back and forth over a net.

bag   1. A container or sack made of paper or other material. June carried the candy home in a **bag**. 2. A purse, handbag, or suitcase. Mother keeps keys and money in her **bag**.

baggage   The trunks or suitcases used by a traveler. Dad picked up his **baggage** at the airport.

bait   Food placed on a hook or trap to attract and catch fish and other animals. Mother used cheese as **bait** in the mousetrap.

bake
baked
baking   To cook or heat in an oven. Janet will **bake** a cake for the picnic. The men **baked** clay to make bricks.

baker
bakery   A person who bakes bread, cakes, and similar foods. The place where a **baker** works is called a **bakery**.

balance
balanced
balancing   To make steady or even; to keep from being too heavy on one side or the other. The waiter **balanced** the tray on one hand.

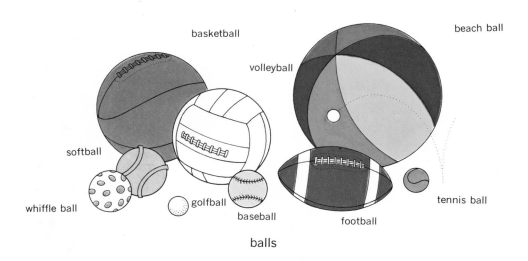

basketball

volleyball

beach ball

softball

whiffle ball

golfball

baseball

football

tennis ball

balls

bale A large bundle of tightly packed hay, cotton, or other material, tied firmly.

ball
1. A round object that is thrown, kicked, or hit in games or sports. Dave kicked the foot**ball.**
2. A game played with a ball. The teams played **ball** in the park.
3. Any round object. The kitten played with a **ball** of string.
4. A pitch in baseball that is not a strike.
5. A special party for dancing. The princess danced with the prince at the **ball.**

balloon

ballad A song or poem that tells a story. The old **ballad** is about a famous hero.

balloon
1. A light, rubber bag filled with air or gas and used as a toy.
2. A very large bag that is filled with gas so that it rises in the air. The **balloon** had a basket underneath for carrying people.

bamboo A tropical grass whose tall, hollow stems are used to make furniture and small huts.

banana A tropical fruit with a smooth yellow or red skin and a soft inside that is good to eat. **Bananas** grow in bunches.

bananas

band   **1.** A group of musicians who play together. The *band* played my favorite song.
2. A group of people or animals. A *band* of thieves robbed the bank.
3. A flat strip of material used to hold something together. The box had a *band* of steel around it to keep it closed.
4. A stripe. Betty's skirt has a *band* of red around the bottom.

bandage   A piece of clean cloth or other material used to cover a cut or wound. The doctor put a *bandage* over the burn on my leg.

Band-Aid   An adhesive bandage with a soft center pad, used to cover cuts.

bamboo

bandit   A robber. A *bandit* robbed the bank.

bang   **1.** A loud, sudden noise. The firecracker made a *bang.*
2. A hit; a blow. Don gave the nail another *bang* with the hammer.

bang
banged
banging
1. To make a loud, sudden noise. The gun will *bang* at the start of the race.
2. To strike; to hit with loud blows. Jim *banged* on the door.

Band-Aid

band (definition 1)

banjo

barge

bangs   (Plural) Hair that is cut straight across the forehead. Mary wore her hair in *bangs.*

banjo   A musical instrument played by using fingers on its strings.

bank   1. A place whose business is the keeping and lending of money. George put his money in the First National *Bank.*
2. A container for saving money. Susan dropped a nickel into her *bank.*
3. The land along the edge of a river, lake, or other body of water.

bar   1. A solid rod of wood or metal. Dad used a steel *bar* to force open the old trunk.
2. A solid piece of something in the shape of a rectangle. Jim washed with a *bar* of soap.
3. A counter where drinks are served. They sell milk shakes at a milk *bar.*

barbecue   1. An outdoor picnic where food is cooked over an open fire.
2. An outdoor fireplace.
3. Meat roasted over an open fire. The chicken *barbecue* was delicious.

barber   A person whose job is cutting hair. The *barber* gave Uncle Ed a haircut and a shave. John got a shampoo at the *barber* shop.

bare   1. Without clothing or covering. The short-sleeved shirt left Dan's arms *bare.*
2. Empty. Mother Hubbard's cupboard was *bare.*

barely   Just; with nothing extra. I had *barely* finished my test when the bell rang.

barge   A large boat with a flat bottom, usually pushed or pulled by another boat and used to carry supplies.

bark
1. The rough covering on the trunks and branches of trees.
2. The short, sharp noise that a dog makes. The dog's **bark** woke me up.

bark
barked
barking
To make the short, sharp noise that a dog makes. A dog will **bark** at cats.

barley
A plant whose grain is used as food.

barn
barnyard
A farm building where grain and hay are stored and cattle or other animals are kept. The cows wandered out of the **barn** into the **barnyard**.

barrel
1. A large container with curved sides and a flat top and bottom. The farmer stored the apples in a **barrel**.
2. The metal tube on the front part of a gun or cannon. The bullet comes out of the **barrel** of a rifle.

base
1. The bottom part of something. The **base** of the lamp rests on the floor.
2. An important place, especially of the army, navy, or air force. The air force built a new **base** for helicopters to land at.
3. A stopping place in some sports and games. The baseball player ran to third **base**.

baseball
1. A game played by two teams with a bat and a ball. A **baseball** field has four bases.
2. The ball used in the game of baseball. Pete hit the **baseball** over the fence.

bark

barn

barrel

baseball

basement A cellar; the area beneath the main floor of a house or other building. Our furnace is in the *basement.*

basin 1. A bowl for holding water.
2. A river and the land that drains into it.

basket 1. A container made of thin strips of wood or other materials that are woven together. Jane put the sandwiches in a *basket.*
2. A hoop through which players try to shoot a ball to score in basketball.

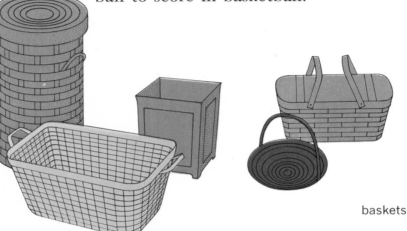

basketball

baskets

basket
(definition 2)

basketball 1. A sport in which two teams of five players each try to score by shooting a ball through hoops at opposite ends of a court.
2. A large, round ball used in basketball.

bat 1. A stick or club used to hit a ball in baseball.
2. A small animal that looks like a mouse with wings and is able to fly.

bat
batted
batting To strike at or hit a ball with a club or bat. My turn to *bat!* The *batter* hit the ball for a home run.

bat

bath 1. A washing of the body, usually in a tub of water.
2. A bathroom.

bathroom   A room that has a tub or shower, a bowl for washing, and a toilet.

bathtub   A large container that holds water for washing the body all over.

battery   A device that makes electricity and stores it for later use. My new toy truck won't run until I put in a **battery.**

bathtub

battle
battlefield   A fight between armed enemies. Many soldiers were wounded in the fierce **battle.** The defeated army left the **battlefield.**

bay   A body of water that sticks out from a larger body of water into land. A **bay** often has land on three sides.

be
been
being   1. To exist or take place. How can that **be?**
2. To have a certain quality or character. Will you **be** happy?
3. A helping word that has many different forms. I **am** going home. **Are** you coming with me? Dick **is** coming later. Karen **was** planning a party. **Were** you invited? The house is **being** painted. John hasn't **been** feeling well.

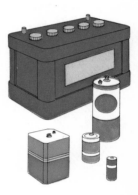
batteries

beach   The sandy shore of an ocean, a lake, or other body of water. Jane collects shells and rocks on the **beach.**

bead   1. A small piece of glass, wood, or other material with a hole in the center, used to make jewelry or to decorate things. Mother wore a string of **beads** as a necklace.
2. A drop of water or any other liquid. A **bead** of water ran down the window.

beagle

beagle   A small dog with long ears and short legs.

beak   The hard, pointed part of a bird's mouth; a bird's bill. The robin had a worm in its **beak.**

beak

beanbag

beam 1. A large, strong piece of wood or metal used to give strength to a building, bridge, or other construction. There are strong *beams* in a ship. 2. A ray of light. We saw a *beam* from the hunter's flashlight.

bean A vegetable plant with pods containing large seeds. George likes to eat lima *beans.*

beanbag A cloth bag filled with dried beans and used in games. Carl tossed the *beanbag* to Sue.

bear A large, strong animal with heavy fur. The polar *bear* lives in a cold climate.

bear

beard The hair that grows on a man's face. Abraham Lincoln grew a *beard* while President.

beast 1. Any animal except man. Linda likes to draw pictures of lions and other *beasts.* 2. A very cruel or wicked person.

beat
beat
beaten
beating
1. To hit over and over. It is cruel to *beat* animals.
2. To defeat. Our team *beat* the other team in baseball.
3. To move in a regular way. The runner's heart *beat* quickly.
4. To blend or stir quickly; to whip. Dad *beat* the eggs for the cake.

beautiful
beautifully
Very pretty; lovely. The roses were *beautiful.* The girls danced *beautifully.*

beauty 1. A quality that gives pleasure. The music has great *beauty.* 2. Someone or something that is beautiful. The horse was a *beauty.*

beaver

beaver A land and water animal with sharp teeth and a flat tail. The *beaver* is an excellent swimmer.

because Since; for the reason that. School is closed today *because* it's a holiday.

become
became
becoming
1. To grow to be. The players will *become* tired by the end of the game.
2. To look nice on. Cathy's dress *becomes* her.

bed
1. A piece of furniture used to sleep on.
2. A sleeping place. The calf slept on a *bed* of hay.
3. A section of ground where plants are grown. Jean planted seeds in the flower *bed.*
4. The ground beneath a body of water. The boat's anchor fell to the *bed* of the river.

bee

bedbug A small insect, sometimes found in beds, that bites people.

bedroom A room where people sleep.

bedtime The time when a person goes or should go to bed. Gail hates *bedtime.*

bee
1. A stinging insect. Some *bees* make honey.
2. A contest; a meeting for work or play. The class had a spelling *bee.*

beef The meat that comes from cattle. We had roast *beef* for supper.

beet

been See **be.**

beer
1. A drink, made from grains, that contains alcohol.
2. A soda made from certain plants. Jack loves to drink root *beer.*

beet A vegetable plant with a large red or white root that is used for food.

beetle A kind of insect that has hard covers to protect its wings when at rest.

beetle

before
1. Ahead of; in front of. At our party, Al arrived *before* Jim.
2. In the past. Karen never sewed *before.*

beg
begged
begging
1. To ask again and again. Tom will *beg* to stay up late tonight.
2. To ask for something without being able to give anything in return. The poor old man had to *beg* for food. A *beggar* is a person who begs.

begin
began
begun
beginning
To start; to take the first step in. The boys will *begin* their trip tomorrow.

behave
behaved
behaving
1. To act properly; to have good manners. Be sure to *behave* at the party.
2. To act in a certain way. Did you *behave* well or badly? How was your *behavior?*

behind
1. At the back or rear of; coming after or later than. The cart was *behind* the horse.
2. Slow or late. The mailman was *behind* in his delivery.

being
1. A person or other living creature. Man is an intelligent *being.*
2. See **be.**

believe
believed
believing
1. To think that something is true. I *believe* that the earth is round. Columbus also had this *belief.*
2. To think that what someone says is true. Do you *believe* me when I say the sky is red?

bell
1. A hollow metal instrument that gives off a ringing sound when it is struck. The *bell* in the church rings every Sunday.
2. Anything that makes a ringing sound. Was that the door*bell?*

bell

belong
belonged
belonging

1. To be the property of. The red car **belongs** to Uncle Bill.
2. To be a part or a member of. Jim **belongs** to the football team.
3. To have a proper place. Milk **belongs** in a refrigerator.

below

In a lower place; lower than; under. A submarine can go **below** the surface of the water.

belt

A strip of material used to hold clothing in place. Dan wore a leather **belt** around his waist.

belts

bench

1. A long seat for more than one person. Three men sat on the park **bench.**
2. The place where a judge sits in a court.

bend
bent
bending

1. To put a curve in. The weight of the fish will **bend** the fishing rod.
2. To curve. The road **bends** to the left.
3. To stoop; to bow. We saw Bob **bend** over to pick up a rock.

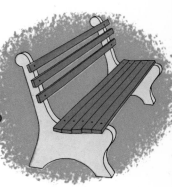

bench

beneath

Under; below. Gail planted the flower seeds **beneath** the ground.

berry

A small, juicy fruit. Tony loves to eat blue**berries** and rasp**berries.**

beside

Next to; near. The salt is **beside** the pepper on the table.

besides

In addition to. **Besides** a bicycle, Jim has a scooter.

best

Most excellent; better than all others. Don won because he was the **best** runner in the race.

bet

A promise to give something to another person if he is right and you are wrong. Dave made a **bet** that he could jump farther than Larry.

better   More excellent; higher in quality. Mary was the *better* of the two tennis players.

between   1. Separating. There was a fence *between* Al's house and Jack's.
2. Owning something together. Alice and Sue had a dime *between* them.
3. Connecting. The road *between* our house and the school is a good one.

beyond   1. Farther on than; on the other side of. The airport was located *beyond* the city limits.
2. After or later than. Mary's party lasted *beyond* three o'clock.

bib   A piece of cloth worn by little children to protect clothing during a meal.

bib

bicycle   A vehicle with two wheels that you ride by moving pedals with your feet.

bid   An amount offered for something that is for sale. Dad's *bid* for the old piano was 20 dollars.

big   Large in size or amount. The hungry boy ate a *big* breakfast.

bike   1. A bicycle.
2. A motorcycle.

bill   1. A paper that shows how much is owed. The waiter gave Dad the *bill* for the meal.
2. A bird's beak.
3. A piece of paper money. I have a dollar *bill.*
4. A plan that may be made into a law. The senators voted on the *bill* to make a new park.

bicycles

billion A number; 1,000,000,000. See page 199.

bin A box-like space in which loose things like apples or potatoes are kept. The farmer poured grain into his *bin.*

bind
bound
binding To fasten or tie together. The students will *bind* their drawings into a book.

bird

bird An animal that has two legs and a pair of wings and is covered with feathers.

birth The act or time of being born. The baby weighed seven pounds at *birth.*

birthday The day on which a person is born, and its celebration each year afterwards. Jody's *birthday* is July 18.

biscuit A kind of bread made in small cakes. Mother served hot *biscuits* with the stew.

biscuits

bit 1. A very small piece. Tony fed the squirrel a *bit* of bread.
2. A tool used for drilling. The *bit* made a round hole in the wooden shelf.
3. A piece of metal that fits into a horse's mouth. The *bit* helps a rider tell his horse which way to go.

bite
bit, bitten
biting 1. To cut with the teeth. Did you see the dog *bite* the man?
2. To sting. A mosquito can *bite.*

bitter
bitterly 1. Having a strong or sour taste; not sweet or pleasant. Tom hated the *bitter* medicine.
2. Angry; full of spite. Carl was *bitter* about losing his bike. He spoke *bitterly* about the unknown thief.
3. Very cold and raw. A *bitter* wind beat against our faces.

black A color. See page 70.

blackberry A small black or purple fruit, or the plant on which it grows.

blackbird A bird that is all or mostly black.

blackboard A surface on which you can write or draw with chalk; a chalkboard. The teacher wrote the word on the *blackboard.*

blade 1. The part of a knife or other tool that cuts.
2. A leaf of grass.

blackbird

blame
blamed
blaming
To say that someone is wrong or at fault. Mother *blames* the other driver for the accident.

blank An empty space, as on a test or other form that asks questions. Please write your name, address, and phone number in the *blanks.*

blanket 1. A large, warm covering for a bed. Joe spread a *blanket* over the sleeping baby.
2. A covering that seems like a blanket. The hills were covered with a *blanket* of snow.

blast
blasted
blasting
To blow up; to destroy. The construction workers will *blast* the huge rock.

blast off To take off in a rocket. We watched the huge rocket *blast off* for the moon.

blaze A very bright fire. The *blaze* destroyed the new house.

blaze
blazed
blazing
1. To burn brightly and quickly. Dry wood makes the fire *blaze.*
2. To shine; to gleam. At night we saw the tall building *blaze* with lights.

blast off

3. To show the way that a trail goes, especially by marking or making cuts in trees. The hunter will *blaze* a trail in the forest.

bleak
bleakly

1. Windy and cold and without much sunlight. The last leaves fell on a *bleak* November day. Winter started *bleakly* with a snowstorm.
2. Without joy. Life in jail is *bleak.*

blackberries

blend
blended
blending

1. To mix very thoroughly. The cook will *blend* flour, milk, and eggs to make a cake. I use our electric *blender* to make milkshakes.
2. To move or flow together. The orange of Ann's dress *blends* into the red.

bless
blessed
blessing

1. To give good fortune to. Good health *blesses* our family.
2. To give thanks and praise to. We met together in church to *bless* God.
3. To pray to make holy. The minister will *bless* the new church tomorrow.

blimp

A balloon-like aircraft filled with gas to make it float. A *blimp* has a small cabin for crew and passengers.

blind

Unable to see. Edna helped the *blind* man cross the busy street.

blink
blinked
blinking

1. To shut and open the eyes quickly. The bright lights made me *blink.*
2. To flash on and off. The light at the lighthouse *blinks* 20 times each minute.

blimp

blizzard

A heavy snowstorm with strong winds and a low temperature.

blob

A drop or lump of soft or sticky material. A *blob* of jam fell on the table.

block

1. A cube of wood, stone, or other material. The baby put one **block** on top of the other.
2. An area in a city or town formed by four streets, usually in the shape of a rectangle. Tom lives in the **block** between Oak and Main Streets and Third and Fourth Avenues.
3. The distance between two streets. It is six **blocks** from Fourth Street to Tenth Street.

blocks

block
blocked
blocking

To stop; to prevent. The thick ice will **block** the boat from reaching the dock.

blood

The red liquid that flows through your body and provides nourishment needed for life. Your heart pumps **blood** to all parts of your body.

bloodhound

A hunting dog with a keen sense of smell.

bloom
bloomed
blooming

To have flowers or blossoms. The rose bush **blooms** in the summer.

blossom

A flower.

blossom
blossomed
blossoming

To have flowers; to bloom. Tulips **blossom** in the spring.

blot

A spot or stain. There was a **blot** of ink on Dave's shirt.

blouse

A piece of clothing worn like a shirt by women or girls.

bloodhound

blow
blew
blown
blowing

1. To move quickly or with force (used in talking about air). The wind will **blow** the leaves across the lawn.
2. To force or send air out of the mouth. Mother told Tom not to **blow** on his hot soup.
3. To make a sound by a rush of air. The Scouts heard the bugle **blow** in the morning.

blue   A color. See page 70.

blueberry   A small, dark-blue fruit, or the bush on which this fruit grows.

bluebird   A small, blue bird.

blue jay   A blue and gray bird that has a crest or narrow crown of feathers on its head. A **blue jay** has a noisy call.

blue jeans   A pair of trousers made from heavy, blue cotton cloth.

blueberries

blush
blushed
blushing
To become red in the face because of feeling shy or excited. The teacher's praise made Joel **blush.**

board   1. A long, flat piece of wood. Dad used a **board** to make a new shelf in the closet.
2. A flat section of material for a special use. Our room has a black**board** and a bulletin **board.**
3. Meals; food. Private schools charge for room and **board.**
4. A committee; a group of people who control or manage things. The **board** of education voted to build a new school.

blue jay

board
boarded
boarding
1. To get on. Passengers can **board** the plane in 20 minutes.
2. To cover with boards or wood. We will **board** up the windows before the storm.

boast
boasted
boasting
To brag; to praise yourself. Tim **boasted** about being strong.

boat   A water craft in which people can travel.

bob
bobbed
bobbing
To move up and down quickly. We watched the block of wood **bob** in the waves.

blue jeans

bobcat

bobwhite

bolt

bobcat   A wildcat; a lynx.

bobwhite   A brown and white bird; a quail. The call of the *bobwhite* sounds like its name.

body   1. The physical part of a person or animal, apart from the mind and spirit. Exercise helps to build your *body.*
2. A mass of anything. An ocean is a large *body* of water.

bog   A swamp or marsh. The ground in the *bog* was soft and wet.

boil
boiled
boiling   1. To heat so hot that bubbles form. *Boil* the water for tea.
2. To cook in boiling water. Let's *boil* eggs for breakfast.

bold
boldly   1. Having courage; brave. The *bold* explorer set off into the wilderness. Karen *boldly* walked home in the dark.
2. Rude or saucy; not quiet or shy. The *bold* boy talked back to the teacher.

bologna   A kind of sausage for sandwiches.

bolt   1. A rod of metal used to hold something in place. A *bolt* screws into a nut.
2. A sliding rod or bar for locking a door.
3. A roll of cloth or other material.

bomb   1. A device used to blow something up. *Bombs* are used in war.
2. A container of liquid under pressure. Mother used an insect *bomb* to kill the flies.

bomber   An airplane made to carry and drop bombs.

bone   One of the hard pieces that make up the skeleton of a person or animal.

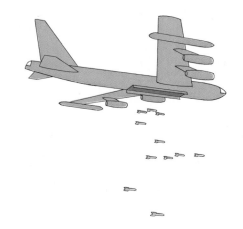

bombers

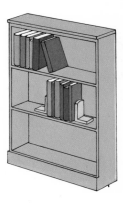

bookcase

bonnet A hat for a baby or woman.

book A group of printed pages bound between covers. A *book* may tell a story or give us information.

bookcase A set of shelves for holding books.

bookkeeper A person whose job is keeping a record of the money taken in or spent by a business.

bookmobile A small library in a truck. A *bookmobile* moves around to serve people in different places.

boom
boomed
booming
1. To make a loud, deep sound. After the lightning, we heard the thunder *boom.*
2. To have a sudden increase in growth and wealth. The discovery of oil made the town *boom.*

boost
boosted
boosting
To raise up from behind or beneath. I can *boost* my little brother up to the cookie shelf.

boot A shoe covering the foot and part of the leg, usually worn in rain, snow, or cold weather.

booth A small room or stand in which a person sells tickets or goods, makes a telephone call, or votes.

boots

bottles

border

1. A boundary or line that separates one thing from another. The Ohio River forms the southern **border** of Ohio.
2. An outside edge. We made a colored **border** to frame our paintings.

bore
bored
boring

1. To make tired and not interested. Long speeches **bore** me.
2. To make by drilling or digging. We will **bore** holes in the board for the screws.

born

Brought forth into life.

borrow
borrowed
borrowing

To use for a time and then return. May I please **borrow** your pencil?

boss

A person who controls or directs others. Ask Jimmy where to put the box; he's the **boss.**

bossy

Telling other people what to do, usually in a rude way or without being asked.

both

1. The two; one and the other. **Both** girls liked to swim.
2. Equally as well (used with "and"). Jim liked **both** candy and ice cream.

bother
bothered
bothering

To be a problem to; to trouble. Don't **bother** Mother when she's talking on the phone.

bottle

A container made of glass or plastic, with a small neck or top.

bottom

1. The part farthest down. Dad was at the **bottom** of the ladder.
2. The under part. The **bottom** of your shoe has a heel on it.

bough

A large limb or branch of a tree. In one nursery rhyme, the **bough** breaks and the cradle falls.

bowling

bounce
bounced
bouncing

1. To strike and spring back from a surface. The ball *bounced* across the floor.
2. To spring or jump. Jed *bounces* out of bed in the morning.

bound
bounded
bounding

1. To leap or spring. Tim *bounds* down the steps two by two.
2. To limit; to be or show the boundary of. The schoolyard is *bounded* by Park Street and West Street.

boundary

The edge or limit of an area or place; a border. The Pacific Ocean is one *boundary* of California.

bow

1. A curved rod fitted to a tight cord and used to shoot arrows.
2. The shape of a ribbon or necktie that has been tied into loops.

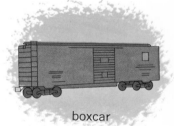

bowls

bow
bowed
bowing

1. To bend from the waist as a sign of honor or thanks.
2. To curve or bend. My poodle's legs *bow* out a little.

bow

A bending from the waist. Kenny made a *bow* when his friends clapped.

bowl

A round, deep dish.

bowling

A game in which players roll a heavy ball down a long wooden floor or alley to try to knock down ten wooden pins.

boxcar

box

A container to hold things, usually made of cardboard, metal, or wood. A *box* has sides shaped like squares or rectangles.

boxcar

A closed car of a freight train.

boxer

1. A person who fights with his fists in the sport of boxing.
2. A large dog with short brown hair.

boxer

Boy Scout emblem

bracelets

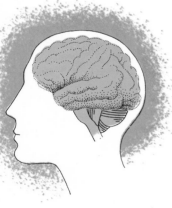

brain

boxing A sport in which two men or boys fight with the fists, wearing large, thick gloves.

boy A very young man; a male child.

Boy Scout A member of a worldwide group that helps train boys in camping and in being good citizens.

bracelet A piece of jewelry worn around the wrist.

brag *bragged* *bragging* To talk too much about oneself; to boast. Tim *brags* about his trip to California.

braid A long band of hair or other material that has been divided into three or more parts and woven together.

Braille A way for blind people to read by feeling a page on which raised dots stand for letters and numbers.

brain The nerve center located in the head, by which you control motions of the body and with which you think and learn.

brake A device that makes a machine stop, slow down, or remain in place. Use your *brake* when you ride your bike down a hill.

branch 1. The part of a tree on which leaves grow. A *branch* grows out from a tree trunk or from another branch.
2. Any part or division running into a main part. This stream is a *branch* of the Ohio River.

brand 1. The official name of a company's product. What *brand* of soup do you buy?
2. A design or mark burned onto cattle with a hot iron to show who the owner is.

brass A yellow-gold metal made from copper and other metals.

brat A child who is always causing trouble.

brave Having courage; ready to face danger. The *brave* firemen saved the child from the fire.

bread A food made by baking dough in an oven. *Bread* is used to make sandwiches.

break
broke
broken
breaking
1. To separate into pieces; to crack. If you drop the glass, it will *break.*
2. To go against. I didn't mean to *break* the rules.
3. To put out of order. Don *broke* his watch by winding it too tight.

breakable Able to be cracked or broken. The glass dish was *breakable.*

breakfast The first meal each day. You eat *breakfast* in the morning.

breast
1. The chest. A robin has a red *breast.*
2. In people and some animals, the part of the mother's body that makes milk for babies.

breath The air you take in and let out of your lungs. On a cold day, you can see your *breath.*

breathe
breathed
breathing
To pull air into the lungs and then let it go out. You must *breathe* to live.

breathless Breathing in short, fast gulps. The race made Paul *breathless.*

breed A certain kind of animal. Collies are a *breed* of dog.

breeze A soft, gentle wind.

brew A drink made by mixing things together. The witch's *brew* was made with a magic powder.

brick A block used in building, made from baked clay, cement, or other hard material.

braid

bread

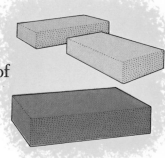

bricks

bride A woman about to be married or just married.

bridegroom A man about to be married or just married.

bridge 1. A walkway or road built over something difficult to cross, such as a river or deep valley. 2. A card game played by four people.

bridegroom and bride

brief Short; not very long. Bob wrote a **brief,**
briefly one-page letter. He wrote **briefly** about camp.

bright 1. Shiny; having much light. The room was **bright** with sunlight.
2. Smart. Jack is a **bright** boy.
3. Glowing in color or sound. Mary's dress was **bright** green.

brilliant 1. Very bright; sparkling. A diamond is a **brilliant** stone.
2. Very smart. The engineer was **brilliant.**

bring 1. To carry or take with you. Please **bring** your
brought sleeping bag on the trip.
bringing 2. To make happen. April showers **bring** May flowers.

bridge

bristle A stiff hair or hair-like part. My toothbrush has many **bristles.**

broad Very wide. The **broad** highway had room for six lanes of traffic.

broadcast A radio or television message or program. We like the six o'clock news **broadcast.**

broadcast 1. To send a radio or television program over
broadcasted the air.
broadcasting 2. To send or scatter over a wide area. Don't **broadcast** my secret to the whole class.

broil To cook directly over or under strong heat.
broiled We **broil** steaks in our oven.
broiling

brook A small stream; a creek. It is fun to wade in the **brook.**

broom A brush fastened to a long handle. A **broom** is used for sweeping.

broth The liquid in which meat is cooked; a thin soup.

brother A boy or man who has the same parents as another person. Tom is Dick's **brother.**

brown A color. See page 70.

brownie 1. A kind of chocolate cookie, usually made with nuts.
2. A helpful elf. The **brownie** in the story did kind things for people.

Brownie A young Girl Scout. **Brownies** are seven and eight years of age.

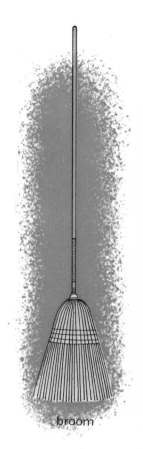

broom

bruise An injury to the body in which the skin isn't broken. A **bruise** often turns black and blue.

brush 1. A tool with bristles fastened to a handle. We use a **brush** to smooth our hair.
2. A group of small trees, bushes, or cut or broken branches. The bunny came out of the **brush.**

brush
brushed
brushing
1. To use a brush on; to clean off. Mary tried to **brush** the crumbs from her dress.
2. To pass and touch lightly. The dog **brushed** by Mary.

brushes

bubble A small ball of air or other gas trapped inside a thin film or liquid. A soap **bubble** looks like a little balloon.

bubble
bubbled
bubbling
To form bubbles. The water will **bubble** when it is hot enough to boil.

buck A grown male of certain animals. The males of deer, rabbits, and goats are called **bucks.**

bucket A deep, round container with a handle; a pail.

bucket

buckle
1. A fastener for a belt.
2. A decoration, especially for shoes. The Pilgrims wore shoes with **buckles** on them.

buckle
buckled
buckling
1. To fasten with a buckle. Be sure to **buckle** your seat belt in a car.
2. To bend under pressure. The shelf **buckled** when Jim put the heavy box on it.

bud A blossom or leaf before it is fully open. In early spring you can see **buds** on the trees.

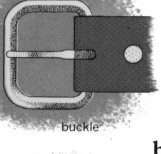
buckle

budge
budged
budging
To move or push from one position; to move even slightly. We could not **budge** the big rock.

buffalo A wild ox-like animal. In Asia, the water **buffalo** is trained to do work.

bug
1. An insect, especially one that crawls. An ant is a **bug.** Some **bugs** can fly.
2. A germ that makes you sick. Tom got a **bug** and doesn't feel well.

buffalo

buggy
1. A carriage pulled by a horse. Before there were cars, many people traveled by horse and **buggy.**
2. A baby's carriage.

bugle A musical wind instrument; a small, brass horn like a trumpet. The **bugle** woke us up every morning at camp.

build
built
building
To make; to put together. Betty likes to **build** model planes. Alex's father is a **builder** of houses.

bugle

building Something built to shelter people, animals, or things. Schools, barns, and skyscrapers are three kinds of *buildings.*

bulb 1. The underground part of certain plants, from which a new plant grows. We eat the *bulb* of an onion plant.
2. A glass globe that gives light when electricity flows through it. Who changed the *bulb* in the lamp?

flower bulb

light bulb

bulge
bulged
bulging
To stick out; to swell up or grow larger. A hamster can fill its cheeks with food until they *bulge.*

bull A male animal, usually of the cattle family. Male elephants and moose are also called *bulls.*

bulldog A short-haired dog with short legs and a square face. The *bulldog* is a good pet.

bulldozer A tractor with a large blade in front used in clearing land. The *bulldozer* pushed trees and rocks from its path.

bulldog

bullet A piece of metal shaped to be fired from a gun.

bulletin A special news statement; a short item about up-to-date news. The news *bulletin* warned about the coming storm.

bullfrog A large frog. The *bullfrog* has a deep voice.

bulldozer

bull's eye The center of a target; a shot that hits the center of a target. The arrow hit the *bull's eye.*

bumblebee A large bee with a loud buzz.

bump 1. A slight blow or knock. The *bump* scratched the car.
2. A raised place; a bulge. Tom's bike hit a *bump* in the road.

bullfrog

bump
bumped
bumping

To run against; to hit. We saw the car **bump** the post.

bumper

A metal bar that protects the back or front of a car. The car's **bumper** was bent in the accident.

bun

A kind of roll, often sweet. We love to eat raisin **buns.**

bunch

A group of similar things; a number of objects fastened together. The fox stole a **bunch** of grapes.

bundle

A package; several things held or tied together. We took a **bundle** of clothes to the laundry.

bunk

A narrow bed, sometimes fastened to the wall.

bunks

bunny

A rabbit.

burglar

A person who breaks into a building to steal; a thief. The **burglar** stole the lady's jewelry.

burn

An injury caused by fire or a hot object. Nell's **burn** came from a hot iron.

burn
burned
burning

1. To be on fire or to set fire to; to blaze. Paper and wood **burn** easily.
2. To give off light or heat. The lamp was **burning** all night.
3. To cause a hot feeling. The red pepper **burned** his tongue.

burro

A small donkey.

burrow

A hole or tunnel in the ground made by an animal. The rabbit family lives in a **burrow.**

burst

1. A sudden effort. In a **burst** of speed, the runner won the race.
2. A sudden breaking forth. A **burst** of laughter filled the room.

burro

burst
bursted
bursting

1. To come apart; to break into pieces. The balloon **burst** with a loud pop.
2. To rush; to appear suddenly. Dick **burst** into the room.
3. To give way to suddenly. Jill **burst** into laughter at the joke.

bury
buried
burying

1. To put in the ground; to cover with earth. We watched the squirrel **bury** nuts.
2. To place in a grave. The family **buried** their pet.

bus

A long motor vehicle for carrying people. The **bus** had seats for 50 passengers.

bush

A plant that has many branches near the ground. A **bush** is not as tall as a tree.

business

1. An occupation; a way of earning a living. Carl's father is in the repair **business.**
2. A store or office or factory. Mr. Smith owns a **business** on Main Street.
3. The amount of buying and selling in a place of business. Tad's father sells cars, and **business** is good.

bus

busy
busily

At work; having something to do. The **busy** dog was burying his bone. Ants always seem to run about **busily.**

but

1. Except; other than. There was no one there **but** Carol.
2. On the other hand; however. Ben is young, **but** he is tall.
3. Only. The twins had **but** one bike.

butcher

A person who cuts up meat; a person who runs a meat market.

butter

A solid yellow fat made from cream. **Butter** is used in cooking and as a spread for bread.

buttercup   A yellow cup-like flower, or the plant on which it grows.

butterfly   An insect with large, brightly colored wings. The *butterfly* flies from flower to flower.

buttermilk   The liquid left when butter is made from cream. Some people like to drink *buttermilk.*

button   1. A kind of fastener on clothes. Tom's jacket is missing a *button.*
2. A round object that you push to make something work. Alice pressed the *button* to make the elevator go.

buttercup

button
buttoned
buttoning   To fasten by using a button. The kindergarten teacher helps the children *button* their coats.

buy
bought
buying   To pay money for. We *buy* lunch in the cafeteria. The *buyer* of our car liked it very much.

butterfly

buzz
buzzed
buzzing   1. To make a sound like a bee. Bees will *buzz* around flowers.
2. To talk with excitement. The class *buzzed* about the trip to the museum.

by   1. Next to; near. The house was *by* a pond.
2. With the use of; by way of; through. Bill's uncle will come *by* plane.
3. During. The owl slept *by* daylight.
4. Not later than. We will be at the party *by* six o'clock.

buttons

Cc

cabbage　A plant whose large leaves grow in a ball and are eaten as a vegetable.

cabin　1. A small, rough house. Early settlers in America lived in *cabins* made from logs.
2. A room on a ship; a section of an airplane.

log cabin

cabinet　A cupboard or piece of furniture that has shelves or drawers to hold things.

cacao　A tree whose nuts are ground to make cocoa.

cactus　A plant that grows in very hot, dry places and has needle-like thorns instead of leaves.

cafeteria　A restaurant where people serve themselves.

cage　A place closed off by bars or heavy wire on one or more sides. Our pet canary sings in his *cage.*

cake　1. A baked dessert made with flour, sugar, eggs, and other materials, usually covered with icing.
2. A solid piece of something. Tom washed with a *cake* of soap.

cactus

calendar　A chart that shows the months, weeks, and days of the year.

calf　1. A young cow; the young of some other animals. A baby elephant is called a *calf.* The plural of *calf* is *calves.*
2. The back of your leg between your knee and your ankle.

cage

call

1. A shout, cry, or other signal to attract attention. Judy heard my *call* for help.
2. A visit in person. We made a *call* on Dick at the hospital.
3. A visit by telephone.

call
called
calling

1. To shout; to speak loudly. We heard the child *call* for his mother.
2. To name. We will *call* the pony Prince.
3. To ask to come. Please *call* the children for breakfast.
4. To telephone. I will *call* Susan from the phone booth.
5. To visit. Did you *call* at the Smiths' house? Dad invited the *caller* to stay for supper.

calm
calmly

Quiet; still. The campers enjoyed the *calm* weather. Mother spoke *calmly* to the dog.

camel

A large animal with one or two humps on its back, used to carry heavy loads. The *camel* helps people to travel over hot deserts.

camera

A device for making photographs, movies, or television pictures.

camp

A place where people take vacations to enjoy the outdoors, often living in tents or cabins.

camp
camped
camping

To live for a while outdoors or in a tent or similar shelter. The cowboys will *camp* near the stream.

camper

1. A person who lives in a camp.
2. A small van to travel and live in.

can

A round, sealed metal container. Dad opened a *can* of beans.

can
could

To be able to. Doris *can* ride a bicycle. I wish we *could* go to the movies.

can
canned
canning
To put food in tightly closed jars or containers for storing. Mother *canned* the fresh peaches.

canal
A waterway built by man for ships to pass through.

canary
A yellow bird that sings beautifully and is a popular pet.

canary

candle
A rod or stick of wax formed around a string that can be burned to give off light.

candy
A sweet food made mostly from sugar.

cane
1. A strong stick that a person uses to help him walk. The lame man had to use a *cane.*
2. A plant from which we get sugar.

candles

cannon
A large gun, usually on wheels.

cannot
To be unable to. Paul *cannot* swim.

canoe
A small, narrow boat that is moved with paddles.

can't
A short form of "cannot."

cantaloupe
A round fruit with a rough, thick covering. The inside of a *cantaloupe* is orange and juicy.

canyon
A deep, narrow valley with steep sides. A river may run through the bottom of a *canyon.*

canoe

cap
1. A small hat. Our team wears red *caps.*
2. A top or covering. Can you get the *cap* off the soda bottle?

cape
1. A piece of clothing that looks like a coat without sleeves. The magician wore a *cape.*
2. A piece of land that stretches out into a body of water. A *cape* is attached to a large body of land and has water on three sides.

capital
1. A city or place that is the center of government for a state or nation. Washington, D.C., is the *capital* of the United States.
2. The larger form of any letter in the alphabet. The first word in this sentence begins with a *capital.*

capitol
A building where laws are made. Leaders of government meet and work in the *capitol.*

capsule
1. A very small container, especially one that holds medicine. The nurse gave me a *capsule.*
2. A section of a spacecraft where spacemen live and work.

captain
1. The man in charge of a boat or ship.
2. An officer in the Army or Navy.
3. A leader. Bob is the *captain* of our team.

capture
captured
capturing
To catch and take by force; to seize. Did the hunters *capture* the wild elephant?

car
1. An automobile.
2. A vehicle that carries passengers, like a railroad *car.*

card
(definition 2)

card
1. A small piece of stiff paper used for a number of purposes. Susan bought a post*card* and a birthday *card.*
2. One of a deck or set of playing cards, used in bridge, "Old Maid," and other card games.

cardboard
A paper-like material, thicker and stiffer than paper. *Cardboard* is used to make boxes.

care
1. Protection; charge. Will you take *care* of my bike next week?
2. Attention. Cross the busy street with *care.*
3. A worry or trouble. Ted doesn't have a *care* in the world.

care
cared
caring
To want; to like. Would you *care* to go to the game?

careful
carefully
Watchful; paying attention. We were *careful* not to wake the baby. Mother drove the car *carefully.*

carpenter

careless
carelessly
Paying no attention; not watchful or thinking. The *careless* player dropped the ball. He played *carelessly.*

cargo
The goods or supplies carried by a ship, train, or other vehicle. The ship carried a *cargo* of oil.

carnival
A show or activity that includes games, rides, and refreshments. We rode the merry-go-round at the *carnival.*

carpenter
A person who works with wood to make or fix furniture and buildings.

carrot
A long, narrow plant root eaten as a vegetable.

carry
carried
carrying
To take from one place to another. *Carry* the package to the car.

carrot

cart
A small wagon for carrying goods or passengers. Our shopping *cart* was full of groceries.

cartoon
cartoonist
A funny drawing or a movie made from funny drawings. A *cartoonist* draws comics for a newspaper.

cartwheel
A flip or turning over of the body sideways with the hands placed on the ground. The acrobat did a *cartwheel.*

carve
carved
carving
To cut; to shape by cutting. Dave can *carve* a boat from a bar of soap.

cartwheel

cascade A waterfall or group of waterfalls.

case 1. A box; a container. My watch came in a plastic *case.*
2. A situation or condition. Don has a bad *case* of sunburn.
3. An action of law. The judge heard the *case.*

cash Coins and paper money. Mother pays her bills in *cash.*

casserole 1. A deep baking dish, usually with a cover.
2. The food baked in a deep dish. Mother made a tuna and noodle *casserole.*

cast 1. A hard molded covering worn to protect an injured part of the body. The doctor put a *cast* on my broken arm.
2. All the actors taking part in a play. Joan is in the *cast* of the school play.

castle A palace; a large building used as a fort or a home.

castle

cat A small animal with smooth fur, often kept as a pet. Our *cat* had three kittens.

catch
caught
catching
1. To take and hold; to grab. Tom will *catch* the football.
2. To seize; to capture. Did you *catch* any fish?
3. To get to in time. Can we *catch* the bus?

caterpillar An insect form that looks like a worm with fur. Every butterfly was once a *caterpillar.*

catsup See **ketchup.**

caterpillar

cattle (Plural) Animals such as cows, bulls, or oxen. The *cattle* ate the long grass.

cause Anything that makes another thing happen. A bad tire was the *cause* of the accident.

cause
caused
causing
To make happen. The heavy rain may *cause* a flood.

cave
A hollow place under the ground or in the side of a hill; a cavern. The bear lives in a *cave*.

cave

ceiling
The top surface of a room. Dad painted the walls blue and the *ceiling* white.

celebrate
celebrated
celebrating
To honor with a party or in another special way. We will *celebrate* the team's victory. The king planned a *celebration* on the queen's birthday.

celery
A plant whose stalks we eat as a vegetable.

cell
1. One of the many very small parts that plants and animals are made of. The doctor looked at blood *cells* with his microscope.
2. A small room, especially one where a prisoner is kept.

celery

cellar
A room under a building; a basement. We keep our tools in the *cellar*.

cement
A building material made from clay and rock mixed with sand and water. Many sidewalks are made of *cement*.

cent
A penny. There are ten *cents* in a dime.

center
1. The middle. Mother put flowers in the *center* of the table.
2. A main or important place. The library is our reading *center*.

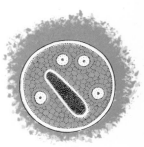

cell

century
A time period of 100 years.

cereal
1. Grain; a plant such as wheat, rice, or oats.
2. A breakfast food made from grain. Oatmeal is my favorite *cereal*.

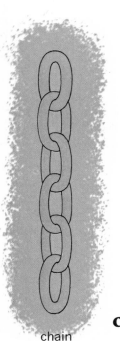

chain

chalkboard

certain
certainly

1. Sure. Are you *certain* that the door is locked? Doris *certainly* is pretty.
2. Some; special. My dog will eat only *certain* foods.

chain

1. A line or row of connected links. The anchor was at the end of a strong *chain.*
2. A group of connected things. The plane flew over a *chain* of mountains.

chair

A piece of furniture with a seat, back, and four legs, for use by one person.

chalk

A material used for writing on a blackboard or chalkboard.

chalkboard

A dark-colored board on which you can write with chalk. Our classroom has a *chalkboard.*

champion
championship

A person or team that wins more often than any other in a sport or contest. The tennis *champion* won every game. The game was a *championship* contest between the two best teams.

chance

1. Luck. She won first place by *chance.*
2. A possible danger; a gamble. The skater took a *chance* by going on the thin ice.
3. An opportunity. George has a *chance* to go to summer camp.
4. A possible happening. There is a *chance* that Charles will go with us.

change
changed
changing

1. To make different. The painter will *change* the color of our house.
2. To replace. After school Jim will *change* his clothes.

character

1. A person in a book, play, or story. Cinderella is a *character* in a fairy tale.
2. The way a person is or thinks; a person's nature. Lincoln had a forgiving *character.*

charge
charged
charging

1. To rush at; to use force against. The soldiers will *charge* the fort.
2. To ask a price. The store will *charge* two dollars for the book.
3. To buy now and agree to pay for later. Did Dad *charge* the radio?
4. To blame. The police will *charge* the robbers with the crime.

chart

1. A sheet or list of information, sometimes in a table or graph form. We made a *chart* to show the number and kinds of all our pets.
2. A map, especially one used by sailors.

chase
chased
chasing

1. To run after; to try to catch. Does your dog *chase* rabbits?
2. To drive away. The cat *chased* the mice out of the barn.

cheap
cheaply

1. Low in price. Fruit is *cheap* at that store. They built their house *cheaply*.
2. Having little value; poor in quality. The *cheap* shoes wore out quickly.

cheat
cheated
cheating

To do something that is not fair or honest. An honest player does not *cheat* in games.

check

1. A close look; a test. Uncle Ed made a *check* of the car's engine.
2. A special piece of paper used instead of money if you have money in the bank. Mother wrote a *check* to pay for the clothes.
3. A bill for food or drink. The waiter brought Dad a *check* for the meal.
4. A mark made to show that something has been done or examined. The teacher made a *check* next to each correct answer.
5. A pattern of small squares. The tablecloth was a red and white *check*.

checkers
A game played by two people who move a number of round colored pieces over a board divided into small squares. *Checkers* is a game in which one player tries to win the other player's pieces.

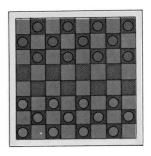
checkers

cheek
Either side of the face above the jaw and below the eye.

cheer
cheered
cheering
1. To show joy or to welcome by shouting. The crowd will *cheer* for the winning team.
2. To raise the spirits of or make happy. After the rain, the sunshine *cheered* us all.

cheerful
cheerfully
Happy; joyful. The gift made Ann feel *cheerful.* The happy boy whistled *cheerfully.*

cheese
A food made from the milk of cows, goats, or other animals.

cherries

cherry
A small, round fruit, usually red, or the tree on which it grows.

chess
A game played by two persons who move figures of different shapes over a board divided into small squares.

chest
1. A large box or piece of furniture in which things are stored. Mother keeps her linens in a *chest* of drawers.
2. The front of the body from the shoulders to the bottom of the ribs.

chestnut
A brown nut that grows inside a hard covering. Not all kinds of *chestnuts* are good to eat.

chew
chewed
chewing
To bite, cut, or grind with the teeth. The mouse will *chew* the cheese into little pieces.

chess pieces

chicken
1. A common farm bird; a hen or rooster. The female *chicken* lays eggs.
2. The meat from a hen or rooster.

chief A leader or ruler of a group of people. Sitting Bull was a famous Indian *chief.*

child A young boy or girl. The plural of *child* is *children.*

chili 1. A food made with meat and hot pepper, usually mixed with beans.
2. A hot, red pepper.

chill Coldness; a cold feeling in the body. We felt the *chill* of the autumn air. The scary stories sent *chills* through us.

chimney A tall, hollow structure, often made of brick, through which smoke from a fireplace or furnace rises.

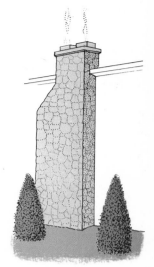

chimney

chimpanzee An ape; a large, intelligent member of the monkey family. A *chimpanzee* can learn tricks easily.

chin The center part of the jaw below the lips. Uncle Bob grew a beard on his *chin.*

chip 1. A small piece; a bit. Jim picked up a *chip* of broken glass.
2. A cut or broken edge where something is damaged. There is a *chip* on the edge of the cup.

chimpanzee

chipmunk A small animal with black and white stripes on its back. *Chipmunks* can carry or store food in their cheeks.

chirp
chirped
chirping To make a short, sharp sound such as some birds and insects make. We heard a cricket *chirp.*

chipmunk

chocolate A drink, candy, or other food made from the ground and roasted nuts of the cacao tree.

choice
1. Something that is wanted or chosen. The red hat was Martha's first *choice.*
2. The chance to choose something. Mother gave us a *choice* of cereal or eggs for breakfast.

choir
A group of people who sing together, especially in a church.

choke
choked
choking
1. To keep from breathing by blocking or squeezing the throat. Small bones may *choke* a puppy.
2. To block, stop, or hold back from moving or growing. Too many weeds will *choke* the flowers in your garden.

chopsticks

choose
chose
chosen
choosing
1. To pick; to select. Which hat did Jane *choose* to wear?
2. To decide. Andy *chose* to go to the movies.

chop
chopped
chopping
1. To cut into pieces with an ax or similar tool. Tom will *chop* the log in half.
2. To cut into small pieces. We watched Susan *chop* the carrot with a knife.
3. To make by cutting. The fireman *chopped* a hole in the roof.

chopsticks
A pair of narrow sticks used in China and some other countries to lift food to the mouth.

chuckle
A quiet or soft laugh.

chum
A good friend.

church
A building where religious services are held.

church

cigarette
A small amount of tobacco packed in a roll of thin paper. A smoker lights a *cigarette* with a flame.

circle
1. A perfectly round ring.
2. A group of people with the same interest. We have a *circle* of good friends.

circus A traveling show in which clowns, acrobats, and animals take part.

citizen A member of a nation, or a person who belongs to a country, state, city, or town. Every **citizen** of our city should be proud of the new park.

city A large or important town. Many people and many businesses are found in a **city.**

claim
claimed
claiming
1. To say or declare as true. Jim **claims** that he is taller than Dave.
2. To demand what is yours. John **claimed** his bike at the lost and found office.

clam A sea animal that has a shell and is good to eat.

clam

clap
clapped
clapping
To make noise by hitting the palms of your hands together. The crowd **clapped** for the winning team.

class
1. A type; a kind. Snakes belong to the **class** of animals called reptiles.
2. A group of students who study and work together. Our **class** has 26 students in it.

claw
1. One of the sharp, curved nails on the foot of certain animals. The kitten scratched me with its **claws.**
2. The end of a limb of a lobster or similar sea animal.

claws

clay A soft substance found in the earth that can be formed and hardened into bricks, dishes, and other objects.

clean
cleaned
cleaning
To remove spots or dirt from; to make neat or tidy. Jim used a wet cloth to **clean** the table. Sally **cleaned** her room yesterday.

clean Free from dirt or spots; neat. My new blouse is bright and **clean.**

clear
cleared
clearing

1. To remove things from; to make neat. Please *clear* the table after supper.
2. To get by without touching. The plane *cleared* the mountain top.
3. To free from blame. The prisoner was *cleared* of the charges.

clear
clearly

1. Easy to see through. The glass was *clear.*
2. Easy to understand. The teacher made the answer *clear* to us. She explained it *clearly.*
3. Bright; not cloudy. The weather is *clear.*
4. Open. There was a *clear* path to the cabin.

clerk

1. A person who sells things or helps shoppers in a store. The *clerk* helped me pick out a gift.
2. A person who keeps records, opens mail, and does similar work in an office.

clever
cleverly
cleverness

Bright; intelligent; having quick wits. The boy is very *clever.* Janet answered the question *cleverly.* Foxes are famous for their *cleverness.*

cliff

cliff

A high, steep hillside of earth or rock.

climate

The usual weather a place or area has. The desert has a hot, dry *climate.*

climb
climbed
climbing

1. To go up or down, using the feet and sometimes the hands. Can you *climb* that tree?
2. To rise. The plane will *climb* above the clouds.
3. To grow. The vine will *climb* up the fence.

clip
clipped
clipping

1. To trim; to cut or cut off. Tell the barber not to *clip* off too much hair.
2. To fasten; to join. The teacher will *clip* the papers together.

clocks

cloak

A loose piece of clothing like a coat or cape.

clock

An instrument that shows what time it is. The alarm *clock* woke me at seven o'clock.

close
closed
closing

1. To shut; to block. Please **close** the door.
2. To finish; to end. The show will **close** with a magic trick.
3. Make complete; to finish. We joined hands and **closed** the circle.

close
closely

1. Near. Jim's house is **close** to Ed's. My dog follows me **closely.**
2. Fond of each other. Jane and Susan are **close** friends.

closet

A small room used for storing things. Hang your jacket in the **closet.**

cloth

1. A material made from cotton, wool, or other fibers.
2. A piece of cloth with a special use. Mother bought a new table**cloth.**

clothes

(Plural) Coats, pants, dresses, and other things that you wear.

clothing

Things that you wear. The store on the corner sells **clothing.**

cloud
cloudy

1. A white or gray mass of moisture in the sky from which rain, snow, or hail sometimes falls. The rain **cloud** grew darker and darker. The skies were **cloudy** during the storm.
2. A floating mass of dust or smoke. The fire sent a **cloud** of smoke into the air.

clover

A low, green plant with small flowers, and leaves that usually grow in three parts.

clown

A person who wears funny clothes and does funny things at a circus or similar show.

club

1. A heavy stick or rod used as a weapon.
2. A stick used in some sports. Dad broke his favorite golf **club.**
3. A group of people who share some interest or activity. I belong to a stamp **club.**

clouds

clover

clown

clue A hint; something that helps to provide an answer. Can you guess the answer if I give you a *clue?*

clumsy Always falling or tripping; not able to move smoothly. The *clumsy* clown sat on his hat.

clutch To hold tightly to. Kate *clutched* the flowers
clutched in her hand.
clutching

coach 1. A closed carriage pulled by horses. The queen's *coach* took her to the ball.
2. A person who teaches sports. The baseball *coach* sent a new pitcher into the game.
3. A railroad passenger car.

coal A hard, black substance that is dug from the earth and burned as fuel.

coal

coarse 1. Rough; not smooth. Some overalls are made from *coarse* material.
2. Rude; not having good manners.

coast The area around the line where ocean and land meet.

coast To move without using power. We like to *coast*
coasted down the hill on our sleds.
coasting

coastline The line or border where land and sea meet. The Atlantic *coastline* forms the eastern boundary of the United States.

coat 1. A piece of clothing with sleeves, used especially in cold weather. You wear a *coat* over other clothing.
2. A thing that covers. We gave the boat a *coat* of red paint.

cob The hard center of an ear of corn. You don't eat the corn *cob.*

coat

cobweb   The web that a spider makes.

cocoa   A drink made from a chocolate powder and hot milk or water.

coconut   The large, hard nut of a tree that grows in warm climates. The white part inside a *coconut* is good to eat.

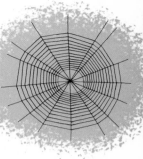

cobweb

cocoon   A covering spun by some insects. A caterpillar comes out of its *cocoon* as a moth or a butterfly.

cod   A food fish that lives in salt water.

code   A system of secret signs or writing. Our club *code* uses numbers in place of letters.

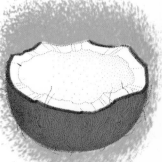

coconut half

coffee   1. The beans of a plant that grows in warm lands.
2. A drink made from these beans after they are roasted and ground.

coin   A piece of metal money made by a government. A quarter is a larger *coin* than a dime.

cold
coldly   Having a low temperature; not warm. Ice is *cold.* The winter wind blew *coldly.*

cocoon

collar   1. The part of a shirt or other piece of clothing that goes around the neck.
2. A strip of leather or other material placed around the neck of an animal.

collect
collected
collecting   1. To gather; to pick up. The campers had to *collect* wood for a fire.
2. To save as a hobby. Dave *collects* old coins. I have a doll *collection.*

college   A school for people who have finished high school.

collie   A large dog with long hair.

collie

Pink	
Red	
Orange	
Yellow	
Green	
Blue	
Violet	
Purple	
Brown	
Black	
Gray	
White	

colors

colonist — A person who lives in a colony or settlement. A *colonist* helps to settle a new land.

colony
colonial — 1. A group of people who settle a new area for their country. A *colony* of men and women landed at Plymouth Rock. Life was often difficult in *colonial* days.
2. An area under the control of a foreign country. England's first *colony* in America was Virginia.

color — Red, yellow, blue, or any similar quality that we see in things.

color
colored
coloring — To put a color on something. Joan used crayons to *color* her drawing orange and green.

colorful — Full of color; having many bright colors. Ann's red and blue dress was very *colorful.*

colt — A young horse, donkey, or similar animal.

column — 1. A row of words, numbers, or other things. I added up a *column* of numbers.
2. A tall post that holds up part of a building.
3. A special section of a newspaper. Dad reads the sports *column.*

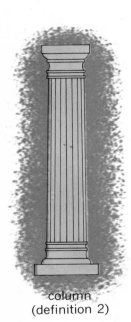

column
(definition 2)

comb — 1. A device used to arrange your hair and keep it neat.
2. A red crest on the head of a bird, especially a rooster.

comb
combed
combing — 1. To arrange the hair with a comb.
2. To search thoroughly. We will *comb* the field for our lost ball.

come
came
coming — 1. To move closer; to approach. Please *come* here.
2. To arrive or attend. Will Ted *come* to the party?

3. To reach. The water will not *come* to the top of the dam.

4. To happen; to take place. The picnic will *come* after school.

comedy
comedian

A play or show that is funny. A *comedy* has a happy ending. A *comedian* is a person who makes us laugh.

comfort
comfortable

A good feeling of being free from pain or worry. Bob likes the *comfort* of taking a warm bath. The bed was *comfortable.*

comic book

A magazine that has cartoons or comics.

comics

Funny or interesting stories shown in a series of drawings or cartoons, usually in newspapers or magazines.

comma

A punctuation mark (,) used in writing to show that a short wait or stop is needed.

command

1. An order. My puppy obeys my *command.*
2. Control. The captain is in *command* of his ship.

command
commanded
commanding

1. To give an order to. A policeman can *command* a driver to stop his car.
2. To be in control of. The pilot *commands* an airplane. A general is the *commander* of an army.

committee

A group of people who do a special job. Bill is on a *committee* to plan for the school fair.

common
commonly

1. Frequent or usual. Bread is a *common* food. Boats *commonly* sail up the river.
2. Owned or used by many people. The park is the *common* property of all citizens.

community

A group of people who live in the same area. Our *community* had a paper drive.

comb

company

1. A business. My uncle's *company* sells autos.
2. Guests; visitors. We had *company* at our house on Sunday.

compare
compared
comparing

To show how things are alike or different. We heard Jim *compare* a zebra with a horse.

compass

A device that shows direction, usually with a needle pointing north.

compass

complain
complained
complaining

To find fault or say why you are unhappy. Sue always *complains* about the cafeteria food.

complete
completed
completing

To finish. Did you *complete* your homework?

complete
completely

Whole; entire. We have a *complete* set of checkers. The ground was *completely* covered with snow.

concert

A musical performance, usually with many musicians or singers.

conch

A curved, cone-shaped seashell.

concrete

A building material made by mixing cement, water, and sand or gravel.

conch

condition

The physical state of a person or thing. Our new school is in good *condition.*

conductor

1. A person who sells or collects tickets on a train.
2. The person who leads a band, orchestra, or choir.
3. A material through which electricity, heat, or sound passes. Copper wire is a good *conductor* of electricity.

cone
1. A shape that is round at one end and pointed at the other.
2. A cake-like holder that can be filled with ice cream. An ice-cream *cone* is round on top and pointed on the bottom.

confuse
confused
confusing
1. To mix up a person's thoughts; to cause a lack of order. Did the puzzle *confuse* you? The storm caused *confusion* among the sailors.
2. To mistake. Did you *confuse* Jan with her twin sister, Jean?

cones

congress
A group of people that makes laws for a nation. *Congress* will vote on the new law.

connect
connected
connecting
To join; to put together. Let me *connect* the lawn sprinkler to the hose. The *connection* between railroad cars is very strong.

conservation
The protecting of or caring for nature. Stopping forest fires is part of *conservation.*

consonant
A letter of the alphabet other than "a," "e," "i," "o," or "u." The letter "b" is a *consonant.*

construct
constructed
constructing
To build; to make; to put together. Dad's company *constructs* houses. I used rocks and sand in my *construction* of a castle.

construction paper
Colored paper, a little stiffer than writing paper but not as stiff as cardboard.

contain
contained
containing
1. To hold. The box *contains* apples. Mother poured milk into a glass *container.*
2. To be partly made of. The soup *contains* chicken and rice.

content
Not needing or asking for anything more.

contents
(Plural) Everything that something contains. What are the *contents* of that package?

contest A game or test; a fight. Who won the spelling *contest?*

continent One of the earth's seven biggest land masses. I live on the **continent** of North America.

continue
continued
continuing
To go on with; to keep going or moving. Did the players **continue** the game during the rain?

continuous
continuously
Without stopping. The band played **continuous** music for two hours. Waves hit the shore **continuously.**

control
controlled
controlling
1. To command; to be in charge of. The captain **controls** the submarine.
2. To hold back. I could not **control** my laughter.

cook Someone who prepares meals in a home or restaurant.

cook
cooked
cooking
To prepare food by heating. Dad will **cook** pancakes for breakfast.

continent

cookie A small, flat sweet cake or biscuit.

cool
cooled
cooling
To lower the temperature of; to chill. The ice will **cool** your soda.

cool Slightly cold. A **cool** breeze made me shiver.

copper A reddish-brown metal with many uses. A penny contains **copper.**

copy Something that looks like something else. The clerk gave us a **copy** of the bill.

copy
copied
copying
To make a copy of; to follow a model or do the same thing. We will **copy** our words from the board.

cord A heavy string. *Cord* is made by twisting several strings together.

cork 1. A very light material made from the bark of some trees. *Cork* will float on water.
2. A stopper for a bottle, made of cork, rubber, or other material.

corks

corn A plant grown for food, or the kernels from this plant. Both people and animals eat *corn.*

corn bread A kind of bread made from dried, ground corn. *Corn bread* and beans are good together.

corner 1. A place where two flat surfaces or lines meet, such as two edges of paper. Put your name in the right-hand *corner* of the paper.
2. The place where two or more streets meet or come together. The school is at the *corner* of Pine and Maple Streets.

correct
correctly Right; exact; proper. Do you know the *correct* time? Mary set the table *correctly.*

corridor A long hall with doors and many rooms opening into it. Do not run in the school *corridor!*

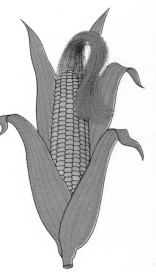

corn on the cob

cost The price; the amount paid for something. The *cost* of the newspaper was ten cents.

costume Clothing not worn every day; a special kind of dress or suit. We wore Halloween *costumes* to the party.

cot A narrow bed, especially one that can be folded up when not in use. There is a *cot* in the nurse's office.

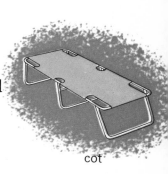

cot

cottage A small house or a vacation cabin. Mark's family went to a *cottage* by the lake.

cotton

cotton	The fluffy white material that grows on certain plants. Cloth can be made from *cotton.*
couch	A sofa; a padded piece of furniture on which three or four people can sit. The *couch* was in the living room.
cough *coughed* *coughing*	To make a noise by forcing air up from the lungs. I *cough* when I have a bad cold.
couldn't	A short form of "could not." Jane *couldn't* go to the movies.
council	A group of people who meet to pass laws, give advice, or govern. Our city is run by a mayor and a city *council.*
counselor	1. A leader in a camp or school; a person who gives advice. The *counselor* taught the campers to swim. 2. A lawyer.
count *counted* *counting*	1. To name numbers in their proper order. Can you *count* from 1 to 1,000? 2. To add up or find a total of. Please *count* the children in our room.
countdown	The act of counting backward toward an exact moment. "10 . . . 9 . . . 8 . . . 7 . . ." went the *countdown* for the launching of the rocket.
counter	A table-like surface on which food is prepared or served. A *counter* is also used to show off goods in a store.
country	1. A nation. My *country* is the United States of America. 2. An open area; not the city or town. Farmers live in the *country.*
county	A division of a state. Ohio has 88 *counties.*

couple
1. Two; a pair. Dad has a *couple* of tickets to the ball game.
2. A man and a woman. Mr. and Mrs. Smith were the first *couple* to arrive.

coupon
A slip of paper that can be exchanged for something. The *coupon* in the newspaper was good for a free ticket.

courage
A lack of fear. Christopher Columbus had *courage* to sail in small ships.

courageous
Brave; not afraid. The pioneers were *courageous* people.

course
1. A subject studied in school. Math is our first *course.*
2. A path or route. The hunters followed a winding *course* through the woods.

court
1. A place where people are brought before a judge. The burglar will be taken to *court.*
2. A palace where a king or queen lives.
3. An area laid out for certain games. There is a tennis *court* at the playground.

cousin
A relative. Any child of your aunt or uncle is your *cousin.*

cover
A thing that is put on top of or around something else. The lid is a *cover* for the pan.

cover
covered
covering
1. To place on top of or around. Mother will *cover* the baby with a blanket.
2. To hide. Clouds *cover* the sun on a dark day.

cow
1. A grown female animal in the cattle family. Our milk comes from *cows.*
2. A grown female of certain other animals. A female elephant is called a *cow.*

COW

cowboy
A man who takes care of cattle on a ranch or range.

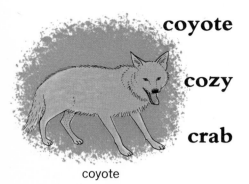

coyote

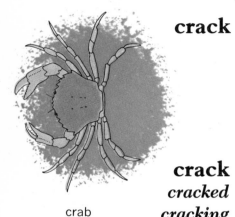

crab

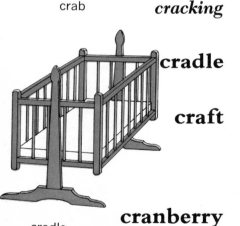

cradle

coyote A dog-like animal that looks like a small wolf. Many *coyotes* live in the western United States.

cozy Snug; warm and comfortable. A fire in the fireplace makes a room *cozy* on a cold night.

crab 1. A small sea animal with a shell-like covering. Some *crabs* are good to eat.
2. A cranky person. Mr. Todd was a *crab* who never smiled.

crack 1. A long, narrow opening. The wind blew through a *crack* in the window.
2. A very thin break. The cup had a *crack* in it.
3. A sudden loud noise. The tree limb broke with a *crack.*

crack
cracked
cracking
1. To break or split without separating. The thin ice will *crack* if you step on it.
2. To break open with a loud noise. The squirrel was *cracking* the nuts.

cradle A bed for a small baby. A *cradle* can usually be rocked.

craft 1. A skill or art; work having to do with skills or arts. Making jewelry is a *craft.*
2. A vehicle, particularly one that moves through water or air. My canoe is a leaky *craft.*

cranberry A red berry used to make jelly.

cranky Hard to please; having a bad temper.

crash
crashed
crashing
To fall, hit, or break with a loud noise. The tree *crashed* to the ground.

crater The hollow in the top of a volcano, or a hole that looks like it. The astronauts explored *craters* on the moon.

crawl   1. To creep; to move on hands and knees. Babies learn to *crawl* before they walk.
2. To move slowly. The cars *crawled* along during the snowstorm.

crayon   A stick of colored wax. *Crayons* are used for drawing and coloring.

crayons

crazy   Foolish; not making sense. That's a *crazy* way to spend money!

cream   The part of milk that is thick and can be made into butter. Whipped *cream* is good on cake.

creamy   Smooth; like cream. The cake was covered with a *creamy* icing.

create
created
creating
To make. A good artist can *create* great pictures.

credit   1. A promise that someone will pay later. The store lets us buy groceries on *credit.*
2. Praise, honor. The team gave Jack *credit* for winning the game.

creek   A small stream; a brook. The *creek* overflows when there is a heavy rain.

creep
crept
creeping
1. To move on hands and knees. A baby will *creep* across the floor.
2. To move slowly and quietly. I *crept* into my seat because the movie had already started.

crescent   The curved shape of a new moon.

crest   1. A grouping of feathers or hair on top of an animal's head. The blue jay has a pointed *crest.*
2. The highest point of something. Jim stood on the *crest* of the hill.

crescent

crib

crew The workers who run a ship, plane, or train; people who work together. The repair *crew* worked on the broken telephone wire.

crib A baby's bed with high sides.

cricket An insect that looks like a small grasshopper. The *cricket* makes a chirping sound.

crime
criminal An act that is against the law. It is a *crime* to steal. The *criminal* was sent to jail for robbing a store.

cripple A lame person or animal. The *cripple* walked with a cane.

crocodile A large reptile that lives in and around water in hot lands. A *crocodile* is somewhat like an alligator.

cricket

crooked
crookedly 1. Bent; not straight. Mary drew a *crooked* line on the paper. The path ran *crookedly* across the field.
2. Not honest or truthful. A burglar lives a *crooked* life.

crop A harvest; a farm product that is gathered at the end of a season. The farmer has a good corn *crop* this year.

cross 1. The figure (+) formed when one line passes over another.
2. An upright post with a second piece crossing it near the top. There is a *cross* on the church steeple.

cross
crossed
crossing To go from one side of to the other. Be careful when you *cross* the street!

crow

crow 1. A large black bird with a loud call.
2. The call of a rooster. The *crow* of the rooster woke the farmer.

crowd   A large number of people in one place. A *crowd* gathered to watch the parade.

crowd
crowded
crowding   To push close together; to force or press. Please do not *crowd* onto the elevator.

crown   A fancy band worn on the head. The king's *crown* has many jewels.

crown

cruel
cruelly   Mean; not kind. Jack killed the *cruel* giant. The boys teased Jane *cruelly.*

crumb   A very small piece; a bit. You dropped a *crumb* of cake on the floor.

crush
crushed
crushing   To press or squeeze out of shape or into small pieces. You can *crush* an eggshell easily.

Cub Scout emblem

crust   1. The pastry shell of a pie.
2. A hard outside layer. The stale bread had a hard *crust.*

cry   A shout; a loud call. We heard the *cry* for help.

cry
cried
crying   1. To weep. Babies *cry* quite often.
2. To call out. "Hello!" *cried* Tom.

lion cubs

crystal   1. An evenly shaped structure formed by certain materials when they harden.
2. Very fine clear glass. Some drinking glasses are made of *crystal.*

cub   A young animal in such families as the bear or lion.

cube   A solid square block with six equal sides.

Cub Scout   A young Boy Scout. A boy may become a *Cub Scout* when he is eight years old.

cuckoo

cuckoo   A bird with a call that sounds like "coo-coo."

cucumber   A crisp green and white salad vegetable.

cuff   1. A band or fold of a sleeve that goes around the wrist. John's shirt has buttons on the *cuffs.* 2. The fold at the bottom of a trouser leg.

cup   A container used for drinking and measuring. Mary drinks milk from a *cup.*

cupboard   A closet or cabinet; a place where things are stored. The dishes are in the *cupboard.*

cure
cured
curing   To make well; to return to health. Doctors work to *cure* sick people.

curious
curiosity   1. Very interested; full of questions. We were *curious* about what was in the package. The ball of string filled the cat with *curiosity.* 2. Strange; odd. An octopus is a *curious* animal.

curl
curly   A curved shape; a twist or circle of hair. Jane cut off a *curl* with the scissors. The pig has a *curly* tail.

curtain   A cloth covering for a window or other opening. The *curtains* are made of lace.

curve
curved
curving   To bend; to turn slightly. Rivers *curve* as they flow to the sea.

cushion   A pillow; a case filled with soft material. The sofa has three green *cushions* on it.

cut   A rip or tear; a break in the skin.

cut
cut
cutting   To divide or separate into pieces with a sharp tool. We *cut* the paper with scissors.

cute   Pretty. Mother took a *cute* picture of the baby.

cyclone   A very bad storm with high winds. The *cyclone* destroyed many buildings.

cucumbers

curtains

Dd

dad   A father. My mother and *dad* are at home.

daddy   A father; dad.

daily   Made or done each day; every day. We get a *daily* newspaper.

dairy   A place that makes or sells butter, cheese, and other milk products.

daisy   A flower, with a yellow center and white or yellow petals, that often grows wild.

daisy

dam   A strong wall built to hold back flowing water. A new *dam* was built on the river.

damage   Harm or injury. The storm caused great *damage* to our barn roof.

damp   Moist; a little wet. My jacket was *damp* after the light rain.

dam

dance   1. Movement in time to music. Our class did a square *dance.*
2. A party for dancing. The school had a *dance* on Friday.

dance
danced
dancing   To move in time to the sound of music. Did the boys *dance* at the party?

dandelion   A weed with bright, yellow flowers.

dandelion

danger
1. A chance that harm may happen. John knows the *danger* of skating on thin ice.
2. Something that might cause harm. Fog is a *danger* for ships.

dangerous
Running a chance of danger; not safe. Playing with matches is *dangerous.*

dare
dared
daring
1. To have courage to do something. Did the sailors *dare* to sail through the storm?
2. To ask someone to prove that he is brave. I *dare* you to ride the wild horse.

dark
darkness
Without light; not bright. The basement was *dark.* At night, the ship sailed through the *darkness.*

dash
dashed
dashing
1. To run or move quickly. We saw the dog *dash* after the rabbit.
2. To splash or sprinkle. The fireman *dashed* water on the small fire.

date
1. The time or day when something happens. What is the *date* of the next game?
2. A social meeting with a friend. My sister enjoyed her *date* with her boyfriend.
3. A small fruit that grows on some palm trees.

dates

daughter
A father's or mother's female child. Mr. Brown has a son and a *daughter,* Ann.

dawn
Very early morning; the beginning of daylight.

day
1. The time between sunrise and sunset. It is light outside during the *day.*
2. A period of 24 hours. Most months have 31 *days.*

daylight
1. The light from the sun; daytime. We hiked during the *daylight.*
2. Dawn. The farmer gets up at *daylight.*

daytime
The hours between sunrise and sunset.

dead Without life. The mouse in the trap is *dead.*

deal 1. A price. The salesman gave Dad a good *deal* on the new car.
2. An amount. Dave spends a great *deal* of money on comic books.

dear 1. Loved; precious. The mother kissed her *dear* child. Jane loves her father *dearly.*
dearly 2. Expensive; not cheap. The steaks were *dear.*

death The end of life. Susan tried not to cry at the *death* of her dog.

December The twelfth month of the year.

decide To make a choice or make up your mind. Did you *decide* to go or stay?
decided
deciding

deck 1. The floor of a ship. The sailor walked across the *deck.*
2. A pack of playing cards.

declare To say; to announce. Bob *declared* that he was saving his money to buy a bicycle.
declared
declaring

deed An act; something done. Cleaning up litter is one of our club's good *deeds.*

deep 1. Far below the surface. Far back. The rabbit lived in a *deep* hole.
2. With a strong, low sound. Uncle George spoke in a *deep* voice.
3. Dark. The coat was *deep* green.

deer A large, fast animal that lives in forests. Only the male *deer* has antlers.

deer

defeat To win a victory over. Did our team *defeat* theirs?
defeated
defeating

defend
defended
defending

To protect; to guard against harm. The soldiers will **defend** the town from the enemy. Is there a **defense** against the disease?

definition

A meaning; an explanation. What is the **definition** of that long word?

delicate

1. Easily broken or harmed; not strong. The glass vase is very **delicate.**
2. Of fine or pleasing quality. The rose has a **delicate** smell.

delicious

Very pleasant to taste. The cake was **delicious.**

delight
delighted
delighting

To please or make happy. The gift will **delight** the children.

deliver
delivered
delivering

1. To hand over; to give over. The messenger will **deliver** the package to Uncle Ed. What was in today's **delivery** of mail?
2. To speak. Did you hear the mayor **deliver** his speech?

demand
demanded
demanding

1. To ask boldly for; to give an order for. The workers will **demand** higher pay.
2. To need; to call for. Doing a puzzle **demands** hard thinking.

democracy
democratic

A nation that is ruled by its citizens. In a **democracy** adults have the right to vote. In America we have a **democratic** government.

den

1. A place where wild animals rest or live. The bear's **den** is a cave.
2. A quiet room for reading or recreation.

den

denominator

The bottom number in a fraction. In "$\frac{2}{5}$" "5" is the **denominator.**

dentist

A doctor who examines and cares for your teeth.

department A part of a business where certain work is done. Mother worked in the jewelry *department* of a big store.

depend
depended
depending To trust; to count on. The players *depend* on the coach for instructions. The settlers were *dependent* upon the stream for water.

depth The distance from the surface to the bottom. The *depth* of the pool is four feet.

describe
described
describing To tell about; to tell how something looks or what it is like. We heard Ellen *describe* her new dress. I read a *description* of the Grand Canyon.

desert A place where little or no rain falls. A *desert* is often sandy.

deserve
deserved
deserving To have a right to. Alice *deserves* the prize for her excellent poem.

design 1. A plan or drawing used as a guide for making something. The workman studied the *design* for the new house.
2. A pattern or arrangement. Jane's skirt has a *design* of colored stripes.

desire A wish. We have a *desire* to travel.

desk A piece of furniture at which you can write, study, or work.

dessert A sweet food eaten at the end of a meal. Pie is my favorite *dessert.*

destroy
destroyed
destroying To ruin; to wreck. The flood will *destroy* the crops.

detergent A cleaning substance used in place of soap.

device An instrument or invention to help you gain a certain result or perform a certain act.

dew Small drops of water that form on things outdoors at night. In the morning, the grass was covered with *dew.*

dial A flat, round device with numbers or letters on it, used to show information or control something. Jim turned the TV *dial* to get a different program.

diamond 1. A very valuable jewel that is clear and colorless. Mother's ring has a *diamond* on it.
2. A baseball field; a shape like that of a baseball field.

diamond

dictionary A book that lists words and their meanings. You are reading a *dictionary* right now.

didn't A short form of "did not." Ann *didn't* go to the party.

die
died
dying
To stop living. Plants need water or they will *die.*

diet 1. Our usual food and drink. You should have milk in your *diet.*
2. A special variety of foods selected for health reasons. Dad lost five pounds on his *diet.*

difference A way in which things are not the same. What is the *difference* between a horse and a donkey?

different
differently
Not alike; not the same. A football and a basketball are *different.* Men and women dress *differently.*

difficult
difficulty
Hard to do; not easy. Chopping down trees is *difficult* work. Mother had *difficulty* carrying the heavy box.

dig
dug
digging

To turn over earth or make a hole. Bill will **dig** for worms with a shovel.

digest
digested
digesting

To turn food, inside the body, into a form that can be used by the body for health and energy.

dim
dimly

Having little light; not clear or bright. The sky became **dim** after sunset. The cabin was **dimly** lit by one lantern.

dime

A coin worth ten cents.

dine
dined
dining

To eat a meal, especially dinner. The guests will **dine** in the cafeteria.

dinner

The main meal of the day. On Sundays we eat **dinner** about noon.

dinosaur

One of a group of huge reptiles that lived on earth many millions of years ago.

dip
dipped
dipping

To put into a liquid and take out quickly. Please **dip** my ice-cream cone in chocolate syrup.

dinosaur

direct
directly

Straight. The bird flew in a **direct** line to her nest. The doctor drove **directly** to the hospital.

direction

1. The act of guiding or leading. Our team is under the **direction** of Coach Harris.
2. Instruction. Follow the **directions** on the box of cake mix.
3. The point or way to which something faces or moves. This bus goes north, in the **direction** of the airport.

dirt
dirty

1. Soil. We covered our seeds with **dirt.**
2. Dust, soil, or anything that makes things not clean. Dave washed the **dirt** from his bike. Susan brushed her **dirty** shoes.

disappear
disappeared
disappearing

To move out of sight; to vanish. The magician made the rabbit *disappear.*

discover
discovered
discovering

To find; to see or learn about for the first time. Astronomers may *discover* a new planet. The *discovery* of America by Columbus was in 1492.

discuss
discussed
discussing

To talk or write about; to speak together about. Bill and Dave like to *discuss* baseball. Mother and Dad often hold *discussions* about money.

disease

An illness; an unhealthy condition. Chickenpox is a *disease.*

dish

1. A container in which to hold or serve food. You will find a *dish* in the cupboard.
2. A food. Apple pie is a delicious *dish.*

dislike
disliked
disliking

To have no liking for. I *dislike* beets.

disobey
disobeyed
disobeying

To fail to obey; to refuse to follow orders. Did Jim *disobey* his parents by staying out late? Jack was punished for his *disobedience.*

distance

The amount of space separating two things. It is a long *distance* from the earth to the sun.

distant

Far-off; not close. The moon is *distant* from the earth.

district

A division or section; an area. Dad's office is in the business *district* of the city.

ditch

A long, narrow opening dug in the ground. Water from the field drains into a *ditch.*

dive
dived, dove
diving

To go into the water headfirst. Water birds *dive* into the ocean to catch fish.

divide
divided
dividing

1. To separate into parts. Let's **divide** the candy bar into three pieces.
2. In arithmetic, to find how many times one number will go into another. Jane **divided** three into six.

dive

dividend

The number that is being divided or separated into parts. If you divide "10" by "5," the **dividend** is "10."

division

1. The act of dividing one number by another. Our teacher gave us four problems in **division**.
2. A section or part. Mr. Smith is with the sales **division** of his company.

divisor

In arithmetic, the number by which another number is divided. If "10" is divided by a **divisor** of "5," the answer is "2."

do
did
done
doing

1. To perform; to finish. Please **do** your homework quickly.
2. A word often used in asking questions. **Do** you know what time it is?

dock

A platform for loading and unloading boats. A **dock** is built out into the water.

dogwood
blossoms

doctor

A person trained to care for people's health. Mother takes the baby to the **doctor** once a month.

doesn't

A short form of "does not." Jim **doesn't** answer the telephone.

dog

A four-legged animal usually kept as a pet. Our **dog** barks at visitors.

dogwood

A tree with pink or white blossoms.

doll

A toy made to look like a person. Jane made a dress for her **doll.**

doll

dollar   A unit of money; 100 cents. Jane paid one *dollar* for her pencil case.

dome   A rounded roof. The Capitol building in Washington, D.C., has a *dome.*

donkey   An animal that looks like a small horse. A *donkey* has long ears.

don't   A short form for "do not." "I *don't* think that I can go," said Mary.

door   1. A flat piece of firm material used to open and close an entrance. Please open the *door.*
2. An opening in a wall through which you can go.

donkey

doorway   The frame of a door; an opening or entrance to a room, house, or other building. "Do not block the *doorway,*" said the teacher.

dot   A very small round mark or spot. The period at the end of this sentence is a *dot.*

double   1. Made for two. The bed was a *double* bed, big enough for two people.
2. Twice as much as usual in size or amount. May I have a *double* helping of ice cream?

dough   A soft mixture used to make bread or pastry. *Dough* is used to make a pie crust.

doughnut   A sweet, fried cake, sometimes with a hole in the middle. I like a jelly *doughnut.*

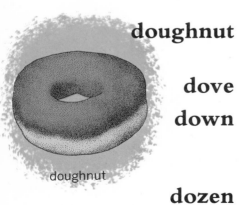

dove   A kind of bird; a pigeon.

down   1. To a lower place. Come *down* to the cellar.
2. In a direction along. We went *down* the street.

doughnut

dozen   A group or set of twelve. Andy bought a *dozen* doughnuts.

drag
dragged
dragging

To pull along. Sam helped Bill *drag* the sled up the hill.

dragon

A make-believe animal that looks like a large fire-breathing lizard with large claws.

dove

drain
drained
draining

To pour off; to empty. The water in the road will *drain* into the ditch.

draw
drew
drawn
drawing

1. To make a picture; to make lines with a pencil, crayon, or chalk. Jean will *draw* on the board.
2. To pull or drag; to move toward you. Please *draw* up a chair and sit down.

drawer

A box-like part of a piece of furniture; a section that slides in and out. The desk *drawer* is open.

dream
dreamed
dreaming

To have thoughts or pictures in the mind while asleep. Did you *dream* last night?

dress

1. A piece of clothing worn by girls and women. Mary got a new party *dress.*
2. Clothing; an outfit. You can tell a clown by his funny *dress.*

dragon

dress
dressed
dressing

1. To put on clothing. Firemen *dress* quickly when the fire alarm sounds.
2. To bandage. The doctor *dressed* Ann's cut.

drift
drifted
drifting

1. To be carried by wind or water; to float away. The boat will *drift* without an anchor.
2. To pile up because of the wind. The heavy snow *drifted* and blocked the highway.

drill
drilled
drilling

1. To use a tool to make a hole. Can you *drill* a hole in this board?
2. To practice by repeating many times. We *drill* our spelling words every day.

drink
drank
drunk
drinking

To put liquid into the mouth and swallow it. We **drink** milk for lunch.

drip
dripped
dripping

To fall one drop at a time. Water began to **drip** through the hole in the roof.

drive

1. A ride, as in a car. We went for a **drive** in the country.
2. A driveway.

drive
drove
driven
driving

1. To steer and operate a car. Many people **drive** to work. Uncle Ted is a good **driver.**
2. To cause to move; to force. Ed used a hammer to **drive** the nail into the wall.

dromedary

dromedary

A camel with only one hump.

drop
dropped
dropping

To fall; to let fall. The ripe apples **drop** from the tree.

drown
drowned
drowning

To die because water keeps one from breathing. People **drown** when water gets into their lungs.

drug

A medicine; a substance given to a person by a doctor. A **drug** can help cure an illness. Some **drugs** are harmful.

drum
drummer

A round, hollow musical instrument with ends covered with skin or thin material. The **drummer** banged on his **drum.**

dry
dried
drying

To remove moisture from; to get rid of water. Wet clothes will **dry** in the sun.

dry

Without moisture; not wet. Mother took the **dry** clothes off the line.

drums

duck One kind of bird that swims. A *duck* has webbed feet.

dull 1. Dim; not bright or shiny. The silver spoon had grown *dull.*
2. Not sharp. It is hard to cut wood with a *dull* ax.
3. Boring; not interesting. Janet didn't like the *dull* story.

duck

dumb 1. Silent; not able to speak. The horse is called a *dumb* animal.
2. Stupid; foolish. John told us a *dumb* joke.

dummy 1. A figure or shape made to look like a person. The *dummy* in the window had on a plaid suit.
2. A foolish or stupid person. Tim felt like a *dummy* when he dropped the ball.

dump
dumped
dumping To drop all at once. The trucks will *dump* gravel on the road.

une buggy A car with very wide tires for driving in sand. We rode in a *dune buggy* at the seashore.

during Throughout; within the time of. *During* the entire game, it was raining.

dust Very small bits of dirt. The wind blew *dust* into our eyes.

dusty Covered with dust or fine dirt. The tabletop was *dusty.*

duty A task or job. His *duty* was to shovel the snow.

dwarf A person, plant, or animal that is smaller than others of the same kind; a midget. The *dwarf* was only three feet tall.

dwarf

Ee

eagle

ear

each   Every single person or thing in a group. **Each** of the boys made a map.

eager
eagerly   Wanting very much; impatient. Jack is **eager** to ride his new bike. Ann opened her gift **eagerly**.

eagle   A large bird that eats other animals. An **eagle** has sharp claws and a strong beak.

ear   **1.** One of the two body organs with which you hear. You have an **ear** on each side of your head.
2. A plant part on which corn grows.

early   **1.** Before the usual time. The teachers arrived at school **early**.
2. First; near the beginning. The **early** part of our trip was exciting.

earn
earned
earning   **1.** To get as pay. My brother **earns** three dollars an hour.
2. To deserve. Jack will **earn** praise for his part in the play.

earth   The ground; soil; land. The man dug his shovel into the **earth**.

Earth   The planet on which we live. See page 222.

earthquake A great shaking of an area of land. An *earthquake* made the building fall down.

east The direction from which the sun rises; the opposite of "west." See picture at **compass.**

easy Not difficult. Picking flowers is an *easy* job.

eat
ate, eaten
eating To chew and swallow. I will *eat* a hamburger for lunch.

echo A sound that repeats another sound, made when the first sound bounces back from a surface. The *echo* of Tom's voice came from the tunnel.

ecology The study of how plants and animals live together in an environment. *Ecology* helps us to understand why some plants and animals live only in certain places.

edge A border; the end of a flat surface. Mother put lace along the *edges* of her scarf.

editor A person in charge of the way a book, magazine, or newspaper is written. The *editor* asked the writer to make the story shorter.

education The teaching and learning of information or ideas. It takes years of *education* to become a doctor.

effect A result of some action. A flood was one *effect* of the heavy rains.

effort A try; the use of strength or energy. Tom made an *effort* to climb the tree.

egg A kind of body from which the young of birds, insects, reptiles, and fish hatch. The *eggs* of birds and most reptiles have hard, thin shells.

egg

eight   A number; 8. One more than 7 and one less than 9. See page 199.

eighteen   A number; 18. One more than 17 and one less than 19. See page 199.

eighty   A number; 80. See page 199.

either   A word used with "or" to show a choice between one thing and another. You can go *either* to the museum or to the movie.

elbow   The place where your arm bends. Your *elbow* joins the upper part of your arm to the lower part.

elephant

election   A method of choosing leaders by voting. The senator won the *election* by thousands of votes.

electric
electrical   Run by electricity. We cook on an *electric* stove. A break in the *electrical* wiring made the light go out.

electricity   A kind of energy used to run machines and to provide heat and light. *Electricity* makes a light bulb glow.

elephant   The largest land animal. An *elephant* has a long tube-like nose (called a trunk) and two long tusks.

elevator   1. A small moving platform or room that lifts or lowers persons or things from one floor to another in a building.
2. A building where grain is stored.

eleven   A number; 11. One more than 10 and one less than 12. See page 199.

elf   A dwarf or fairy. An *elf* stole the magic ring from the princess. The plural of *elf* is *elves*.

elm   A tall shade tree with long, curved branches.

elf

else
1. Other thing; other. What *else* is there for lunch?
2. Otherwise. Run, or *else* you will be late.

elsewhere
In another place. Look *elsewhere* for your book.

emblem
An object or picture used as the special sign of a certain group, thing, or idea. You will find the Girl Scout *emblem* on page 123.

emergency
A situation that needs special or fast action. The fire caused an *emergency* at the school.

empty
emptied
emptying
To remove the contents of; to pour out. Did you *empty* the waste basket?

elm

ncyclopedia
A book or set of books that tells about many things. I read about dinosaurs in my *encyclopedia.*

end
ended
ending
1. To be finished; to be complete. School will *end* in June.
2. To finish. Our teacher *ended* the lesson.

enemy
A person or thing that is not friendly or acts in a harmful way.

energy
Power; the strength to do something. You get your *energy* from food.

engine
1. A machine that supplies power. The car's *engine* makes the wheels turn.
2. A machine that pulls a train; a railroad engine.

engineer
1. A person who runs a railroad engine.
2. A person who designs new structures. The *engineer* made plans to build a new bridge.

enjoy
enjoyed
enjoying
1. To like. Tim *enjoys* all sports.
2. To have or use with pleasure. I hope you will *enjoy* good weather on your trip.

enormous   Huge; very big. A whale is an *enormous* animal.

enough   In the amount or number that is needed. Did you have *enough* money?

enter
entered
entering   To go into; to come into. We saw Judy *enter* the library. The clown's *entry* made the children laugh.

entire
entirely   Whole; total; all. Did you finish the *entire* book? The room was *entirely* empty.

entrance   1. A doorway or place where you can enter. The *entrance* to the library is on Main Street. 2. A going or coming into. The king's *entrance* was greeted with cheers.

envelope   A paper covering in which a letter is sent.

environment   The area and conditions around a person or thing. The polar bear lives in a cold *environment.*

envelope

envy   A desire to own or have what someone else has. Jane felt *envy* at the sight of Ellen's new dress.

envy
envied
envying   To have a strong desire to own or have. The boys will *envy* Bob's ten-speed bike.

equal
equally   In the same number, quality, or amount; even. The two cakes are *equal* in size. Dad divided the candy *equally* among us.

equation   A statement showing that one amount equals another. An *equation* might state: $5 + 3 = 4 + 4$.

equator   An imaginary line that circles the earth exactly halfway between the North Pole and the South Pole.

equipment   Things that are needed for a certain activity. A rod and reel are fishing *equipment.*

erase
erased
erasing

To remove by rubbing out; to wipe away. Please *erase* the words on the blackboard.

eraser

Anything used to rub out marks. There is a red *eraser* on the end of my pencil.

erasers

erosion

A wearing away, as of soil by water. Heavy waves can cause *erosion* along the shore.

errand

A trip made to get or deliver something. Mother sent me on an *errand* to buy milk.

error

A mistake; something that is wrong. Jim made an *error* in subtraction.

escape
escaped
escaping

To get away; to get free. The prisoner tried to *escape* from jail.

especially

In a special way; just. Doris baked the cake *especially* for your party.

even

1. Steady. The horse ran at an *even* gallop.
2. Equal; in the same position. The two runners are *even* at the end of one mile.
3. Flat; level. The floor was *even*.
4. Able to be divided by two without anything being left over. Six is an *even* number.

evening

The end of the day and the early part of night. It becomes dark during the *evening*.

ever

1. At any time. Did you *ever* meet my Uncle Ed?
2. Always. Ellen is *ever* friendly.

every

1. Each one of the group. *Every* member of our class wants to win the art contest.
2. All that is possible. Tim had *every* chance to win the race.

everybody

Each person in the group; every person. *Everybody* in our room likes cake.

everyone Each person; every person. Has *everyone* a piece of paper?

everything All things. Pat's family lost *everything* in the fire.

everywhere In all places. We looked *everywhere* for the lost kitten.

exact
exactly Correct; just as it should be. The *exact* weight of the box is $6\frac{1}{4}$ pounds. Ed remembered the poem *exactly.*

exam A test or quiz at school.

examination A test of knowledge or skill.

examine
examined
examining To look at or study carefully. The dentist will *examine* your teeth.

example 1. A sample or model. This painting is a good *example* of a water color.
2. A problem in arithmetic.

excellent Very good; of the best quality. The movie was *excellent.*

except But. Ann likes all colors *except* blue.

excite
excited
exciting To stir up or cause strong feelings, such as joy or anger. The parade *excited* the children. Don showed his *excitement* by jumping up and down.

!

exclamation point

exclamation point A punctuation mark (!) used in writing after a statement of strong feeling or excitement. Look out for that car!

excuse A reason given to explain something. Do you have an *excuse* for being absent?

excuse
excused
excusing 1. To forgive. Please *excuse* me for being late.
2. To let go; to free, as from a duty. "I will *excuse* you from class," said the teacher.

exercise   1. An activity that makes your body healthy and strong. Running is good *exercise.*
2. An activity that helps you learn something. We have a spelling *exercise* for homework.

exit   A way out. The rear door of the school bus is used as an emergency *exit.*

expect
expected
expecting   To look forward to. I *expect* a package from Grandma on my birthday.

expensive   Costing much money. A car is *expensive.*

experience   1. A happening; something that happens to a person. We enjoyed the *experience* at the zoo.
2. Practice; time spent learning or doing. Ted's dad had four years of *experience* as a truck driver.

experiment   A test or trial to see if something works. The *experiment* proved that air takes up space.

explain
explained
explaining   To tell about; to make clear or easy to understand. Dad *explained* the rules of football.

explore
explored
exploring   To examine something not known; to travel in order to discover new things. The astronauts *explored* the moon. An astronaut is an *explorer.*

extra   More than is needed. This ticket to the play is an *extra* one.

extreme
extremely   In the highest amount. We have had *extreme* heat this summer. I am *extremely* hungry.

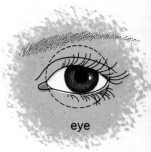

eye

eye   A body organ in the head of people and animals with which they can see. You have two **eyes.**

eyelash   One of the tiny hairs on the edge of an eyelid.

eyelid   The piece of skin that moves to cover the eye.

Ff

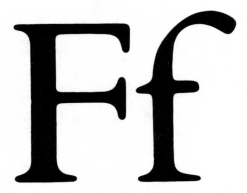

face

fable   A story or fairy tale that teaches a lesson.

face   1. The front part of the head, where the eyes, nose, and mouth are.
2. The front part of anything. The hours of the day are on the *face* of a clock.

fact   Something that is true. It is a *fact* that we breathe air.

factory   A place where things are made. My brother works in a *factory* where airplanes are made.

fade
faded
fading   1. To become lighter in color. Every time my blue jeans are washed, they *fade* a little.
2. To become weaker, or not as strong. Bill's voice *faded* as he walked away.

fail
failed
failing   1. Not to do as well as you could. I may *fail* my math test today.
2. To do poorly, or not as well as expected. Since we sold only two glasses, our lemonade stand was a *failure.*

faint
faintly   Weak. If I don't eat breakfast, I feel *faint.* The starved kitten cried *faintly.*

fair
fairly   1. Not too bad, but not very good. Your work is *fair,* but you can do better.
2. Pretty; beautiful. The prince fell in love with the *fair* princess.

3. Clear and bright. Today is sunny and *fair.*
4. Treating all equally. Dan divided the apples *fairly,* giving two to each of us.

fair
1. A show or festival, usually one with contests for animals, vegetables, flowers, and goods made by hand. A *fair* often has food stands and carnival rides.
2. A show or sale of some special things. We had a book *fair* at our school.

fairy
A small imaginary person thought to have magic powers.

fairy tale
A story about fairies or other imaginary creatures. The story of Cinderella is a *fairy tale.*

fairy

fake
False; not real or true. The *fake* fur looked real.

fall
fell
fallen
falling
1. To drop suddenly or tumble down. Someone will *fall* over the pipe.
2. To come down. Rain *falls* to the ground.

fall
The season between summer and winter.

false
Not right or true; not honest; fake. Is it true or *false* that Nan is moving away?

family
1. A group of people who are relatives. There are 16 aunts and uncles in our *family.*
2. A group of similar plants or animals.

famous
Very well known by many people. Sally's uncle is a *famous* circus clown.

fan
1. A machine or object that moves the air, often used to make air seem cooler.
2. A person who greatly likes a famous person or an activity such as a sport.

farm

faucet

fawn

fancy Especially nice; not plain. Jane's *fancy* dress was covered with flowers and designs.

far A long way. China is *far* away.

fare An amount of money needed to ride something. How much is the bus *fare* to the city?

farm An area of land used to raise food, other crops, or animals. Ted's uncle has a chicken *farm.*

farmer A person who owns or works on a farm.

farther More distant. Jim's house is *farther* from school than Ed's house.

fast Speedy; moving or doing quickly. Bill ran so *fast* that he won the race.

fasten
fastened
fastening 1. To close firmly; to lock. Please *fasten* the gate.
2. To tie. Don *fastened* his bicycle to the fence.

fat Round and plump.

father 1. A male parent.
2. A priest. The mass was said by *Father* Paul.

faucet A spout through which water flows into a sink or tub. The handle on a *faucet* turns water on and off.

fault A mistake; a weakness. It was your *fault* that we lost our money.

favor 1. A kind act. Jim did a *favor* for the old lady.
2. A treat or gift. The *favors* at the party were filled with candy.

favorite Most liked. Chocolate is my *favorite* ice cream flavor.

fawn A baby deer.

fear A frightened feeling; a worry. Some people have a *fear* of ghosts.

fear
feared
fearing

To be afraid of. Do you *fear* thunder and lightning?

fearful

1. Scared or frightened. I am *fearful* of barking dogs.
2. Frightening; causing fear. A tiger is a *fearful* sight.

feast

A large meal, often a holiday meal.

feat

An act of skill or daring. Saving the child from the bear was a brave *feat.*

feather

One of the soft, light growths that make up the coat of a bird.

feather

February

The second month of the year.

feed
fed
feeding

To give food to. I *feed* my cat three times every day.

feel
felt
feeling

1. To touch, especially with the hands. *Feel* the puppy's soft fur.
2. To experience. I *feel* happiness when someone smiles at me.

feeling

What you feel or sense inside yourself. Joy, fear, and sadness are different *feelings.*

fellow

A boy or man. Jack is a good *fellow.*

female

1. A girl or woman.
2. An animal that can have babies or lay eggs.

feminine

Having to do with girls and women; female.

fence

fence

A wall of wood or wire to keep something closed in or to keep other things out. We built a *fence* around the yard to keep the dog in.

fender

A metal covering over a wheel. A *fender* stops water from splashing up.

ferry A boat that regularly carries people and cars across a body of water, especially a lake or river. The *ferry* took us to an island.

festival A celebration. The spring *festival* marked the end of winter.

fever A high body temperature caused by illness. Jamie had a cold and a *fever.*

few A small number; not very many. We have only a *few* trees on our lot.

fib A lie that doesn't seem important. My sister told a *fib* about her age.

fiction A story in which the people and happenings are not true, but are thought up by the writer; a made-up story. *Charlotte's Web* is *fiction.*

fiddle A violin.

field 1. A piece of land used for growing crops and raising cattle.
2. A piece of land used for a sport. The boys went to the baseball *field.*

field trip A visit by a class to a place away from school, such as a museum, farm, or factory.

fierce Strong and wild. Wildcats are *fierce* animals.

fifteen A number; 15. One more than 14 and one less than 16. See page 199.

fifty A number; 50. See page 199.

fig A small fruit that has many small seeds. *Figs* are eaten fresh or dried.

fight A quarrel or battle.

ferry

figs

fight
fought
fighting

To battle; to quarrel. The dogs will **fight** for the bone.

figure

1. A shape. A circle is a **figure**.
2. A number that is not written in words. The number "12" is a **figure**.

file

1. A metal tool used to make things smooth or sharp. Susan smoothed her broken fingernail with a **file**.
2. A cabinet or other container used to keep papers in order. Mother keeps recipes in a **file**.

fill
filled
filling

1. To put as much into something as it can hold. I hope I can **fill** my bank with money.
2. To supply or give what is called for. **Fill** in the blank spaces with your name and address.

film

1. A movie. We saw a **film** on how to brush our teeth.
2. A special material that changes when light reaches it. The **film** in our camera makes 12 color pictures.
3. A thin layer or covering. There was a **film** of dust on the piano.

filth
filthy

Dirt and garbage. The trash can is the place for **filth**. Bill's clothes get **filthy** when he climbs trees.

fin

1. A thin, flat part on a fish's body used to balance it and help it move through the water.
2. Something that looks like a fish's fin, as on a car or airplane.

final
finally

Last. I like the **final** song in our music program. It's June, and school is **finally** out.

find
found
finding

To discover or come upon. Did you **find** your lost ring?

file

fin

fine
1. Good; excellent. He is a *fine* boy.
2. Not coarse; made of very small pieces.

fine
fined
fining
To punish a person for breaking a law or rule by making him pay money.
The judge will *fine* Dad ten dollars for parking by a fire hydrant.

finger
1. One of the five long, slender, jointed parts on your hand.
2. Something that looks like a finger. My gloves have *fingers.*

fingernail
A hard growth that protects the tips of your fingers.

finish
finished
finishing
To get through with; to complete. When you *finish* your work, you may do anything you want.

fire
Burning with flames, heat, and light. A forest *fire* can be started with only one match.

firecracker
A paper object holding powder that will blow up and make a loud noise when lit. *Firecrackers* can be very dangerous.

fire escape

fire drill
A practice that prepares you to know what to do in case of fire. We marched out of the school during the *fire drill.*

fire engine
A large truck with special equipment for fighting fires. Firemen ride on a *fire engine.*

fire escape
An outside staircase used as an exit when there is a fire.

firefly
A small beetle that makes a flashing light at night.

fireman
A person whose job is putting out fires.

fireplace
An open place, often at the bottom of a chimney, in which a fire can be made.

fireplace

fireproof Not able to catch on fire. The brick building is *fireproof.*

fire station A building that houses firemen and fire engines.

firewood Wood that is collected for burning. The farmer chopped *firewood* for the old stove.

fireworks Firecrackers or skyrockets. *Fireworks* are set off on the Fourth of July.

firm
firmly
1. Solid; not soft. Is the ice cream *firm* or is it melting?
2. Strong; not easily moved. The cowboy had a *firm* grip on the rope. Drive the stake *firmly* into the ground.

first Coming before all others. Jay was the *first* one to enter the classroom.

fish A kind of animal that lives in and can breathe under water. Many *fish* are important to man as food.

fish
fished
fishing
To catch or try to catch fish. Dad likes to *fish* in the lake.

fist A hand that is closed tightly in a ball. Don pounded his *fist* on the table.

fireworks

fit
fitted
fitting
To be the correct shape, size, or kind for. The small shoes did not *fit* Dad's large feet.

five A number; 5. One more than 4 and one less than 6. See page 199.

fish

fix
fixed
fixing
1. To repair. Did the man *fix* our leaking roof?
2. To get ready; to arrange. Let's *fix* lunch.

flag

flag
1. A piece of cloth with a colored design that stands for a nation, place, or group. The American *flag* has red and white stripes and, on a blue square, a white star for each state.
2. A piece of cloth used as a signal. The workman used a red *flag* to stop cars.

flair
A special skill; an ability. Susan has a *flair* for making people happy.

flake
A small, thin piece or bit of material. George picked a *flake* of dried paint from the wall.

flame
A blaze from a fire or burning object. The candle *flame* was yellow.

flap
flapped
flapping
To keep moving up and down or back and forth. Birds *flap* their wings in order to fly. The flag *flapped* in the wind.

flare
A bright light used as a signal. The *flare* at the airport guided the plane through the fog.

flash
A sudden streak of bright light. We saw a *flash* of lightning.

flash
flashed
flashing
To give off a sudden bright light or fire. Lightning will *flash* during a storm.

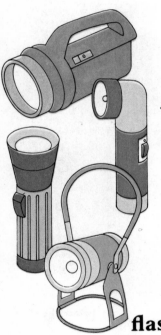

flashlights

flashlight
An electric light that you can carry in your hand.

flat
1. Level or even; not curved. The top of a desk is *flat.*
2. Stretched out. Jim fell *flat* on his back.
3. Out of tune. The singer sounded *flat.*

flavor
A taste or smell. Lemons have a sour *flavor.*

flea
A tiny insect that lives in the fur of animals and bites their flesh.

flea

flee
fled
fleeing

To run away; to escape. Most people will *flee* from an angry dog.

fleet

1. A group of ships under one leader. Columbus had only three ships in his *fleet.*
2. A group of cars or trucks belonging to one company. Uncle Joe owns a taxi *fleet.*

flesh

1. The part of the body that covers the bones; the meat of animals. The lion ate the *flesh* of a zebra.
2. The part of a fruit or vegetable that you eat. The *flesh* of a peach is soft and juicy.

flight

1. A trip through the air. The plane's *flight* lasted two hours.
2. A group of birds or planes. A *flight* of ducks flew south.
3. A set of stairs that connects two floors in a building. We live one *flight* up.

flip
flipped
flipping

To toss or turn over quickly. We watched Dad *flip* the pancakes.

float
floated
floating

1. To stay on the surface of a liquid, such as water. The raft *floats* on the lake.
2. To drift or be carried along in the air. The clouds *floated* gently across the sky.

flock

A group. We saw a *flock* of sheep.

flood

A great amount of water which has come over buildings and land that are usually dry. The heavy rains caused a *flood* on the roads.

floor

1. The part of a room or building where you walk. There is a rug on the *floor.*
2. A level in a building. The doctor's office is on the third *floor.*

flounder   A flat fish that is used as food.

flounder

flour   A fine substance made by grinding grain and used to make bread and cakes.

flow   To pour; to move along steadily. The stream *flows* into a lake.
flowed
flowing

flower   The part of a plant in which its seeds grow. I like the shape and color of this *flower.*

fluffy   Soft and light. The kitten has *fluffy* fur.

fluid   A liquid or gas. Water is a *fluid.*

flute   A tube-like musical instrument with holes in the side.

flower

fly   1. A flying insect that often spreads germs.
2. A ball batted high in the air in baseball.

fly   1. To move through the air on wings. Birds *fly* by moving their wings.
flew
flown   2. To operate a plane or kite. The pilot will *fly*
flying   to Chicago.

foam   A light mass of small bubbles. Dad spread a *foam* of shaving cream on his face.

fog   A cloud-like mist settling close to the ground or sea. The sailors could not see in the *fog.*

fly

fold   1. To turn or bend over so that one part covers
folded   another. Please *fold* the blanket.
folding   2. To place across each other. Jim *folded* his arms.

follow   1. To move along behind. Did your dog *follow*
followed   you to school?
following   2. To obey. Please *follow* the directions.
3. To come after. Monday *follows* Sunday.
4. To move along the path of. *Follow* that street to my house.

fond
fondly

Having feelings of love. The prince is *fond* of the princess. The mother spoke *fondly* of her child.

food

1. What people and animals eat or drink to keep healthy. Milk is an important *food* for children.
2. Materials that plants take from the soil to help them to grow.

fool

A very silly or stupid person. Only a *fool* would skate on thin ice.

fool
fooled
fooling

To trick. Did you *fool* Bob by pretending to be someone else?

foolish
foolishly

Very silly; stupid. It is *foolish* to play with matches. The jaywalker acted *foolishly*.

foot

1. The bottom part of the leg, below the ankle. I put the shoe on my *foot*. The plural of *foot* is *feet*.
2. The bottom; the lowest part. The cabin is at the *foot* of a hill.
3. A measurement; 12 inches.

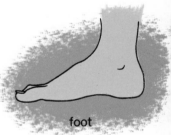

foot

football

1. A game played by two teams with 11 players each on the field at one time.
2. The ball used in the game of football.

for

1. To the distance of. From the top of a hill, you can see *for* miles.
2. In the amount of. Mother received a check *for* five dollars.
3. In place of. Dave traded his baseball glove *for* Jim's kite.
4. Given to. The birthday gift is *for* you.
5. Because of. Mary is liked *for* her kindness.
6. Toward. We should start *for* home.
7. In order to find. We looked *for* Dad's coat.

football

forest ranger

force

1. Power; strength. It took great *force* to move the huge rock.
2. A group that works together for a special purpose. Jan's father is on the police *force.*

force
forced
forcing

1. To move by using strength or power. Ed tried to *force* the door open.
2. To cause; to make. Rain may *force* us to stop the game.

forehead

The front of the head between the hair and eyes.

foreign

From or describing a country other than your own. Uncle Ed bought a *foreign* car.

forest

A large woods; a land covered with trees. Many animals live in the *forest.*

forest ranger

A person whose job is to prevent fires and to do other things to take care of a forest.

forever

All the time; without an end. Jill is *forever* telling Bill what to do.

forget
forgot
forgotten
forgetting

To fail to remember. Don't *forget* your phone number.

forgive
forgave
forgiven
forgiving

To excuse or to pardon. Please *forgive* me for my rude behavior.

fork

1. A tool used for eating or for handling food.
2. A branch of a road or river. One *fork* in the road takes you to school; the other takes you to the center of town.

form

1. A shape or figure. We made cookies in the *form* of animals.
2. A kind or type. Ice is a *form* of water.

fork

form
formed
forming
To make or shape. The children began to *form* a line at the drinking fountain.

fort
A place from which to fight; an area protected by strong walls. The soldiers defended the *fort.*

fort

forth
Forward; ahead. The swing goes back and *forth.*

fortune
1. Wealth; a large amount of money. The king's jewels are worth a *fortune.*
2. Luck. Ted had good *fortune* when he found his book.

forty
A number; 40. See page 199.

forward
Ahead; toward the front. The train moved *forward* slowly.

fossil
A trace or the remains of an animal or plant that lived long ago. We saw the *fossil* of a fish at the museum.

fossil

foundation
The base of a building; a part that supports. A skyscraper needs a strong *foundation.*

fountain
A stream of water that goes up into the air, or a device that makes water flow. The drinking *fountain* is in the hall.

four
A number; 4. One more than 3 and one less than 5. See page 199.

fourteen
A number; 14. One more than 13 and one less than 15. See page 199.

fox

fox
A wild animal that belongs to the dog family and is thought to be very clever.

fraction
A part of something; a portion; in arithmetic, a figure such as "$\frac{1}{4}$" or "$\frac{1}{2}$."

frame 1. A rim or border. The artist put his picture in a wooden *frame.*
2. The skeleton or support around which a thing is made or built. The *frame* for the new building is made of steel.

frank Honest; truthful. Tom is a *frank* person who
frankly cannot lie. Mary told us *frankly* about her problem.

frankfurter A long, slender, sausage-like roll of chopped meat and spices.

free 1. Without charge; costing nothing. The baker gave the children *free* cookies.
2. Not locked up or controlled by others. The lion in the cage would like to be *free.*

free To turn loose; to give liberty to. If you *free* a
freed canary, it will fly away.
freeing

freedom Independence; liberty; a state of being free. The judge gave the prisoner his *freedom.*

freeze To turn into ice; to become very cold and get
froze hard. Cold weather will make the pond *freeze.*
freezing We keep ice cream in the *freezer.*

French fries

French fry A long narrow piece of potato fried in deep fat. Ken put salt on his *French fries.*

French toast Bread slices that have been dipped in milk and eggs and fried.

frequent Happening often; close together in time. The
frequently bus makes *frequent* stops. We watch TV *frequently.*

fresh Clean; new; recently made or picked. We need
freshly *fresh* air. The bread is *freshly* baked.

Friday   The sixth day of the week.

friend   A person whom you know and like.

friendly   Kind; pleasant; nice to others. Our mailman is a *friendly* person.

friendship   A warm feeling between two people; the condition of being friends. Pat and Mike have a great *friendship.*

frighten
frightened
frightening   To scare; to cause one to be afraid. The loud noise will *frighten* the baby.

frog   A small animal that spends part of its life in the water and part on land. *Frogs* eat flies and other insects.

frog

front   The forward part or face of something; the opposite of "back." Put the stamp on the *front* of the envelope.

frontier   1. An area that is not fully explored. The settlers built a cabin on the *frontier.*
2. A border between countries.

frost   Very small bits of ice; frozen dew. There was *frost* on the grass that cold morning.

fruit   The part of a plant that has seeds and is usually good to eat. Limes and apples are *fruits.*

fruit

fry
fried
frying   To cook in hot fat. Mother showed us how to *fry* an egg.

fudge   A kind of soft candy, often made at home. Mary made chocolate *fudge* for the party.

fuel   Something that is burned to make heat or supply power. Gasoline and oil are two kinds of *fuel.*

full
1. Filled to the top; containing all it will hold. The bucket is *full* of water.
2. Whole or complete; entire. We spent a *full* day at the museum.

fume Gas or smoke, especially evil-smelling smoke. The *fumes* from the fire made us cough.

fun A good time; pleasure. We have *fun* playing.

funny Amusing; causing laughter. The cartoon show was *funny.*

fur
1. The soft coat or hair that covers an animal. The cat's *fur* is fluffy and smooth.
2. A piece of clothing made of animal fur. Mother wore a *fur* around her neck.

furious Rage; wild anger. The man was *furious* over the broken window.

furnace A closed place where fuel is burned. An oil *furnace* heats the apartment building.

furniture Items in a house or building that can be moved, such as tables, beds, and chairs. We moved our *furniture* in a truck.

further More; in addition. The teacher will talk *further* about safety tomorrow.

furthermore Besides; in addition. Jane did not like the dress; *furthermore,* it didn't fit her.

fuss A small quarrel; a difference of opinion. The boys had a *fuss* over who would pitch.

future The time to come; not the present or past. We all may ride in spaceships in the *future.*

fuzzy
1. Covered with very short soft hair. A caterpillar has a *fuzzy* body.
2. Not clear. We get a *fuzzy* picture on our TV set.

Gg

gain
gained
gaining

To get, especially to get more. Jeff wants to *gain* five pounds.

gallon

A measurement of volume equal to 4 quarts or 128 ounces.

gallop
galloped
galloping

1. To ride a horse fast. Tom likes to *gallop* on his pony.
2. To run fast. Ruth *galloped* through the house.

gallop

gamble
gambled
gambling

To play a game in which you can win or lose something; to take a chance.

game

A contest; a sport; a kind of play with rules. The baseball *game* was exciting.

garage

1. A building or part of a building where cars are kept.
2. A place where cars, trucks, or buses can be fixed.

garbage

Leftover food that is of no use, usually thrown away.

garden

A piece of ground used for growing vegetables or flowers.

garden

garment

A piece of clothing.

gas
1. A substance such as air: not a solid, not a liquid. Our stove burns natural **gas.**
2. Short for "gasoline." Our car needs **gas.**

gasoline
A fuel used to make cars, trucks, and some other machines run. A car won't run without **gasoline.**

gasp
gasped
gasping
1. To catch your breath quickly. The monster in the movie made me **gasp.**
2. To speak between gasps. Jane **gasped,** "I'm . . . I'm afraid!"

gate
A door-like opening in a wall or fence. Close the **gate** to keep the dog at home.

gate

gather
gathered
gathering
1. To bring together; to come together. The boys **gathered** newspapers for the paper drive.
2. To pick or harvest. Let's **gather** berries.

gay
gaily
1. Merry, lively, joyful. Everyone was **gay** at the party. Children called **gaily** to each other.
2. Bright in color.

gear
1. A wheel with a toothed rim that fits against and moves another toothed wheel in a machine.
2. The tools or equipment needed for doing something. The Scouts carried camping **gear.**

gerbil

gem
A precious stone; a jewel.

general
A very important army officer. A **general** commands many troops.

generally
Nearly always; usually. I am **generally** at the bus stop on time.

gentleman
A polite, honest, kind man.

geography
The study of the earth and its people. *Geography* tells us what the land and the seas are like.

gerbil
A small mouse-like animal. My pet **gerbil** eats lettuce and seeds.

germ   A tiny bit of living matter that can grow. You need a microscope to see a *germ.* Some *germs* make people sick.

get   1. To become the owner of; to receive. We *get*
got   new books every month.
gotten   2. To go for. I'll *get* your coat for you.
getting   3. To catch. I don't want to *get* a cold.
4. To earn. Ted *got* one dollar for raking leaves.

geyser   A hot spring that shoots water and steam high in the air.

ghost   The spirit of a person who is dead and who, some believe, can visit the living; a spook.

giant   1. An imaginary person of great size and power.
2. A thing that is unusually large. Some airplanes are *giants* beside others.

gift   A present; something given to someone. Everyone took a *gift* to Jan's birthday party.

giraffe

giraffe   A tall, spotted animal with a long neck. A full-grown *giraffe* can be more than 15 feet tall.

girl   A female child who will grow up to be a woman. Are there more *girls* or boys in your class?

Girl Scout   A member of a worldwide group that trains girls in camping and in being good citizens.

Girl Scout emblem

give   1. To hand over; to make a present of. Nan
gave   wants to *give* her book to Scott.
given   2. To present. The President will *give* a
giving   speech on television.
3. To grant. I *give* you permission to use my bike.
4. To make happen. Our club will *give* a show next week.
5. To pay. How much do you *give* for lunch?

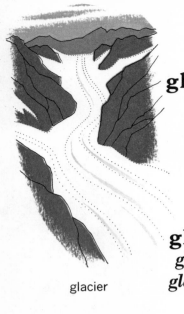

glacier

glacier   A giant field of ice moving slowly down mountains and across land.

glad
gladly
   1. Happy or pleased. I am **glad** you are here. I will **gladly** play with you.
   2. Bright or gay. Wilma is wearing a **glad** smile.

glance
glanced
glancing
   1. To give a quick look. Will you **glance** at my paper?
   2. To hit at an angle. The ball **glanced** off the wall and hit Greg.

glare
glared
glaring
   1. To shine with a blinding light.
   2. To stare at in an angry or mean way.

glass   **1.** A hard material you can usually see through. Windows are made of **glass.**
   2. A drinking container made of glass. I poured milk into a **glass.**

gleam
gleamed
gleaming
   To glow with light; to shine faintly. A small fire **gleamed** in the darkness.

glider

glide
glided
gliding
   To move smoothly and gently. Watch my paper airplane **glide** to the floor.

glider   An aircraft that has wings but no engine. A **glider** stays in the sky by riding on air drifts.

globe

globe   **1.** Anything round like a ball.
   2. A round model of the earth. The United States is one country shown on a **globe.**

glory   **1.** Great honor. The astronaut's moon trip brought him **glory.**
   2. Beauty. The peacock spread its wings in bright **glory.**

glossy   Shiny and smooth. Our cat's fur is **glossy** black.

glove   A covering for the hand with a separate place for each finger.

glow
glowed
glowing
   1. To shine with heat, especially without a flame. Ashes *glow* after a fire dies down.
2. To look pleased. Alice *glowed* when she became class president.

glue   A substance used for sticking things together. Fix the chair leg with *glue.*

gloves

go
went
gone
going
   1. To change position; move from one place to another. The rocket will *go* to the moon.
2. To start off; leave. When will you *go?*

goal   1. The place on a sports field or floor where scores are made. The *goal* in basketball is a hoop with a net.
2. An aim or purpose. My *goal* is to be a teacher.

goat   A grass-eating animal with horns, often having a beard. *Goats* are livelier than sheep.

goat

gobble
gobbled
gobbling
   1. To make a sound like a male turkey.
2. To eat in a hurry; to gulp. A hungry boy may *gobble* his food.

goblin   A make-believe, naughty elf.

go-cart   1. A carriage or wagon that children can ride in or pull.
2. A small motor-driven car for young people.

go-cart

god   1. (God) The being in some religions believed to be the maker or creator of everything.
2. A being thought to have special powers. Indians prayed for water to the *god* of rain.

gold   1. A valuable yellow metal. My ring is made of *gold.*
2. The bright yellow color of this metal.

goldenrod

golden   Made with gold or having the yellow color of gold. The king wore a *golden* crown.

goldenrod   A plant with small yellow flowers and a long stem. *Goldenrod* grows wild in many places.

goldfish   A small orange-gold fish.

golf   An outdoor game played with a small ball and a set of clubs with long handles.

good   1. Behaving well. The *good* baby didn't cry.
2. Pleasant; enjoyable. Everyone had a *good* time at the party.
3. Fine; excellent. That is a *good* painting.

good-by   A word used when you leave or part from someone.

goods   (Plural) Something that you can buy. The store has many *goods* for sale.

goose   A long-necked water bird that looks something like a duck. The plural of *goose* is *geese.*

gorilla   A large ape.

govern
governed
governing   To guide; to direct; to rule. Parents try to *govern* how their children act.

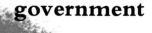

goldfish

government   The ruling body of a community or nation. The *government* of the United States is in Washington, D.C.

governor   A person who directs a state or territory.

gown   1. A long party dress worn by a woman.
2. A loose robe or nightgown.

grab
grabbed
grabbing   To reach out and take quickly; to snatch. Did you see Dave *grab* the candy?

gorilla

grade
1. A class in school. Lou is in the first *grade.*
2. A score or mark. Anne got the highest *grade* in the class.
3. A slope. The steep *grade* made the hill hard to climb.

graffito
Writing on a wall. The plural of *graffito* is *graffiti.*

grain
1. A very tiny bit or piece. The boys swept every *grain* of sand out of the clubhouse.
2. The seeds of certain food plants such as wheat or corn. Wheat *grain* is eaten as a cereal.

grapes

grand
1. Splendid; large. Ann's home was *grand.*
2. Of high character; fine. Abe was a *grand* person.

granite
A hard rock, often used as a building material.

grant
granted
granting
To give; to allow. Tom hopes his parents will *grant* him permission to stay up late.

grapefruit

grape
A small green, purple, or red fruit that grows in bunches on a vine.

grapefruit
A large yellow fruit that grows in warm climates.

graph
A drawing or chart that shows a relation between two things, such as rainfall and time. You can see from the *graph* that there was more rain in June than in May.

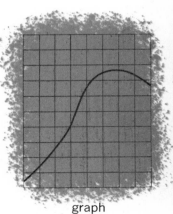

graph

grasp
1. A firm hold. Sally had a *grasp* on the ropes of the swing.
2. Understanding. Bill has a good *grasp* of math.

grass
A green ground cover with narrow blades.

grasshopper An insect with strong hind legs that moves by flying or hopping. Some *grasshoppers* cause damage to plants.

grave A place where a dead person or animal is buried.

grave Serious. Bill's brother said it would be a *grave* mistake to drop out of school.

gravel A mixture of small stones or pebbles. The rough road was covered with *gravel.*

gravity The force that pulls things together, especially down toward the center of the earth. When you throw a ball into the air, *gravity* brings it down.

gray A color. See page 70.

graze 1. To feed on grass. Cows *graze* when they are
grazed hungry.
grazing 2. To touch lightly while passing. The ball *grazed* Ed's face.

grease Very thick oil or fat. Mother spilled bacon
greasy *grease* on the floor. Now the floor is *greasy.*

grease To put grease on something. Sam *greased* his
greased bicycle wheel to make it move more easily.
greasing

great 1. Very large; big. The stars are a *great* distance from the earth.
2. Fine; excellent. He is a *great* teacher.

greatly Very much. We were *greatly* excited by the good news.

greedy Wanting, using, or asking for more than you need.

green 1. Not yet ripe. *Green* apples are sour.
2. A color. See page 70.

grasshopper

graves

greet
greeted
greeting

To welcome; to speak to someone in a friendly way. My sister ran to **greet** me.

grin

A broad smile. The clown had a big **grin** on his face.

grin
grinned
grinning

To smile broadly. Do you **grin** when you see a funny hat?

grind
ground
grinding

To crush into powder or break into very small pieces. A mill **grinds** wheat to make flour.

grinder

1. A machine used to crush or cut something into small pieces. The butcher put meat through his **grinder** to make hamburger.
2. A big sandwich; a hero sandwich.

grip

A firm hold. Joe has a **grip** on the rope.

groan
groaned
groaning

To make a low sound, as if in pain; to moan. The sick man began to **groan.**

grocery

1. A store where food and household supplies are sold. We went to the **grocery** for bread.
2. (Plural) Things bought at a grocery. I carried the **groceries** home in a bag.

grouch
grouched
grouching

To grumble; to find fault. Try not to **grouch** when things go wrong.

ground

1. The solid surface of the earth; land. The kite fell to the **ground.**
2. (Plural) Land that has a special use. We will eat at the picnic **grounds.**

groundhog

groundhog

A small, brownish animal with short legs; a woodchuck.

group   Two or more persons or things that are together. A *group* of children was playing.

group
grouped
grouping   To bring several persons or things together. Try to *group* the new books on the same shelf.

grove   A number of trees; a small woods.

grow
grew, grown
growing   1. To get bigger. Kittens *grow* very fast.
2. To plant and raise. I want to *grow* flowers in my garden.

growl
growled
growling   To make a deep sound, as of an angry dog; to say in an angry way. Jack heard the giant *growl,* "Fee-fi-fo-fum."

grownup   An adult; a person who is fully grown.

growth   The act of growing or becoming bigger. Dick watched the *growth* of the new kittens.

gruel   Thin, cooked cereal or porridge.

gruff   Rough, rude. The man spoke in a *gruff* voice.

grumble
grumbled
grumbling   To find fault in a low voice; to complain. We *grumble* when it rains.

grunt
grunted
grunting   To make a short, deep, rough sound in the throat. Pigs *grunt* when they eat.

guard   1. A person who protects persons or things. A *guard* carried the money into the bank.
2. A watching over. Dogs kept *guard* in the store at night.
3. A thing that protects. Jane had a chain *guard* on her bicycle.

guard
guarded
guarding   To protect; to watch over; to keep from harm. A shepherd *guards* his flock.

guess
An opinion or answer that you give without being sure it is correct. Janet's *guess* was that the box contained candy.

guess
guessed
guessing
To judge or give an answer without being sure. *Guess* who was wearing the mask at the party!

guest
An invited or welcome visitor.

guide
1. A person who leads or shows the way. A sailor was our *guide* when we visited the ship.
2. A list, book, or example that instructs or gives information. The book about the museum was a good *guide.*

guide
guided
guiding
To show the way or lead; to direct. The control tower *guided* the jet to a safe landing.

guitar
A musical instrument whose strings are picked with the fingers to make music.

gulf
A large body of water branching off from an ocean. A *gulf* has land around it on several sides.

gulp
gulped
gulping
To swallow quickly, often in a noisy manner. Bob was late and had to *gulp* his lunch.

guitar

gum
1. A soft, sticky material that is pleasant to chew. Don is chewing bubble *gum.*
2. (Often plural) The parts of the mouth from which teeth grow.

gun
A weapon that shoots bullets or other objects; a rifle or a pistol.

gym
A class for physical training or learning sports. We have *gym* on Monday.

gymnasium
A large room or building for games or exercise.

Hh

habit   A thing that a person does over and over again. Abe has a **habit** of getting up early.

hadn't   A short form of "had not." Jill **hadn't** seen Mary for two weeks.

hail   Small bits of ice that fall from the sky.

hair
hairy   One or all of the thread-like growths from the skin, especially on top of the head. Maria combed her **hair**. A monkey is a **hairy** animal.

haircut   1. The act of cutting hair.
2. The way in which hair is cut. Bob had a short **haircut**.

half   One of two equal parts. An orange can be cut in **half**. The plural of **half** is **halves**.

hall   1. A small or narrow room that connects larger rooms. Ruth walked down the **hall** to her classroom.
2. A building or very large room where public groups may meet. A meeting was held at the town **hall**.

ham

halt
halted
halting   To stop; put an end to. We had to **halt** our game when it got dark.

ham   Meat from the upper part of a hog's back legs. Carl likes **ham** and eggs for breakfast.

hamburger 1. Beef that has been ground up. The butcher sold Jane a pound of *hamburger.*
2. Cooked chopped beef, usually served on a bun.

hammer A hand tool used for hitting nails.

hammer
hammered
hammering To pound or hit with a hammer or other object. Dad *hammered* a nail into the board.

hamster A small animal that has a short tail, puffed cheeks, and soft fur. *Hamsters* are often kept as pets.

hand 1. The part of a person's arm from the wrist to the end of the fingers. We have five fingers on each *hand.*
2. One of the finger-like pieces on the face of a clock or watch that point to the time. At noon both *hands* of a clock are on 12.
3. A worker. The farmer hired a new *hand.*

handbag A small bag used to carry money and other things; a purse.

handkerchief A small, square piece of cloth used to dry the nose or other parts of the face. Brian dried his tears with his *handkerchief.*

handle The part of something you hold to lift it or to move it from place to place. I carry my record player by the *handle.*

handle
handled
handling 1. To touch with the fingers; to hold in the hand. *Handle* eggs carefully.
2. To manage or control. Pat will *handle* tickets for the class play.

handsome Pleasing to look at; having a nice appearance. Ben is a *handsome* boy.

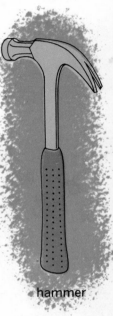

hamburger on bun

hammer

hamster

hang
hung
hanging

1. To fasten or attach. Let's *hang* a picture on the wall.
2. To be attached so as to swing but not drop. I can *hang* from the tree by my legs.

happen
happened
happening

To take place; to come about; to occur. When did the car crash *happen?*

happiness

A very good feeling; joy. Tony's new bike will bring him *happiness.*

happy
happily

Having a feeling of joy. Tony is *happy* when he rides his new bike. He sings *happily* as he rides.

harbor

A protected body of water where ships can anchor; a port. A *harbor* is a safe place for ships to dock.

hard

1. Very firm; very solid; not soft. Rock is *hard.*
2. Difficult; not easy. Building a house is *hard.*
3. With much power or effort. Dave tried *hard* to win the race.

hardly

Just; barely. Bill had *hardly* finished dinner when he was hungry again.

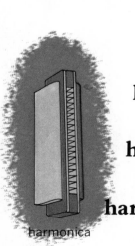

hare

hare

A four-legged animal somewhat like a large rabbit.

harm

Injury; hurt; damage. Sunburn can do *harm* to the skin.

harmful

Causing injury or damage. Too much sun is *harmful* to the skin.

harmless

Safe; not dangerous; not harmful. The gun is *harmless* because it is empty.

harmonica

harmonica

A small flat musical instrument. You play a *harmonica* by blowing into holes in its side.

harvest
harvested
harvesting

To gather, pick, or collect. The farmer will *harvest* corn next week.

hasn't

A short form of "has not." Bill *hasn't* been to school this week.

hat

A cover for the head. A *hat* protects your head from rain and snow.

hatch

A small door or opening in a floor or wall. The sailor went through the *hatch* on the ship's deck.

hatch
hatched
hatching

To come out of an egg by breaking through its shell. The baby ducks will *hatch* soon.

hate
hated
hating

To dislike very strongly. Meg *hates* beans.

have
had
having

1. To be the owner of; to be in charge or control of. We *have* a puppy!
2. To be sick with. I *have* a cold.
3. To hold. Can we *have* a party?
4. To contain. The dish *has* flowers in it.

haven't

A short form of "have not." We *haven't* eaten dinner yet.

hawk

A large bird that has strong claws and hunts smaller birds and animals.

hay

Tall grass that is cut and dried to be used as feed for animals. Cows and horses eat *hay.*

hazel

A small tree that produces sweet nuts.

he

A word used in place of the name of a male person or animal. Herb was sleepy because *he* stayed up late.

hawk

head
1. The top part of the body, above the shoulders and neck.
2. The one in charge or control; the leader. The President is the **head** of our country.

headache
A pain in your head.

headlight
A light on the front of a vehicle like a car, bus, or bicycle. The broken **headlight** made night driving hard.

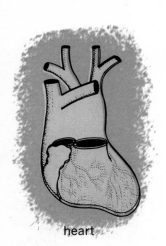

headlight

health
healthy
The condition of your body. A well-balanced diet helps to keep you in good **health.** Susan is a **healthy** baby.

heap
A pile. I left my clothes in a **heap** on the floor.

hear
heard
hearing
1. To listen to; to take in sounds through the ears. Can you **hear** my radio?
2. To learn; to be informed. Did you **hear** about the robbery?

heart
1. The part or organ in the body that pumps blood to all other parts.
2. An object with a shape something like a heart; a valentine heart.
3. A center for feelings such as love or sorrow. Tim's new dog made his **heart** glad.

heart

heat
Warmth; the energy given off by fire or the sun. **Heat** from the furnace keeps our house warm in winter.

heaven
1. The sky above; the wide area of space around the earth.
2. The place where God is thought to be.

heavy
1. Having much weight; not easy to lift. This box of books is **heavy.**
2. Big; great in size or number. It was a **heavy** snowstorm.

he'd   A short form of "he had" or "he would."

heel
1. The back part of the foot.
2. The back, bottom part of a shoe or sock.

height   The distance from the bottom to the top of something. The **height** of this wall is four feet.

helicopter   A kind of airplane that has large propellers on top. **Helicopters** can go straight up and come straight down.

helicopter

he'll   A short form of "he will" or "he shall."

hello   A greeting. Do you say *"hello"* when you meet people or answer the phone?

helmet   A hard hat worn to protect the head.

help   Aid; support; comfort or service. I got **help** from my brother in doing the puzzle.

help
helped
helping
1. To give your time, work, or money; to aid. You can **help** clear the table.
2. To ease the pain of; to make better. Rest in bed **helps** a cold.
3. To serve. **Help** yourself to some pie.

helmet

helper   A person who does something for another person. Gail was the teacher's **helper**.

helpful
helpfully
Useful; giving benefit to others; Ben is **helpful**. He **helpfully** offered to do the dishes.

helping   An amount one person can eat; a serving. Steve had another **helping** of potatoes.

hen   A female bird, especially a chicken. **Hens** lay eggs.

her   A word used in place of the name of a female person or animal. The mother dog is feeding **her** puppies.

hen

herd A large group or number of animals that are together. Cows and elephants move in **herds.**

here At this spot or in this place. Look! **Here** is the money I lost.

hero 1. A person who is very brave or does many good things for others.
2. A big sandwich, usually containing meat, cheese, lettuce, and other kinds of food.

hers That which belongs to her. Al ate all his candy, but Susie shared **hers** with me.

herself 1. Her own self. Sally often talks to **herself.**
2. Her usual, normal self. When Kay was sick, she was not **herself.**

he's A short form of "he is" or "he has." Tim says **he's** sleepy.

hey A word used to attract attention or show surprise. **"Hey!"** Jake yelled. "Don't touch the wet paint."

hi A short form of "hello"; a greeting.

hide-and-seek

hidden Out of sight; not easily seen.

hide The skin from an animal. Some animal **hides** make fine leather.

hide
hid
hidden
hiding
1. To go out of sight. Let's **hide** from Gus.
2. To put out of sight or into a secret place. Where did the dog **hide** his bone?

hide-and-seek A game in which children who hide are caught by one person who is "it."

high 1. Very tall; reaching up a great distance. Some **high** buildings are called skyscrapers.
2. With a definite height. Our fence is three feet **high.**

highway A public road, usually a main road.

hike A very long walk, often taken where there are no roads. A *hike* can be good exercise.

hill A place where the earth rises above the ground around it. A *hill* is not as high as a mountain.

him A word used in place of the name of a male person or animal. Give Ed this book and ask *him* to return it soon.

himself 1. His own self. Don served *himself* a second helping.
2. His usual, normal self. When Joe is sad, he is not *himself.*

hind Back or rear. The dog hurt its *hind* leg.

hint A clue; a suggestion. Mother gave me a *hint* about what my birthday present would be.

hip The part of the body around and including the joint formed where the upper leg is attached to the main part of the body.

hire
hired
hiring
1. To give a job to. The factory wants to *hire* three new workers.
2. To rent; to pay for the use of. Dad will *hire* a truck to move our furniture.

his Belonging to him; that which belongs to him. Ed had *his* raincoat. Ted forgot *his.*

historic
historical
Belonging to history. The old fort was a *historic* place. My favorite books are *historical* stories.

history 1. A record of things that happened in the past.
2. The study of the past. In *history* we learned that Indians were the first Americans.

hit
hit
hitting
To strike. Dad *hit* the nail with a hammer.

hitch
hitched
hitching

To fasten or connect; to tie. Let's **hitch** your wagon to my bike.

hitchhike
hitchhiked
hitchhiking

To travel by getting rides from passing cars and trucks. A person holds out his thumb when he **hitchhikes.**

hive

1. A box or container built for bees to live in.
2. A large number of bees that live together.

hobby

An occupation that you enjoy doing apart from your usual studies or work; something done for fun. Cooking is my father's **hobby.**

hockey

A game played on ice or on a field by players who move a ball or flat object with long sticks. Players in ice **hockey** wear skates.

hoe

A garden tool with a small blade and a long handle. A **hoe** is used for digging in soil.

hoe

hog

1. A pig, especially a large one.
2. A greedy or selfish person.

hold
held
holding

1. To keep in your hands or arms; to clutch. Mother asked me to **hold** her purse.
2. To contain; to have enough room for. This glass **holds** a pint of water.
3. To keep together; to fasten. The nail is not strong enough to **hold** the picture on the wall.
4. To keep. This TV program **holds** my attention.
5. To have. The class will **hold** a book fair next week.

hog

holdup

1. A robbery; the taking of money or other property by force.
2. A stopping or a slowing down. The accident caused a **holdup** of traffic.

hole 1. An open or torn place on a surface. Water dripped through a *hole* in the tent.
2. A pit; a hollow. The workmen dug a *hole* in the street.

holiday A day celebrated in honor of some historical or holy happening. Thanksgiving is a national *holiday* in the United States.

hollow With nothing inside; not solid. The fox hid in a *hollow* log.

holster A leather case for a pistol. The sheriff wore his *holster* on his hip.

holster

holy Having to do with religion.

home 1. The place where a person or family lives. Martha went to her uncle's *home* for supper.
2. The place where a player stands to bat in baseball.

home run A hit in baseball that allows the batter to circle the bases and score a run.

homesick Lonely or unhappy because of being away from home. Nan was *homesick* at camp.

homework Schoolwork done at home. Tonight, I have to study 15 spelling words for *homework.*

honest Truthful; not lying. An *honest* person tells the truth.

honey 1. A sweet, thick syrup made by bees. *Honey* is good to eat.
2. A way of saying "dear." "*Honey,*" said Dad, "I'm glad you are my daughter."

honeymoon A vacation that a man and woman take soon after they are married.

honk
honked
honking

To make a sound like that of a goose or a horn. Drivers **honk** their horns when the traffic stops.

honor

1. Good character. The mayor is a man of **honor** who is fair and just.
2. Respect. The mayor is treated with **honor** by the people in our town.
3. (Plural) A student's award for excellent work. Ellen's sister won **honors** in high school.

honor
honored
honoring

1. To show respect for. The class will **honor** the flag by saluting it.
2. To give an award to. The President **honored** the astronauts.

hood

1. A piece of clothing that covers the head and neck, usually part of a coat.
2. The cover over the engine of an auto.

hoof

hoof

A hard covering on the feet of horses, cows, and many other animals.

hook

A curved piece of metal or other material, used to fasten things together or to hold things up. Hang your hat on the **hook**. A pointed **hook** is used to catch fish.

hoop

A circle or band of metal or other material. Linda shot the basketball through the **hoop**.

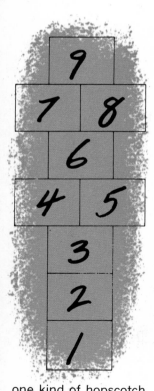

one kind of hopscotch

hop
hopped
hopping

1. To jump or leap. A frog can **hop** from one rock to another.
2. To jump on one leg. You **hop** when you play hopscotch.

hope

A desire; a wish. It is our **hope** that the world will have peace.

hope
hoped
hoping

To desire or wish. I **hope** that Don finds his lost dog.

hopeful   Desiring that something good will happen. Ted was *hopeful* that his team would win.

hopeless   Impossible to get done; without hope. Trying to save the sinking ship was *hopeless*.

hopscotch   A game in which players hop into squares marked on the ground. In *hopscotch* you try not to touch the lines between squares.

horizon   The line where the earth and sky seem to meet. A rainbow formed just above the *horizon*.

horizontal   Running from left to right on a level line; not up and down. Book shelves are *horizontal*.

horn   1. A hard, pointed body part that grows out of the heads of cattle and many other animals. A deer's antler is one type of *horn*.
2. A musical instrument that a person blows into to make sounds. A bugle is a *horn*.
3. A device that makes a loud noise as a signal. Dad blew his car's *horn*.

horrible   Causing fear or terror; alarming; very bad. The Halloween mask was *horrible*.

horror   A feeling of great dislike, fear, or terror; a feeling of not liking something. Janet was filled with *horror* when she saw the monster movie.

horns

horse   A large four-legged animal used for riding or for pulling heavy loads.

hose   A rubber or plastic tube through which water or other liquids are carried. Peggie sprayed the lawn with a *hose*.

hose   Socks or stockings.

hospital   A building where sick or injured people are cared for by doctors and nurses.

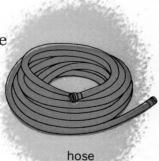

hose

hot
1. Having great heat; very warm. Boiling water is very **hot.**
2. Burning or very sharp to the taste. Red pepper makes food taste **hot.**

hot dog
A frankfurter, often served in a long roll.

hotel
A place where travelers rent rooms and buy meals; an inn. We stayed in a **hotel** on our vacation.

hour
A measurement of time; 60 minutes.

house
1. A building in which a person or family lives. Sarah's **house** has six rooms in it.
2. A building that has a special use. A school**house** is a building for teaching and learning.

hot dog on roll

household
All of the people who live in the same house, especially a family. The entire **household** ate supper together.

how
1. In what way. **How** did you learn to swim?
2. In what condition. **How** is your sister?
3. In what amount or number. **How** many brothers do you have?
4. For what reason; why. **How** can you call George lazy?

however
1. In what way; by what manner. **However** did Ben fix the fence?
2. Whatever amount. **However** much you spend, get a good bike.
3. Yet; even so. I don't like beans; **however,** I will eat them.

howl
howled
howling
1. To wail or make a long, deep cry. Dogs often **howl** at night.
2. To cry out loudly. I **howled** with laughter.

huddle
huddled
huddling

To gather close together; to move close. The ice skaters **huddled** near a fire.

hug

A close, tight hold with the arms. Peg's aunt gave her a **hug** and a kiss.

huge

Very large; enormous. A whale is **huge.**

hum
hummed
humming

1. To make a low, long sound, much like that made by bees. The air conditioner will **hum** when it is on.
2. To sing while one's lips are closed.

humming- bird

A very small bird with a long bill that makes a humming sound when it flies.

hump

A round lump. A camel has a **hump** on its back.

hundred

A number; 100. See page 199.

hunger

A feeling caused by a desire or need for food. Kay's **hunger** was satisfied by a hot dog.

hummingbird

hungry

Needing or wanting food. The **hungry** boy ate four sandwiches for lunch.

hunt
hunted
hunting

1. To try to kill. The men will **hunt** deer for food. The **hunter** shot a bear.
2. To try to catch. Police **hunt** criminals.
3. To look or search. We helped Dad **hunt** for the missing keys.

hurrah

A cheer; a cry of joy, excitement, or victory. *"Hurrah!"* I shouted when my team won.

hurricane

A storm with strong winds and heavy rain. Several ships were sunk by the **hurricane.**

hurry
hurried
hurrying

To move quickly; to rush. **Hurry** up or you will be late!

hurt
hurt
hurting
To cause or to suffer pain or injury. The bad fall *hurt* my wrist.

husband
The man to whom a woman is married. Mr. Cook is Mrs. Cook's *husband.*

hush
A period of quiet; a stillness. After the storm there was a *hush* in the forest.

hushpuppy
A small cake made from fried ground corn.

hut
A small, roughly made cabin or house; a shack. The poor old man lived in a *hut.*

hydrant
A stump-like pipe whose spout can be opened to release water from underground pipes. Firemen connect long hoses to *hydrants* to fight fires. A *hydrant* is also called a "fireplug."

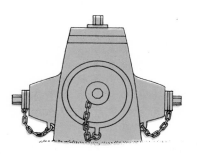

hydrant

Ii

I   A word used in place of a person's own name. Nan said, "*I* am Nan Clark."

ice
icy   1. Water that is frozen solid. The rain froze into slippery *ice*. The *icy* trees look like glass.
2. A dessert of crushed fruit-flavored *ice*.

iceberg   A large mass of ice floating in the ocean. An *iceberg* can be a danger to ships.

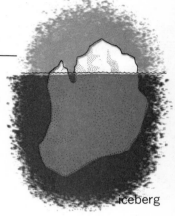
iceberg

ice cream   A sweet frozen food made with cream or milk. *Ice cream* makes a delicious dessert.

ice skate   A shoe with a metal runner for skating on ice.

icicle   A hanging stick of ice formed by water freezing as it drips. An *icicle* grows longer as each drop of water freezes.

ice skate

icing   A sweet covering on cakes or baked goods. Mother put chocolate *icing* on the cake.

I'd   A short form of "I had," "I would," or "I should."

idea   A thought; a plan; an opinion. I have an *idea* that it will rain tomorrow.

if   1. Whether. Josie didn't know *if* Ruth was at home.
2. In the event that. *If* the rope breaks, he will fall.

icicle

igloo

igloo	A hut built by Eskimos from blocks of snow or ice.
ill *illness*	Sick; not in good health. John is *ill* from eating too much. His *illness* kept him from sleeping.
illustrate *illustrated* *illustrating*	To make clear by using pictures or examples. Ellen will *illustrate* her story of the zoo with photographs. She also will use a drawing for an *illustration.* Ellen is a good *illustrator.*
I'm	A short form of "I am." "*I'm* hungry," said Joan.
image	A picture, reflection, or other likeness of a person or thing. Look at your *image* in the mirror.
imaginary	Make-believe; not real. Snow White is an *imaginary* person.
imagine *imagined* *imagining*	To form a picture of in the mind. Can you *imagine* what a giant is like? Tim used his *imagination* to make a new kind of toy.
immediate *immediately*	Without waiting; happening right away. The class had an *immediate* need for pencils. The teacher gave out new ones *immediately.*
imp *impish*	A playful, teasing child. My little brother is an *imp.* His *impish* behavior makes me angry.
impatient	Not able to wait; not patient. The kids were noisy and *impatient.*
important *importance*	1. Having great value. Signs are *important* on highways. Safety is of *importance* to everyone. 2. Having power or high social position.
impossible	Hopeless; not able to be done. It was *impossible* to stop the flood.

in
1. Into. Come *in* the house.
2. At home or indoors. On wet days we stay *in*.
3. Inside. He held the ball *in* his hand.

inch
A measurement of length. There are 12 *inches* in a foot.

inch

income
The money earned from doing work, from the sale of goods, or from investment. Dad's *income* took care of the family bills.

increase
increased
increasing
To become bigger; to grow. The storm *increased* in strength.

indeed
In fact; truly. The boys sang very well *indeed*.

dependence
The ability to act without control by others; freedom. The people wanted *independence* from their ruler.

ndependent
Without the help of others; free from the control of others.

Indian
1. A person who is a native of America and belongs to the so-called red race. *Indians* lived in North America before white people came.
2. A person who is a native of India.

indoor
indoors
Inside a building. The *indoor* swimming pool was used in bad weather. When it rained, Gil stayed *indoors*.

Indian

industry
industrial
1. Business; manufacturing. In the steel *industry,* workers make steel. An *industrial* city has many factories.
2. Hard work. His *industry* in working on his project made Brian's teacher happy.

inform
informed
informing
To tell or report to; to give news to. *Inform* Sue's teacher of her illness. Her friends will also want this *information.*

injure
injured
injuring

To hurt; to harm. Don't fall and *injure* yourself. An *injury* can be painful.

ink

A liquid used for printing and writing. These words are printed in black *ink.*

inland

Away from the coast; toward the inner part of a country. The weather is warmer *inland.*

inn

A hotel where travelers can eat and sleep. The small *inn* was on a mountain road.

inner

Inside; farther within. Ted found himself in the *inner* part of the castle.

inning

A division of a baseball game; the time it takes for each of two teams to get a turn at bat. A baseball game usually has nine *innings.*

insect

insect

A tiny animal with three pairs of legs and one or two pairs of wings. Bees, ants, flies, and beetles are *insects.*

inside

1. The inner part. The *inside* of the box is red.
2. Into or in the inner part of. We played *inside* the house.

instant

1. A very short time. In an *instant* the bird was out of the cage.
2. A moment. Come here this *instant!*

instead

In place of; rather than. Bring cake *instead* of ice cream.

instruct
instructed
instructing

1. To give knowledge to; to teach. Dad *instructs* me on how to bowl. I listen to his *instruction.* He's a good *instructor.*
2. To order or command. The Boy Scout leader *instructed* the boys to put up their tents.

instrument

1. Something that helps you to do a kind of work; a tool. A knife is an *instrument* for cutting bread.
2. A device that produces music. Barbara's *instrument* was the piano.

intelligence
intelligent

The ability to get and use knowledge; the ability to understand and to think. Sally has *intelligence.* She's a good thinker. An *intelligent* person has a bright mind.

intercom

A system of loud-speakers for speaking from one room to another. The principal spoke to our class over the *intercom.*

interest
interested
interesting

To attract or hold the attention of. Stories of dogs *interest* me.

international

Having to do with two or more nations. Ten nations sent people to the *international* meeting.

into

Toward the inside of; in. Sandy went *into* his house.

introduce
introduced
introducing

1. To make known face to face; to present. Be sure to *introduce* your friends to your mother. In your *introduction,* say their names clearly.
2. To tell about or show for the first time. The boys will *introduce* their plan for lending books.

invent
invented
inventing

To think up; to plan or design. Many people *invent* useful machines. The telephone was a good *invention.*

invite
invited
inviting

To ask, usually politely. Andy *invited* his friends to his house. The family has an *invitation* to a picnic.

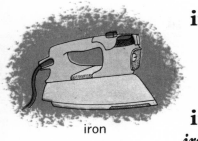

iron

iron
1. A common metal found in many building materials.
2. A tool that can be heated to press clothes smooth.

iron
ironed
ironing
To press clothes smooth with a heated iron.

is See **be.**

island Land with water on all sides. An *island* is much smaller than a continent.

it A word used in place of the name of a thing or animal already mentioned. Where's my book? I had *it* just a minute ago.

item Each thing named in a group or list. Mother forgot one *item* on her market list.

it's A short form of "it is." *It's* a nice day.

itself A word used in place of the name of a thing already mentioned. The door seemed to move by *itself.*

I've A short form of "I have." Ken said, "*I've* got an idea."

ivy A climbing or trailing vine. *Ivy* makes a good ground cover for a garden.

ivy

Jj

jacket   A short coat reaching to the hips.

jack-o'-lantern   A hollow pumpkin with a face cut into it and a light or candle inside.

jack-o'-lantern

jail   A building used to lock up people who break laws. A person locked in a *jail* is a prisoner.

jam   1. People or things crowded together. A traffic *jam* kept cars from moving.
2. A spread for bread made from fruit and sugar.
3. A difficult situation. Alice was in a *jam* when she broke the window.

January   The first month of the year.

jar   1. A wide-mouthed glass container. Open a *jar* of peaches.
2. A sudden shake. The car gave us a *jar* when it hit the hole in the road.

jars

jaw   The bones of the mouth, in which the teeth grow

jaywalk
jaywalked
jaywalking   To cross a street against a traffic signal; to cross a street at a dangerous spot. If you *jaywalk,* a car might hit you.

jeep   A small car first used by the U. S. Army.

jelly   A sweet spread for bread, made of fruit juice boiled with sugar. I like grape *jelly.*

jeep

jets

jerk
jerked
jerking
To move with a sudden, quick motion. A loud noise made me *jerk* my head.

jersey
1. A soft, knitted cloth.
2. A pull-over knitted shirt, usually tight-fitting.

jet
1. A strong stream of gas or liquid. A *jet* of water spouted high from the fountain.
2. An engine in which burning fuel releases a stream of hot air and gases from the rear to produce forward motion. An airplane with such an engine is called a *jet.*
3. A glossy black color.

jewel
A valuable stone such as a diamond. A pearl is another kind of *jewel.*

jewelry
Ornaments to wear, made of gold, silver, or other metal, and sometimes set with gems or stones.

jigsaw
1. A saw with a small blade that can cut tiny curves and other unusual shapes.
2. A puzzle made by cutting a picture into unusual shapes that must be fitted together again.

jigsaw

job
1. Work that is done for pay. My brother's *job* is driving a truck.
2. A piece of work that has to be done; a task. Bob's *job* was to clean the blackboards.

jog
jogged
jogging
1. To run at a steady slow pace. Many people *jog* to keep healthy.
2. To give a little push to. Mother *jogged* me to wake me up.

join
joined
joining
1. To put together; to fasten. Use glue to *join* the two blocks of wood.
2. To become a part of. A new pupil will *join* the class next week.

joint A place in the body where bones are joined together. Your knee is a *joint.*

joke 1. A short funny story.
2. A funny trick played on someone.

joke
joked
joking To tell or play jokes; to kid or tease. Uncle Jim *joked* about his funny old car.

jolly Cheerful, merry, gay; full of happiness.

journey A trip from one place to another. Our *journey* to Arizona took five days.

joy A feeling of happiness; delight; gladness. Linda's new bike filled her with *joy.*

joyful Happy; gay; full of joy.

judge A person who decides questions in a court. A *judge* tries to be fair.

judge
judged
judging To decide what is right or wrong about something; to decide what should be done. Our teacher *judges* our finger paintings.

jug A container for liquids. A *jug* has a handle and a narrow mouth.

juggler A person who can keep several balls or other things in the air at one time by tossing and catching them. A *juggler* has to be quick.

juice
juicy A liquid found in vegetables, fruits, and other foods. Lemon *juice* is very sour. A watermelon is *juicy.*

July The seventh month of the year.

jump
jumped
jumping 1. To spring into the air; to leap.
2. To move suddenly because of a surprise or a scare. Terry *jumped* at the sound of the loud bell.

juggler

jumper
1. A person or animal that jumps.
2. A sleeveless dress worn over a blouse or sweater.

June
The sixth month of the year.

jungle
A thick, tangled growth of trees and plants growing in a hot land; a tropical forest.

junk
Anything thrown away or a collection of things thrown away because they are worn out.

Jupiter
The largest planet in the solar system. See page 222.

just
1. Honest; fair. The storekeeper's prices are *just.*
2. Only. The baby is *just* two months old.
3. Exactly. The bus came *just* at 8 o'clock.
4. Certainly. Peg's party was *just* great!

jungle

Kk

kangaroo   An animal with large hind legs, small front legs, a long, strong tail, and a pouch for carrying its young.

kangaroos

keen   1. Sharp. The knife has a *keen* blade.
2. Bright; eager. Sue has a *keen* mind.

keep
kept
keeping
   1. To hold or have. I *keep* my pencils in my desk.
2. To take care of. Will you *keep* my dog for me while I'm away?
3. To stay or remain. She told the dog to *keep* quiet.

kernel   1. A piece of grain such as wheat, corn, or rye; a seed. This ear of corn has yellow *kernels*.
2. The inside of a nut. The squirrel ate the *kernel* but not the acorn shell.

ketchup   A tomato sauce used to add flavor to foods.

kettle   1. A big pot or pan. Mother makes soup in a *kettle*.
2. A kettle for boiling water; a tea*kettle*.

kettle
(definition 2)

key   1. Something that will fit into and turn a lock. We use a *key* to open the door.
2. Something that explains. The *key* on the map tells where the mountains are.

key in keyhole

keyhole   The opening into which a key fits.

kick
kicked
kicking

1. To strike out with the foot quickly. The dancers learned to **kick** very high.
2. To hit or strike with the foot. Can you **kick** the football?

kid

1. A young goat.
2. A child or young person. The **kids** like to play baseball.

kid
kidded
kidding

To tease; to make fun of. Bill likes to **kid** his sister.

kidney

One of two organs in the body that help clean the blood.

kidney bean

A large, dark red bean. Chili has meat and **kidney beans** in it.

kidney beans

kill
killed
killing

To put to death. Did the cat **kill** the mouse?

kind

A type, sort, or variety. My mother baked two **kinds** of cookies.

kind
kindly

Good, helpful, friendly. My uncle is a **kind** man. He treats us **kindly.**

kindergarten

A class for children before first grade.

kindness

A good act; a way of helping. It is a **kindness** to feed the birds.

king

A man who rules a country. A **king** may have great power.

kingdom

1. A land ruled by a king or queen.
2. A division of the natural world. The animal, vegetable, and mineral **kingdoms** are parts of the world of nature.

king of the hill A game in which one person tries to keep the others from climbing to the top of the hill.

kiss
kissed
kissing To touch with the lips as a sign of love or greeting. Nan ran to **kiss** her mother.

kit A container for special equipment. The workman has a tool **kit.**

kitchen A room in which food is prepared. Our **kitchen** has a big stove in it.

kitchenette A small kitchen or room where food is prepared.

kitten

kite 1. A plaything, made of wood and paper, cloth, or plastic. You fly a **kite** on the end of a long string.
2. A bird of prey. Some **kites** are as big as eagles.

kitten A young cat. Our **kitten** likes milk.

kitty A kitten; a young cat.

knee The place where your leg bends. Your **knee** joins the upper and lower parts of your leg.

kneel
knelt
kneeling To rest on your knees. Some people **kneel** to pray.

knickers (Plural) Short pants that are gathered just below the knee. Grandfather used to wear **knickers** to school.

knife A tool with a flat blade. This sharp **knife** is for cutting meat. The plural of **knife** is **knives.**

knight Long ago, a special soldier who fought for a king. The **knight** rode a horse and carried a sword or spear.

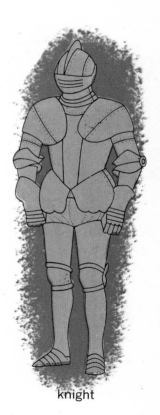
knight

knit
knitted
knitting

To make by using long needles or special machines to join loops of yarn together. Grandmother knows how to **knit** sweaters.

knob

A round handle. Turn the **knob** to open the door.

knock
knocked
knocking

To strike or hit. We will **knock** on your door to wake you up.

knockout

A hard blow that sends a fighter to the floor so he can't get up. The fighter won the fight by a **knockout.**

knot

1. A way to tie two or more pieces of string or rope together. The Cub Scouts learned to tie a square **knot.**
2. A measure of speed in boating.

know
knew
knowing

1. To be sure; to be certain. I **know** that two and two are four.
2. To understand; to have knowledge of. I **know** how to ride a bicycle.
3. To be familiar with. I **know** all the children on our street.

knots

knowledge

Information that is known.

knuckle

One of the joints of a finger.

koala

A bear-like animal found in Australia. The **koala** has no tail.

Ll

label   A piece of paper or a tag that gives information about the item on which it is placed. The **label** said that the jar contained grape jelly.

labor   Work; effort. The farmer's **labor** made him very tired.

laboratory   A room or building where science experiments are done.

lace   **1.** A fancy delicate cloth with open weave, usually used as trimming.
2. A cord or string used to tie a shoe.

lack
lacked
lacking   To be without or have too little. I **lack** the strength to lift the heavy box.

lad   A boy; a young man.

ladder   A device used for climbing up or down, made by attaching wood or metal steps to long side pieces.

lady   A woman, especially one with good manners.

ladybug   A small flying beetle, usually red or orange with black spots.

lake   A large body of water. A **lake** is closed in by land on all sides.

ladder

ladybug

lamb

lamb
1. A young sheep.
2. The meat from a young sheep.

lame
Not able to walk in a normal way. The *lame* woman limped because of an injured ankle.

lamp
An object used to produce light. An electric *lamp* has a bulb, and an oil *lamp* has a wick.

land
1. The solid surface of the earth. After weeks at sea, the ship reached *land.*
2. A country or area. Alaska is a *land* of many lakes and mountains.
3. The soil; the ground. The farmer plowed his *land.*

land
landed
landing
1. To reach land after traveling on water or through the air. We watched the plane *land* at the airport.
2. To catch. Susan *landed* the fish.

landslide
A huge amount of rocks and soil that slides down a hill or mountain. The *landslide* came across the road and blocked traffic.

lane
1. A narrow road or path. The horse pulled the cart along the *lane.*
2. A section marked on a road to show where a line of cars should move. The car went into the left *lane* in order to pass a truck.

lamps

language
1. The speech, writings, or signs that people use to make ideas known to each other. The *language* in a high school book may be hard for a young child to read.
2. The words used in speaking and writing by the people of a country. English is the *language* people speak in the United States.

lantern
An object with a glass cover that contains a flame or bulb that gives off light.

lap The front part of a seated person from the waist to the knees. Barbara petted a kitten sleeping on her *lap.*

lard Hog fat that is melted down and used for cooking.

large Big; having great size or amount. An elephant is a *large* animal.

lark
1. A bird with a pleasant song.
2. A happy adventure; good fun. The boys had a *lark* building a dam across the stream.

last
lasted
lasting
To continue or remain. The ice on the lake will *last* until spring.

last
1. Coming after all the others; final. December is the *last* month of the year.
2. Most recent. The *last* rain was yesterday.

late
1. Tardy; not on time. Hurry or you will be *late!*
2. Happening after the usual time or near the end. They had a *late* snack at midnight.
3. Recent. What's the *late* news?
4. Having died recently. The *late* mayor was buried on Monday.

laugh A happy sound that you make when something is funny. Gail has a loud *laugh.*

laugh
laughed
laughing
To make a happy sound with the voice. We *laugh* at a good joke. We heard the *laughter* of the children watching the clowns.

launch
launched
launching
1. To move into the water. We will *launch* our boat soon.
2. To fire, as a rocket; to start. They will *launch* a rocket to the moon.

lantern

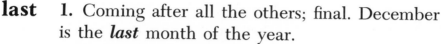

lark

launch pad   A special place from which rockets are shot into space.

Laundromat   A store where a person can wash and dry his own clothes in coin-operated machines.

laundry   1. Clothes that need to be washed. Jim put his *laundry* in the washing machine.
2. A room or building in which clothes are washed, dried, and ironed.

lava   Very hot, melted rock that pours from a volcano, or the same material when it cools and hardens.

lava

law   A rule or rules of a city, state, or country. *Laws* are designed to keep good order, safety, and fair play.

lawn   An area of ground covered with short grass. Mr. Jackson cuts his *lawn* every week.

lawyer   A person whose job is to know and explain laws. The *lawyer* presented a case before the judge in court.

lay
laid
laying   1. To put down; to rest on a surface. *Lay* the packages on the kitchen table.
2. To produce eggs. Chickens *lay* eggs.

layer   A sheet or single thickness of any material. A *layer* of ice formed on the lake.

lazy   Not willing to work. The *lazy* boy rested while his friends rowed the boat.

lead
led
leading   1. To guide or direct; to show the way to. The hunter will *lead* us through the forest.
2. To be in front of or in first place in. The red car *led* the race.
3. To experience; to live. An explorer *leads* a life of adventure.

lead   A common metal used to make such things as bullets.

leader   A person in charge; one who leads or shows the way.

leaf   One of the thin, flat parts that grow on trees, bushes, and flowers. That *leaf* is green. The plural of *leaf* is *leaves.*

leak
leaked
leaking
To pass through a crack or hole in a surface by accident. The rain will *leak* through the rip in the tent.

lean
leaned
leaning
1. To place or rest at a slant. The ladder is *leaning* against the wall.
2. To bend. Bob had to *lean* over to pick up the box.

leap
leaped
leaping
To jump. Can you *leap* across the stream?

leapfrog   A game in which a person leaps over one or more other persons who are bent over.

learn
learned
learning
To get knowledge; to find out. Children *learn* to read and write in school.

least   The smallest in size, amount, or number. The cheapest book in the store costs the *least.*

leapfrog

leather   A material that is specially made from the skins of cattle and other animals. Some shoes and belts are made of *leather.*

leave
left
leaving
1. To go away from. The travelers will *leave* Chicago tomorrow.
2. To let stay. Did Jack *leave* his lunch at home?

left   The direction to the west when you are facing north; the opposite of "right."

leg
1. A part of the body from the foot to the hip. We need our **legs** for walking.
2. One of the parts on which a chair or other piece of furniture stands.

lemon
A yellow fruit whose juice has a sour flavor.

lemonade
A drink made from water, sugar, and the juice of lemons.

lend
lent
lending
To allow the use of for a time. Please **lend** me your bicycle for an hour.

less
1. Smaller in amount or number. The small glass holds **less** milk than the big one.
2. Minus. Five **less** three is two.

lesson
1. A thing that is taught. Did you understand today's math **lesson?**
2. A thing that is learned by experience. The accident taught the driver a **lesson** about speeding.

let
let
letting
To allow; to give permission to. Mother **let** us stay up late last night.

let's
A short form of "let us." **Let's** go swimming.

letter
1. A sign or mark used in writing. "A" is the first **letter** of the alphabet.
2. A written message. Dad mailed his **letter.**

lettuce
A green vegetable. **Lettuce** leaves are used for making salads.

level
1. Flat; not on a slant. The land was **level** with no hills.
2. Even; equal. The two piles of bricks are **level** with each other.
3. Calm; not excited. During the fire drill, the children kept **level** heads.

lemon

lettuce

liberty A freedom; the right to do as you want. A prisoner does not have the *liberty* to go where he wants.

librarian A person in charge of a library. The *librarian* helped me to find the book.

library A building or room where books are kept for reading or borrowing. Our town has a public *library.*

lick
licked
licking 1. To move the tongue over. Ann watched Bill *lick* his ice-cream cone.
2. To move around in a fluttering manner. We saw flames *lick* at the edge of the log.

lid A top or cover that can be raised or removed. Dad pressed the *lid* of the paint can back into place.

lie A statement that is false, or not true. Kate's story about a flying cow was a *lie.*

lie
lied
lying To say or write something that is not true. Some people will *lie* to get out of trouble.

lie
lay
lain
lying 1. To place yourself in a horizontal position; to stretch out flat.
2. To be in a special place or condition. A huge rock *lies* at the bottom of the lake.

life 1. The quality of being alive. Breathing is a sign that an animal has *life.*
2. The time from birth to dying. The old man had a long *life.*
3. The story of a person's deeds. I read about the *life* of Columbus.
4. Spirit; energy. The puppy is full of *life.*

lifeboat

lifeboat A boat used to save passengers from a sinking ship or to rescue swimmers along the shore. The sailor used a *lifeboat* to save the boy.

lighthouse

lift
lifted
lifting

To raise to a higher place or position. *Lift* the box onto the table.

liftoff

The start of a rocket flight when the rocket blasts off from earth. The *liftoff* of the rocket to the moon was exciting to see.

light

1. A form of energy that gives off brightness; the opposite of darkness. The sun gives us *light* in the daytime.
2. A lamp or other object that gives off brightness. The *light* in the hall needs a new bulb.

light
lightly

1. Easy to lift or hold; not heavy. A bag of feathers is very *light*. The snow fell *lightly* on the field.
2. Bright; not dark. The sun makes this room very *light*.

light
lighted or lit
lighting

1. To cause to flame; to set on fire. Uncle George will *light* the candle.
2. To cause to give out light. Jim *lighted* the lamp in the dark room.

lighthouse

A building or tower near the sea with a bright light that warns ships of rocks or other dangers.

lightning

A flash of light caused by electricity in the air during a storm. A crash of thunder followed the flash of *lightning*.

lightning bug

lightning bug

A tiny insect that seems to glow or flash on and off when it flies at night.

like
liked
liking

To be fond of; to enjoy. I *like* play more than work.

likeness

The quality of being similar to something; a copy or image.

lily   A plant with flowers usually shaped like a trumpet.

lima bean   A round, almost flat, green or white bean that is eaten as a vegetable.

limb
1. A branch of a tree.
2. An arm or leg. The tall boy had long *limbs.*

lime
1. A green fruit that looks like a small lemon.
2. A white powder that has many uses, especially on farms and in building. *Lime* is used in plant foods and cement.

lily

limerick   A funny poem that has five lines.
   A fat man named Jonathan Blake
   Went skating one day on a lake.
   But the ice was too thin;
   The fat man fell in.
   Oh, wow! Did he shiver and shake!

limit
1. The most that is allowed or possible. What is the speed *limit* on this highway?
2. An edge or border; a boundary. A fence showed the *limit* of the farmer's land.

limp
limped
limping
To walk as a lame person walks. Bobby *limped* after he hurt his ankle.

limp   Weak; not straight or stiff. The heavy rain made the flowers look bent and *limp.*

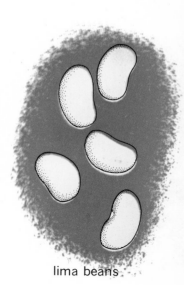

lima beans

line
1. A narrow mark along a surface. There is a *line* painted down the center of the road.
2. A row of people or things. A *line* of boys waited to enter the gym.
3. A string, cord, or wire. Mother hung the clothes on the *line* to dry.

link   One of the loops or rings that form a chain. Jane's bracelet is made of gold *links.*

lion A large, powerful, cat-like animal of a dull yellow color. Many *lions* live in Africa.

lion

lip One of the two edges of the mouth. Mother touched her *lips* to the baby's face.

liquid A substance such as water, ink, or milk that is not a solid or a gas. *Liquids* make things wet.

liquor A liquid that contains alcohol.

list A row or series of words or numbers that are written down. There are ten words on our spelling *list.*

listen
listened
listening
To pay attention; to hear. *Listen* carefully to the teacher's instructions. The teacher told Jack that he was a good *listener.*

literature Poems, stories, and similar writings. Our city library has one big room to hold children's *literature.*

litter 1. Paper, cans, or other trash that is carelessly left about. After the parade, workmen swept *litter* from the street.
2. All of the babies that a mother animal has at one time. Our cat had a *litter* of five new kittens.

litterbug A person who leaves trash around. Don't be a *litterbug!*

little Small; not big. A mouse is a *little* animal.

Little League An organization or group of baseball teams for young boys.

live
lived
living
1. To be alive; to have life. Some people *live* to be very old.
2. To have a home in a place. Jim and Joan *live* in Arizona.

3. To feed on, in order to stay alive. Hawks *live* on mice and other small animals.

live
1. Having life; not dead. There are many *live* animals in a zoo.
2. Carrying electricity. You can get a dangerous shock from a *live* wire.

lively
Full of action or excitement. We played a *lively* game of ball.

liver
An organ in the body that helps people and animals to get energy from the food they eat.

lizard
A small long-tailed animal that looks like a snake with four legs. A *lizard* is a reptile.

lizard

llama
An animal that lives in South America and looks like a small camel with no hump. A *llama* is used to carry heavy loads.

load
What is carried or held. The donkey carried a *load* of grain on its back.

loaf
Bread, cake, or other food baked in one piece. Dad made a meat *loaf* for supper. The plural of *loaf* is *loaves.*

loaf
loafed
loafing
To do nothing; to be lazy. We *loaf* on the beach on hot summer days.

loafer
1. A person who loafs or is lazy.
2. A shoe without laces that looks like a moccasin.

loan
Money or anything else that is borrowed or used for a certain time. Dad got a *loan* of $100 from the bank.

llama

lobby   A room inside the entrance to a building. They sell popcorn in the **lobby** of the theater.

lobster   A large shellfish with two large front claws. **Lobsters** are very popular as food.

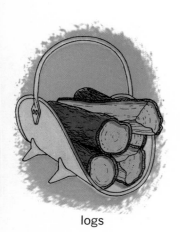

lobster

local   Nearby; belonging to a neighborhood or small area. Our **local** library is larger than the one in the next town.

locate
located
locating
1. To find. Did Linda **locate** her lost book?
2. To place. Let's **locate** our lemonade stand here.

lock   1. A device for fastening a door or a box or a gate to keep it from opening. Dad opened the trunk **lock** with a key.
2. A section of a canal in which boats can be raised or lowered by letting water in or out.

lock
locked
locking
1. To close or fasten with a lock. Dad will **lock** the door of his car.
2. To shut in with a lock. The zoo keeper **locked** the wolf in a cage.

lodge   A country inn or cabin where sportsmen or people on vacation can stay. The skiers warmed themselves by the fireplace in the **lodge.**

log   A piece of a tree that has been cut up, for burning or building. A **log** burned in the fireplace.

logs

lone   Single or alone; without company. The **lone** cowboy had no one to talk to.

lonely   1. Having a sad feeling because you are alone; lonesome. The **lonely** woman wished that someone would visit her.
2. With few or no people nearby. The mountain cabin was a **lonely** place.

lonesome   Sad because you are alone; lonely.

long
1. Having much distance from one end to the other; not short. The highway was *long* and straight.
2. In length. The ruler is 12 inches *long.*
3. With much time between. It is a *long* time from March to July.

look
looked
looking
1. To use your eyes in seeing. *Look* at that pretty red bird.
2. To search. Joan *looked* for the lost money.
3. To appear to be; to seem. The ship *looks* far away to me.

lookout
1. A person who watches. The *lookout* on the ship saw a raft in the water.
2. A tower or other place from which people watch. We took pictures of the valley from a *lookout* on the mountain.
3. A careful watch. The children were on the *lookout* for the ice cream truck.

loop
A rounded figure that is made when a line or rope is crossed over itself.

loose
1. Free; not fastened. Eileen's dog got *loose* and ran away.
2. Not tight or close. Dad's tie was *loose* around his collar.

lose
lost
losing
1. To be unable to find. You cannot see the movie if you *lose* your ticket.
2. To be unable to keep. The farmer *lost* his crops because of the snowstorm.
3. To be defeated; to not win. Did our team *lose* the game?

loss
1. A losing or failing to keep something. The *loss* of her mittens made Lucy sad.
2. A thing that is missed. The library that burned down is a great *loss.*
3. A defeat. Our team's *loss* ended the season.

lot
1. A large number or amount. The box contained a *lot* of buttons.
2. A piece of land. The boys played ball on the *lot* next to our house.

loud
loudly
Noisy; not quiet. The jet engine made a *loud* noise. The crowd cheered *loudly*.

loudspeaker
A machine that makes voices or sounds louder than usual. The mayor used a *loudspeaker* to talk to the crowd.

love
A very strong liking. Juan shows *love* for his little sister.

love
loved
loving
1. To have a very strong liking for. The prince *loves* the beautiful princess.
2. To enjoy greatly. Tom *loves* chocolate candy.

lovely
1. Beautiful; very easy to love. The baby was a *lovely* child.
2. Very pleasant. We had a *lovely* picnic.

low
1. Short; not high or tall. Jim jumped over the *low* fence.
2. Soft or deep in sound; not loud. The bees made a *low* humming sound.
3. Of a small amount or number. The price of the dress was very *low*.

lower
lowered
lowering
1. To pull or let down. We will *lower* the flag at sunset.
2. To make less. The farmer is going to *lower* the price of his corn.

luck
What happens by chance. Sue had good *luck* when she won the prize.

lucky
Having good fortune. The *lucky* driver was not hurt in the accident.

lullaby   A soft song used to help a baby fall asleep.

lumber   Wood used for building, such as boards. It took a lot of *lumber* to build the house.

lump   1. A bump or raised spot. The fall caused a *lump* on Ted's head.
2. A small mass of material that has no special shape. Jan had a *lump* of clay.

lunar   Having to do with the moon. The spaceship made a *lunar* landing.

lunch   A meal eaten near the middle of the day. We eat *lunch* in the school cafeteria.

lung   One of the two body organs within the chest used for breathing.

lynx   A wildcat found in North America.

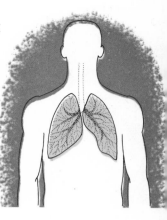

lungs

lynx

Mm

macaroni A food made from flour paste and shaped into little tubes. We had *macaroni* and cheese for lunch.

machine A device used by a person to help do work. Mother sews with a sewing *machine.*

machinery The parts of a machine; a group of machines. The *machinery* in the factory is very noisy.

mad 1. Angry. Ted often gets *mad* at his brother.
2. Having a sick mind.
3. Having a strong liking for. Bill is *mad* about comic books.

magazine A publication that is printed at regular times, such as once a week or once a month. The *magazine* contains stories, jokes, and puzzles.

magic A mysterious power to make things change or appear to change.

magician A person who can do tricks of magic. The *magician* pulled a rabbit out of his hat.

magnet An object that pulls iron and some other metals toward it. Tom picked up nails with his *magnet.*

maid A female servant; a girl or woman who is paid to do housework.

magnets

mail
Letters or packages sent from one place to another through the postal service. Our *mail* today included two letters for Jane.

mail
mailed
mailing
To send by using the postal service. The store is going to *mail* the shoes to Sue.

mailbox
A box used only for mail. The postman puts our letters in the *mailbox.*

mailman
A person who carries and delivers the mail. In the country, *mailmen* deliver mail by car.

main
Most important; chief; first. Corn is the *main* crop in Iowa.

mailboxes

make
made
making
1. To build; to construct. Tom will *make* a kite.
2. To cause or cause to become. The boat ride *made* me sick.
3. To force. No one can *make* the waves stand still.
4. To earn. Lisa *made* one dollar by washing windows.

make-believe
Pretending; imagination. Fairies live only in the land of *make-believe.*

male
A boy or man; an animal that is masculine. A bull is a *male;* a cow is a female.

mall
A place where people may walk; an open area. The *mall* is lined with stores.

mama
Mother.

mammal
An animal that has a backbone and a warm body, the female of which produces milk for its babies. Dogs and cats are *mammals,* but fish are not.

man
1. A grown male person. A boy grows up to be a *man.* The plural of *man* is *men.*
2. People in general. *Man* has invented many things to make life easy.

manage
managed
managing
To control; to be in charge of. Jim's uncle will *manage* the new store. The *manager* of the business was the boss.

mane
The long hair that grows on the neck and head of some animals. Black Beauty has a black *mane.*

manner
1. A way of acting; behavior. The sales clerk had a nice *manner.*
2. (Plural) Polite behavior. It is good *manners* to say "Please" and "Thank you."

manufacture
manufactured
manufacturing
The business of making things, especially by machines. Auto factories *manufacture* cars. Henry Ford was one of the first auto *manufacturers.*

map
A drawing that shows the earth or a section of it. Joan found her state on the *map* of the United States.

maple
A kind of tree. The seeds of the *maple* look like little wings. One kind of *maple* tree gives sap for *maple* sugar.

maple

marble
1. A small round glass object or stone used in playing certain games.
2. A kind of hard stone. The statue was made of white *marble.*

marble

March
The third month of the year.

march
marched
marching
To walk in time to a beat; to walk with even steps. The school band will *march* in the parade.

margin The white border around the printing or writing on a page. Your dictionary has a *margin* on each page.

marine A person who belongs to the Marine Corps of the United States. Soldiers, sailors, and *marines* marched in the parade.

mark 1. A written or printed figure or line. Put a check *mark* next to your name.
2. A line or spot left by something that is no longer there. John's rubber heel left a *mark* on the floor.
3. A grade. Hal received a good *mark* on his spelling paper.

market A place where goods are bought and sold, often an outdoor space. We bought apples at the fruit *market.*

marry
married
marrying To become husband and wife; to have a wedding. Sarah is going to *marry* Walter.

Mars The fourth planet from the sun. See page 222.

marsh An area of low land partly covered by water. Many kinds of grasses grow in a *marsh.*

marshmallow A soft, sweet, candy-like food, usually white.

masculine Having to do with boys and men; male.

mash
mashed
mashing To crush or press together; to change into a soft mixture. Pat *mashed* the potatoes.

mask 1. A covering to hide the face; a false face. We wore Halloween *masks* to the party.
2. A covering to protect the face. The worker wore a *mask* while cutting steel.

masks

mass 1. A large number of people or things in one place. A *mass* of people watched the parade.
2. A lump. The ice cubes stuck together in a *mass.*
3. A kind of Catholic church service. Mary's family goes to the ten o'clock *mass.*

mast A long upright pole on a sailboat. The *mast* holds up the sails.

master The head person; the person in charge. Bill is the dog's *master.*

mat 1. A small rug. Wipe your feet on the *mat.*
2. A pad. We use thick *mats* in gym.

mast

match 1. A small stick of wood or cardboard tipped with a substance that burns when scratched against a rough surface. A *match* is used to light a fire.
2. A person or thing that is exactly like or almost like another. This sock is not a *match* for the other sock.
3. A contest or game. The fighters had a boxing *match.*

material 1. Cloth or yard goods. Alice's dress is made of soft *material.*
2. A substance used in making something else. Wood and brick are building *materials.*

math A short word for mathematics; arithmetic.

mathematics Arithmetic; the study of numbers, size, and form. *Mathematics* is Jan's favorite subject.

May The fifth month of the year.

may
might 1. To have permission to; to be allowed to. You *may* leave when your work is finished.
2. To be possible to; to be likely to. It *may* rain.

maybe Perhaps; possibly. *Maybe* it will rain tomorrow.

mayor The person at the head of a city or town. The *mayor* is elected by the people.

me A word used in place of one's own name. Janet said, "Call *me* tomorrow."

meadow A field of grass. The sheep are in the *meadow.*

meal 1. Food eaten at a regular time each day. Breakfast is the first *meal* of the day.
2. Grain that is coarsely ground. *Meal* is not so fine as flour.

mean Cruel or rude; not kind. The boy was *mean* to the cat.

mean
meant
meaning
1. To say the same thing as. The word "small" *means* "little."
2. To do on purpose. The boy did not *mean* to slam the door.

meanwhile At the same time; while something else is happening. The cake was in the oven; *meanwhile* Jane made the icing.

measure
measured
measuring
1. To find the size, amount, time, or weight of. The shoe salesman will *measure* your foot.
2. To have a certain measurement. The table *measures* six feet long.

**measure-
ment**
Size; how large or small something is. Do you know the *measurements* of a football field?

meat 1. The flesh of animals that is used for food. Bacon, lamb, and beef are kinds of *meat.*
2. The part of nuts that is eaten. Mother put nut *meats* into the cookies.

medal A small flat piece of metal with a design that is an award for a special act. The runner was given a *medal* for winning the race.

medal

medicine
1. A substance given to a sick person to help him get well. Pills are one kind of *medicine.* 2. The science of treating sick people. Dr. Adams studied *medicine.*

meet
met
meeting
1. To come together; to come upon face to face. Lucy and I plan to *meet* at the corner. 2. To be introduced to; to get to know. You will *meet* new people at a new school.

meeting
A gathering; the coming together of two or more people. We have a Scout *meeting* each Monday night.

melody
A tune; a series of musical notes that follow each other in a pleasing way. The *melody* of that song is easy to sing.

melon
A fruit with juicy flesh inside and a hard, thick skin outside.

melon

melt
melted
melting
To change from a solid to a liquid. Ice will *melt* quickly in warm weather.

member
A person who belongs to a club or other organized group. Wanda is a *member* of the Brownies.

memo
A short note, report, or reminder. Our school sent a *memo* home about our field trip.

memorize
memorized
memorizing
To learn and be able to repeat word for word. Our teacher asked us to *memorize* a poem.

memory
The ability to remember. Granddad has a good *memory* of the past.

mend
mended
mending
To fix or repair; to put in good condition again. Mother will *mend* the rip in your coat.

mention
mentioned
mentioning
   To speak of or talk about briefly.

menu   A list of foods served. The waiter in the restaurant gave each of us a *menu.*

Mercury   The planet nearest the sun. See page 222.

mercury   A heavy, silver-white metal, usually a liquid. *Mercury* is often used in thermometers.

mermaid   An imaginary creature that lives in the sea. The top half of a *mermaid* looks like a woman and the bottom half looks like a fish.

merry   Jolly; gay; full of fun. The children had a *merry* time at the party.

merry-go-round   A round platform that turns, with wooden animals and seats for children to ride on or in, usually to the sound of music. We will ride horses on the *merry-go-round.*

merry-go-round

mess   A lack of order; a dirty or mixed-up condition. My brother's room is usually a *mess.*

message   A note or information that is sent from one person to another. Tom gave the teacher a *message* from his father.

metal   A substance found in the earth. *Metal* is usually hard and shiny and can be shaped into different forms when hot. Iron and gold are *metals.*

meteor   A burning meteoroid which leaves a streak of light in the sky as it enters the atmosphere. Sometimes *meteors* are called shooting stars.

meteor

meteoroid   A stone or metal object in space. A *meteoroid* becomes a meteor or shooting star when it falls through Earth's atmosphere.

microphone   A piece of equipment used in TV or radio broadcasts or with a loudspeaker. An announcer talks into a *microphone.*

microscope   An instrument that makes very small objects easier to see. A fly's wing looks big under a *microscope.*

middle   1. At the same distance from all sides or between the first and the last.
2. A central area. We live in the *middle* of the city. Jan is the *middle* child, with an older brother and younger sister.

midget   1. A person who does not grow nearly as big as most people; a dwarf.
2. Something much smaller than others of its kind. John went to see the *midget* autos race.

microscope

midnight   The middle of the night; twelve o'clock at night.

might Strength; power; force. Tim pushed with all his *might* to open the door.

mild 1. Kind or gentle; not rough.
2. Not strong in taste or smell. There is a *mild* smell of smoke in the air.

mile A measurement of length; 5,280 feet.

milk 1. A white liquid produced by some female animals to feed their young.
2. The milk of animals used as food by people. *Milk* comes from cows and goats.

milkman A man who sells or delivers milk.

milk shake A drink made by shaking a mixture of milk, flavoring, and sometimes ice cream. Sue likes a chocolate *milk shake.*

Milky Way Millions of faraway stars, seen as a white trail of light in the sky at night.

mill 1. A building with machinery for grinding grain into meal or flour.
2. A factory. Dad works in a *mill* that makes rugs.

Milky Way

miller 1. A person who owns or runs a grain mill.
2. A kind of moth. At night you may see a *miller* fly around a lamp.

million A number; 1,000,000. See page 199.

mind The ability to think, learn, and reason. Pat uses her brain; she has a good *mind.*

mind
minded
minding 1. To obey; to do as you are told. "*Mind* your teacher," said Mother.
2. To take care of. Sally will *mind* her baby sister after school.
3. To be bothered by. Did Al *mind* the cold?

minibike

mine 1. A hole in the earth from which ores or minerals are removed. The old cowboy discovered a gold *mine.*
2. A kind of bomb, usually hidden from sight. The tank blew up as it went over the *mine.*

mine Belonging to me. This book is my book and the pencil is *mine,* too.

mineral A chemical substance found by digging in the earth. Gold is one kind of *mineral.*

minibike A small bicycle or motorcycle.

minister 1. The person in charge of a church.
2. In some countries, an official of the government. The head of the education department may be called a *minister* of education.

minor A person who is not old enough to be given all the rights of an adult. A *minor* is not old enough to vote.

minus 1. Less. Ten *minus* five is five.
2. Without; lacking. It began to rain but Mike was *minus* his umbrella.

mirror Any surface in which you can see yourself, especially a piece of glass with a metal film on the back.

mirror

mischief A person's playful act that makes trouble for others. Dan's *mischief* made Ann break a dish.

Miss A title used before the name of an unmarried woman or of a girl. *Miss* Johnson works in the bank.

miss
missed
missing

1. To fail to hit, reach, or catch. The sun in my eyes made me **miss** the ball.
2. To feel lonesome for. I **miss** my old friends.
3. To fail to attend. Roy will **miss** the party next week because he will be away.

missile

An object that can be thrown or fired at a target. A rocket is a **missile.**

mission

1. A person or a group of persons sent some place to do special work. A **mission** of Americans went to help people in Africa.
2. The work to be done by a group of people. Their **mission** was to teach new ways of farming.

mission control

In a space center, the people who control a space flight. **Mission control** directed the moon landings.

mist
misty

Very fine bits of water in the air. Sometimes the air is **misty** and cloudy.

mistake

An error; something done wrong. I made a **mistake** on one arithmetic problem.

mitt

A baseball glove.

mitten

A covering for the hand with one part for four fingers and another part for the thumb.

mix
mixed
mixing

To stir and blend two or more materials together. Dad will **mix** cement with sand, gravel, and water. This **mixture** will be concrete.

mitten

moan

A low sound of pain; a low sad sound.

mob

A crowd of people, sometimes acting in an angry way. The **mob** pushed at the iron gate.

mobile home

A house trailer, usually a large one. Our friends moved their **mobile home** to a new state.

moccasin   A soft shoe or slipper with no laces. Indians made *moccasins* out of animal skins.

moccasin

model
1. A small copy of an object. Chris made a clay *model* of a horse.
2. A person who acts as a subject for an artist or a photographer. The picture was of a *model* wearing the new fashions.
3. An object of a certain design. Dad's car is a new *model.*

modern   Having to do with present times; up-to-date. Flying is the *modern* way to travel.

moist   Wet; damp. Dot's face was *moist* from tears.

moisture   Slight dampness or wetness. The *moisture* in the air made the clothes slow to dry.

mold
1. A hollow form for giving shape. We have a cake *mold* in the shape of a heart.
2. A fur-like substance that grows on old wood, paper, leather, or food. Don't eat bread with *mold* on it.

moment   A very short time; an instant. Our TV program will start in just a *moment.*

Monday   The second day of the week.

money   Coins and paper bills used in buying and selling and as a payment for work.

monkey   A long-tailed, tree-climbing animal that lives in tropic lands.

monorail
1. A kind of train that travels on one rail.
2. The rail or track that a monorail runs on.

monorail

monster
1. An unusually large animal or object. A bulldozer is a *monster* compared to a lawn mower.

2. A huge, frightening imaginary person or animal. The dragon was a *monster* with teeth like a lion's and eyes like fire.

month   A period of time; usually 30 or 31 days.

monument   A thing built in memory of a person or a happening. The Washington *Monument* honors George Washington.

moon   The body in space that orbits the earth; a satellite. The *moon* is not as large as the earth.

moonlight   Light that seems to come from the moon. *Moonlight* is made by reflection of the sun's light shining on the moon.

moonwalk   A walk by astronauts to explore the moon's surface. The astronauts picked up lunar rocks on their *moonwalk.*

moose   A large animal of the deer family. The plural of *moose* is *moose.*

mop   A floor-cleaning tool with a cloth, sponge, or other material at the end of a long handle.

more   A larger amount. We need *more* meat for the hamburgers.

morning   The early part of the day; the time from midnight to noon or from sunrise to noon.

Morse code   A code for sending telegraph or radio messages by dots and dashes or long and short sounds that stand for letters and numbers.

mosquito   A flying insect. The female *mosquito* bites people and animals.

moss   A tiny green plant that grows in patches on the ground, on trees, and on stones. Sometimes *moss* looks like a soft rug.

moose

mop

mosquito

most
mostly
The biggest part. *Most* of the bread was eaten. The candies are *mostly* chocolate.

motel
A hotel where guests can park their cars near their rooms. A *motel* may be called a "motor inn" or a "motor court."

moth
An insect something like a butterfly. A *moth* is usually a night insect.

moth

mother
1. A woman who has one or more children.
2. A female animal that has babies.

motion
1. Movement; activity. Don't leave your seat while the bus is in *motion.*
2. A suggestion to be voted upon. Al made a *motion* that everyone should fight pollution.

motion picture
A series of filmed pictures shown on a screen. Things appear to move in a *motion picture* because many single pictures are shown quickly, one after another.

motor
An engine; a machine that creates energy. Our car has a *motor.*

motorboat
A boat that has a motor to move it. A *motorboat* moves faster than a rowboat.

motorcycle
A two-wheeled motor vehicle. A *motorcycle* is a type of bicycle moved by a motor.

motto
A short saying or rule to follow. My *motto* is "Always take time to be safe."

mountain
A place where the earth rises very high above the level of the ground around it. A *mountain* is higher than a hill and often has steep sides.

mouse
A small, gray, brown, or white animal that lives in buildings, fields, or woods. The plural of *mouse* is *mice.*

mouse

mouth The opening in the face through which a person or animal eats food and makes sounds.

move
moved
moving
1. To change the position or place of. *Move* your arms above your head. I like to watch the *movements* of a musician's hands.
2. To cause motion of. The wind will *move* the boat.
3. To go to another place to live. The family will *move* to a big city.

movie A motion picture.

mow
mowed
mowing
To cut down grass or other plants. My sister *mowed* our yard when I was at camp. She likes our new lawn *mower*.

muffins

Mr. A title used before the name of a man.

Mrs. A title used before the name of a married woman.

Ms. A title used before the name of a married or unmarried woman.

much Great in amount. *Much* snow falls in the North.

mud A mixture of water and earth. Debby's shoe came off in the thick *mud.*

muddy Full of mud; covered with mud. Don't come inside with your *muddy* shoes.

mug

muffin A kind of bread baked in the shape of a cup. This sweet *muffin* is like cake.

mug A thick, heavy drinking cup.

mule A work animal that is half horse and half donkey. A *mule* has longer ears than a horse.

mule

multiply
multiplied
multiplying
To increase greatly in number. Without birds to eat them, insects will *multiply. Multiplication* is a quick way to add the same number many times.

murder The crime of killing a person.

muscle A rope-like inner part of the body that makes other body parts move. Baseball players need strong *muscles.*

museum A building where interesting objects from many places are kept for people to see. We saw the skeleton of a huge dinosaur at the *museum.*

mushrooms

mushroom A small, spongy, leafless plant that grows close to the ground. Some *mushrooms* are good to eat. Wild *mushrooms* may be poisonous.

music
musical Pleasing sounds made by singing, or by instruments such as the piano, flute, or guitar. Our school will put on a *musical* show.

musician A person who plays a musical instrument. Our school band has 30 *musicians* in it.

must To have to. I *must* hurry to catch the bus.

mustard A yellow or brown spread used on foods to season them. People often put *mustard* on ham sandwiches.

my Belonging to me. The dog is *my* dog and lives with *my* family.

myself My very own self. I can read a book by *myself.*

mysterious
mysteriously Hard to explain; full of mystery. There are *mysterious* things happening at our house. Things are disappearing *mysteriously.*

mystery An unexplained happening or situation.

Nn

nail
1. A slim piece of metal, pointed on one end and having a flat head on the other. You can hammer a *nail* to fasten two pieces of wood together.
2. The hard covering that grows at the end of a finger or toe. Your *nails* help to protect your fingers.

naked   Bare; not wearing any clothes.

name
1. A word by which a person or thing is known. My dog's *name* is Lady.
2. An unkind word spoken about someone. The big boys called Ted *names.*

nap
1. A brief or short sleep. The cat took a *nap* in the sun.
2. The soft surface on certain cloths or materials. The rug had a thick *nap.*

napkin   A piece of cloth or paper used to wipe the lips and fingers while eating.

narrow   Of a short distance across; not wide. The path is *narrow.*

nation
national   A land or country and the people who live there. The United States is a *nation.* The eagle is the *national* bird of the United States.

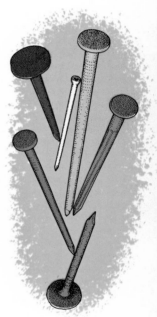

nails

native A person born in a certain place. Abe Lincoln was a *native* of Kentucky.

native Describing an animal, plant, or person first found in one part of the world. The kangaroo is *native* to Australia.

natural Found in nature; not made by man. Honey is a *natural* food made by bees.
2. Created by nature; not the result of training. Pete has a *natural* singing voice.
3. Happening in an expected way. It was *natural* for Dot to want to go on the trip.

nature The world and all things not made by man, especially the outdoors and living things. We see *nature* all around us; in plants and animals, the sea, the land, and in our weather.

naughty Bad; not well behaved. The *naughty* child would not go to bed on time.

navy A nation's sea force of ships, planes, and men. A warship is part of a *navy*.

near Not far off in space or time; close by. When birds go south, winter is *near.* We will walk *near* the water.

nearby Close by; not far away. The baby's mother is *nearby.*

nearly Almost; close to. The baby is *nearly* a year old.

neat
neatly In good order; tidy, clean. Mary likes a *neat* room. She hangs up her clothes *neatly.*

necessary Needed. Warm clothes are *necessary* in cold weather.

neck The part of the body between the head and shoulders. The giraffe has a long *neck.*

necklace A kind of jewelry worn around the neck.

necktie A narrow piece of cloth worn around the neck and tied in a knot or a bow.

need
needed
needing To have to have or do; to be unable to do without. We **need** money to pay for food.

needle 1. A thin piece of steel used for sewing.
2. A pointer showing direction on a compass.

needn't A short form of "need not."

Negro A person with black or brown skin whose ancestors lived in Africa. Dr. Martin Luther King, Jr. was a **Negro.** He led and helped other **Negroes.**

neighbor A person who lives near or is located next to another person.

neighbor-hood An area; a section of a town or city. The children in our **neighborhood** like to play ball together.

neither Not either; not one or the other. **Neither** Alice nor Frank will go.

Neptune The eighth planet from the sun. See page 222.

nest A home made by a bird or other animal.

net A web-like material with many holes in it. Tom caught a fish with his **net.**

never At no time; not ever. You will **never** see a purple cow.

new 1. Recently made or grown; not old. Each spring, the trees have **new** leaves.
2. Different from before. The family moved to a **new** town.

compass needle

sewing needle

knitting needle

bird's nest

newborn Very young; born recently.

news 1. Something that has just happened; new information. The report that the boy saved the baby's life was *news.*
2. Reports presented on radio or television and in newspapers about current happenings. We listened to the six o'clock *news.*

newspaper Sheets of paper on which news and other information are printed.

next 1. Nearest; closest. My friend lives in the house *next* to mine.
2. Following in time or order; after this. What book will you read *next?*

nibble
nibbled
nibbling To eat in small bites. The mice will *nibble* the cheese.

nice Good, pleasant. The weather is *nice* today.

nickel 1. A United States coin worth five cents. A *nickel* is equal to five pennies.
2. A hard, silver-colored metal.

nickname A name used in place of a real name. "Billy" is a *nickname* for "William."

nifty Great; pleasing; up-to-date. Jim has a *nifty* new bike.

night The hours of darkness. *Night* comes between sunset and sunrise.

nightgown A loose garment that is worn to bed.

nightmare A horrible dream. Dan's *nightmare* was about men from space.

nine A number; 9. One more than 8 and one less than 10. See page 199.

nineteen A number; 19. One more than 18 and one less than 20. See page 199.

ninety A number; 90. See page 199.

no
1. Not so; the opposite of "yes."
2. Not any. There are *no* cookies in the jar.

nobody
1. Not one person; not anyone. *Nobody* was in the room.
2. A person who is not important.

nod
nodded
nodding
1. To say "yes" by bowing the head forward or moving it up and down slowly. Nan *nodded* to show she agreed with Tim.
2. To let the head fall forward in sleep. The tired child began to *nod.*

noise A sound, especially a loud one. That *noise* was the slamming of the door.

noisy Loud; easy to hear. A *noisy* truck woke the sleeping baby.

none
1. Not one. We saw *none* of our friends at the game.
2. Not any. *None* of the cake is left.

nonfiction Written facts or information; stories that are true and not made up. This book about dogs is *nonfiction.*

nonsense Foolishness; something that doesn't make sense. It is *nonsense* to say that elephants fly!

noodle A thin strip of dough, often used in soup. We had chicken soup with *noodles* for dinner.

noodles

noon Twelve o'clock in the daytime. We eat lunch at *noon.*

nor And not either; and not. Neither Gail *nor* Kate can go to the movies.

nose

normal Regular, usual; the way things are most of the time. We had the *normal* amount of rain this year.

north The direction on your left when you face the sunrise. See illustration at **compass.**

nose 1. The middle part of the face, standing out above the mouth and below the eyes. The *nose* is used for breathing and smelling.
2. The front part of anything that moves. The pilot put the *nose* of the plane down to land.

nostril One of two openings in the nose. Air and smells come into the body through the *nostrils.*

not In no way. *Not* is used to change a word to its opposite meaning. The paint is *not* dry.

note 1. A short letter; a few words.
2. A musical sound. The singer sang the first *notes* of the song.

note
noted
noting 1. To observe or notice carefully. Please *note* that the sun is setting.
2. To write down or put in writing.

nothing Not anything; no thing. There was *nothing* in the empty box.

notice A message or sign. Our teacher put a *notice* on the bulletin board.

notice
noticed
noticing To look at or see; to pay attention to. *Notice* how the bird flies.

noun A word that gives a name to a person, place, or thing. *John, America, book,* and *luck* are *nouns.*

nourishment Something necessary for life and growth. Milk provides *nourishment* for our bodies.

novel A long, make-believe story.

November The eleventh month of the year.

now 1. This time. Ben should be here by *now*.
2. At once; right away. Do it *now!*
3. Since; being that. *Now* that the sun is shining, we can go outside.
4. With things as they are; as it is. Sally walked too slowly; *now* she will be late for school.

nowhere In no place. *Nowhere* could we find the lost kitten.

number 1. A word or figure used to tell how many. *Numbers* are shown in the chart on this page.
2. Several; more than one. A *number* of children are playing in the park.

number
numbered
numbering
1. To add up to or make a total of. Our club *numbers* 22 members.
2. To put numbers on. Please *number* the lines on your paper from one to ten.

numeral A number; a figure that stands for a number.

NUMBERS

0	zero		10	ten			
1	one	first	11	eleven			
2	two	second	12	twelve	20	twenty	100 one hundred
3	three	third	13	thirteen	30	thirty	1,000 one thousand
4	four	fourth	14	fourteen	40	forty	10,000 ten thousand
5	five	fifth	15	fifteen	50	fifty	100,000 one hundred thousand
6	six	sixth	16	sixteen	60	sixty	1,000,000 one million
7	seven	seventh	17	seventeen	70	seventy	10,000,000 ten million
8	eight	eighth	18	eighteen	80	eighty	100,000,000 one hundred million
9	nine	ninth	19	nineteen	90	ninety	1,000,000,000 one billion

nurse A person trained to take care of sick people. The *nurse* works at the hospital.

nursery 1. A baby's room.
2. A place where babies and small children are cared for.
3. A place where plants are grown and sold. They don't have pine trees at this *nursery.*

nut

nut 1. The fruit or seeds of certain plants. Some *nuts* have hard shells.
2. A piece of metal that fits on a bolt.
3. A foolish person. Some *nut* threw trash on the sidewalk.

nutrition Food; the way the body uses food. We learn about *nutrition* in our health class.

nylon A synthetic material, like silk, used mostly for clothing.

Oo

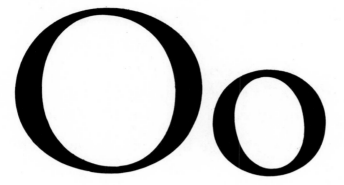

oak   A kind of tree. The *oak* has acorns.

oar   A pole with a wide, flat end. *Oars* are used to row a small boat through the water.

oasis   A place in the desert where water and plants are found. Palm trees grow at this *oasis.* The plural of *oasis* is *oases.*

oat   A kind of grass grown for its cereal grain. We eat cereal made from *oats.*

oatmeal   A cooked cereal made of oats. Tom eats hot *oatmeal* for breakfast.

obey
obeyed
obeying   To mind; to do as you are told. Steve taught his dog to *obey* commands. The dog won a prize for *obedience.*

object   1. A thing that can be seen or touched. There are three *objects* on the table: a ball, a ring, and a pencil.
2. The aim; the point or plan of. The *object* of the game is to throw the ball into the basket.

object
objected
objecting   To refuse to agree; to be opposed to. Why do you *object* to my riding your bike?

observe
observed
observing   To see; to take notice; to watch carefully. *Observe* how the spider builds a web.

oak

oasis

occupation A person's work or business.

occur
occurred
occurring
1. To happen; to take place. When will the game *occur?*
2. To come to the mind or the attention of. It *occurred* to John that he was late.

ocean A very large body of salt water; the sea.

o'clock Time of day. We eat dinner at six *o'clock.*

October The tenth month of the year.

octopus An animal with eight legs that lives in the ocean. Most *octopuses* live in warm, shallow waters.

octopus

odd
oddly
1. Strange; queer; unusual. The lady had on an *odd* hat. Some clouds are *oddly* shaped.
2. Not able to be divided exactly by two. Three and five are *odd* numbers.
3. Extra; not part of a pair. Bob found an *odd* sock in his drawer.

odor A smell. The flowers have a pleasant *odor.*

of
1. From; with. My coat is made *of* wool.
2. About. The story was *of* Cinderella and the prince.
3. Connected with. Holidays are a time *of* joy.
4. Named or called. Bob lives in the city *of* Los Angeles.

off
1. Away. The robin flew *off.*
2. Down or away from. The ball rolled *off* the table.
3. Not on or in. Please keep *off* the grass.
4. Not in use. Turn *off* the light.

offer
1. To try to give. The children *offered* peanuts to the squirrel.
2. To say that you are willing. Bob *offered* to wash the dishes.

office 1. A place where business or a certain kind of work is done. The doctor is in her *office.*
2. A special job or public position. Mr. Wilson holds the *office* of mayor.

officer 1. A person with a special position in a club or company. The president is one of the *officers* of a club.
2. A policeman. Ask the *officer* for directions.
3. A person who commands others in forces such as the Army or Navy.

official A person holding a high position in business or government. The governor is an *official* of a state.

often Again and again; many times. I *often* listen to the radio.

ogre A make-believe monster; a very ugly person. In the story, the *ogre* frightened the princess.

oh A word showing surprise or feeling. *"Oh!"* said Sue. "That puppy is cute."

oil A greasy liquid. *Oils* are used in paints, salads, and on machine parts.

O.K. All right; correct. The teacher marked *"O.K."* on Mike's math paper.

old 1. Having lived long or been used for a long time; not young or new. Our *old* dog sleeps much of the time.
2. Of age. Tina is three years *old.*
3. Of past time or place. Jim's *old* house was in another state.

olives

olive The small, green or ripe fruit of a tree that grows in warm countries. Ripe *olives* are dark purple in color.

on
1. Touching the surface of. Your gloves are *on* the table.
2. By means of. Alice talked to Ken *on* the telephone.
3. A member of. Bob is *on* the safety patrol.
4. Along or at the side of. The ranch was *on* a river.
5. In use; not off. The TV is *on.*
6. At the time of. Henry was sick *on* Friday.

once
1. One time. Mother shops *once* a day.
2. In the past. Ed's dad was *once* a printer.
3. As soon as; after; whenever. *Once* you've read the book, you'll want to read it again.

one
1. A number; 1. *One* comes before two. See page 199.
2. Any person or thing. *One* can hope for peace.
3. The same; alike. The cars were moving in *one* direction.

onion

onion
A vegetable with a strong odor and taste. Tony puts *onion* on his hamburger.

only
1. One; alone. Ted lost his *only* pencil.
2. Except that; but. She is nice, *only* she always wants her own way.
3. Just. Paul lived *only* a block from the school.

onto
1. On the top of. He threw the ball *onto* the roof.
2. Upon; on. Gail jumped *onto* the bus.

onward
Ahead; forward. The band marched *onward* to the city hall.

open
openly
1. Allowing entrance or exit; not closed or covered. The window is *open.*
2. Not secret or hidden. Tim showed *open* sorrow. He cried *openly.*

open
opened
opening

1. To move from a closed position. Please **open** the door.
2. To begin or start. The show will **open** with music.
3. To remove a cover. **Open** your birthday gift.

opera

A kind of play in which the actors sing instead of talk most of their parts. An **opera** needs an orchestra.

operate
operated
operating

1. To work; to run. John can **operate** the camera. He will explain the **operation** of the camera to you.
2. To manage or control; to be in charge of. Alice's dad **operates** a gasoline station.
3. To cut into the body to remove or repair an injured part. The doctor **operated** on the boy.

opinion

A thought that something is so or will be so. In my **opinion,** it will rain.

opposite

1. Placed right across from. The store is **opposite** the fire station.
2. In all ways different from. "Good" is the **opposite** of "bad."

or

On the other hand. You may ride your bike **or** take a walk.

orange

1. A round, juicy fruit. An **orange** is a good breakfast food.
2. A color. See page 70.

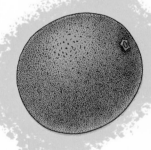

orange

orbit

The path followed by a heavenly body or spaceship. Our earth is in an **orbit** around the sun.

orchard

A group of fruit or nut trees. The farmer has an apple **orchard.**

orchestra

A group of musicians playing together under one leader. Many different instruments are needed in an **orchestra.**

organ

order
1. A list of things that are wanted. We gave our *order* to the waiter.
2. A command or instruction. Kathy must follow the doctor's *orders.*
3. The way things are placed or happen. We put the books in the right *order.*

ordinary
Usual; regular. We will not wear our *ordinary* clothes in the school play.

ore
A kind of rock or mineral that contains valuable material, especially metal.

organ
1. A part of the body which does a special and important job. The heart is an *organ.*
2. A large musical instrument with sounding pipes. Many churches have *organs.*

organization
A group of people working together. The U.N. is an international *organization.*

organize
organized
organizing
1. To arrange or put in order. Please *organize* the books on the library table.
2. To form. Let's *organize* a chess club.

original
The first form of something, one from which copies can be made. This copy of the painting looks very much like the *original.*

ornament
A fancy button, ribbon, pin, or other object added to make something more beautiful. A ring is an *ornament* for the finger.

other
Different; not the same. Bill liked the *other* drawing best.

ought
Should. Everyone *ought* to learn to swim.

ounce
1. A unit of measurement for liquids, about equal to what can be held in two soup spoons.
2. A unit of measurement for weight. Two big spoonfuls of sugar weigh about one ounce.

our
ours Owned by or belonging to us. *Our* car is red.
That house is *ours.*

ourselves Our own selves or us. By playing with matches, we can burn *ourselves.*

out
1. Away from the inside of something. Come *out* and play.
2. On or along. The car went *out* Main Street.
3. No longer burning. The campfire was *out.*
4. Into view or able to be seen. I hope the sun comes *out* today.

outdoor
outdoors Outside of a house or building; in the open air. Jim likes *outdoor* games. He likes to be *outdoors* instead of indoors.

outfit A set; a number of things that belong together. Each Scout has a new camping *outfit.*

outlaw A person who breaks a law.

outside
1. The surface; not the inside. A ripe watermelon is green on the *outside.*
2. Outdoors; not inside. Jim went *outside* to play.
3. Beyond the area or limits of. He played *outside* the park.

oven A closed place in which things are heated or cooked. The bread was baked in the *oven.*

over
1. In a higher place; above in place or power. The light was *over* the sink.
2. Across and above. The plane went *over* the mountains.
3. Throughout or during. Sandy stayed home *over* the holidays.
4. Finished; at an end. The play is *over.*
5. So as to cover. Jill put a blanket *over* the bed.

overalls

| **overalls** | (Plural) Loose, heavy work pants. Some *overalls* have bib-like fronts and straps over the shoulders. |

overboard From the side of a boat or ship. The sailor fell *overboard* into the water.

overcoat A warm coat worn over other clothes. An *overcoat* is worn in cold weather.

overcome
overcame
overcoming
1. To defeat; to do better than. The crippled boy will *overcome* his handicap.
2. To make helpless. The hunter was *overcome* with fear as the tiger sprang.

overflow
overflowed
overflowing
To run over; to spill out. Do not let the water in the sink *overflow* onto the floor.

overhear
overheard
overhearing
To hear something by accident or without being noticed. Whisper so no one will *overhear* you.

overlook
overlooked
overlooking
To miss; to fail to see. Jack's teacher will not *overlook* a spelling error.

overseas Beyond or across the ocean. Mike's dad made an *overseas* telephone call.

overshoe A covering for the foot worn over a regular shoe; a boot or rubber. We wear *overshoes* when it rains or snows.

overshoes

overweight Too heavy; weighing too much. The fat boy is very much *overweight.*

owe
owed
owing
To need to pay or give. Maria borrowed a quarter from Bill. Now she *owes* Bill 25 cents.

owl　A bird of prey with large eyes and sharp claws. The *owl* usually flies at night and sleeps during the day.

own　To have as property. Tom *owns* an old bike. Ed
owned　is the *owner* of a new ten-speed bicycle.
owning

ox　An animal in the cattle family. An *ox* can be trained to pull a cart or plow. The plural of *ox* is *oxen.*

oxygen　A gas that all people and animals need in order to live. *Oxygen* is in the air we breathe.

oyster　A small animal found in the sea, which is used as food. The *oyster* is a shellfish with a soft body inside a two-part shell.

owl

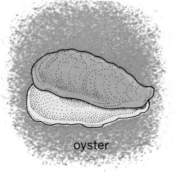

oyster

ox

Pp

pace
1. A walking step. An adult *pace* is three feet.
2. The speed at which something is done. The carpenter worked at a rapid *pace.*

pack
packed
packing
1. To put in a container or a bundle. I will *pack* my clothes in this suitcase.
2. To fill. A crowd will *pack* the circus tent.
3. To crowd together. The people were *packed* into the crowded train.

package
A bundle or box and its contents. The big *package* contained a doll.

pad
1. A tablet of paper for writing or drawing. I took a sheet of paper from my *pad.*
2. A thick piece of soft material used to protect something. The football player wore *pads* to protect his knees.

paddle
A small oar. You use a *paddle* to move a canoe through water.

page
1. One side of a printed piece of paper in a book, magazine, or newspaper. You are reading a *page* in your dictionary now.
2. A person who carries messages or runs errands. The *page* called the senator to the telephone.

paddle

pageant A costume show or parade about things that happened long ago. I saw a *pageant* about the discovery of America.

pail A metal or plastic container with a handle, used for carrying things or liquids; a bucket.

pail

pain A feeling you get when something hurts you; an ache. I have a *pain* in my left foot.

painful
painfully Hurting; causing pain. A burn is a *painful* injury. The injured dog limped *painfully* down the road.

paint A colored liquid that dries when brushed on something. Jane used red *paint* on her bed.

paint
painted
painting To color with paint. My big brother *painted* the walls of my room blue.

pair A set of two things that belong together. Joe left a *pair* of gloves on the table.

pajamas A light, loose suit worn when sleeping.

palace A large and grand house in which a king or queen lives.

pans

pale 1. Having little color. Your face is *pale.*
2. Without much brightness. The stars in the sky are *pale* tonight.

palm 1. The inside surface of your hand between your wrist and your fingers. Mary held the frog in the *palm* of her hand.
2. A tall tree with big, fan-like leaves at its top. *Palms* grow in warm places.

pan A container used for cooking.

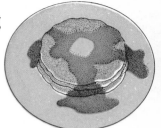

pancakes

pancake A thin, round cake that is fried. I like *pancakes* for breakfast.

pansy

pansy　A low garden plant with colorful flowers. Yellow, violet, and white flowers grow on my *pansy* plants.

pantry　A small room in which food, kitchen supplies, and dishes are stored.

papa　Father.

paper　Thin sheets of material used for writing or wrapping. *Paper* can be made from wood or rags.

parachute　A large, strong cloth and metal frame, which can carry a person or thing safely from a plane in the air to the ground below. A *parachute* opens like an umbrella.

parade　A group of people marching or riding in line through the streets. There is a big *parade* with marching bands on the Fourth of July.

paragraph　A group of sentences that tells about one idea or thing. Read about the lion in the first *paragraph* of the story.

pardon　The act of forgiving someone or something. Ann said, "I beg your *pardon* for being late."

parachute

parade

pardon
pardoned
pardoning

1. To forgive. Will you *pardon* me for not calling you?
2. To excuse from punishment. The robber was *pardoned* and sent home.

parent A mother or father.

park An outdoor place with grass and trees where people can sit on benches or play.

park
parked
parking

To put or leave for the time being. *Park* your bike behind the school.

parka A heavy, warm jacket with a hood.

parrot A brightly colored tropical bird which can be taught to speak.

parka

part
1. A piece of something. Here is *part* of my sandwich.
2. A role in a play. Who will play the *part* of the king?

part
parted
parting

To separate, one from another. Jack and his friend had to *part* for the summer.

partly Not entirely or completely. Our tree house is *partly* built.

partner
1. A person who owns part of a business.
2. One of two people who do something together. Who is your *partner* for the dance?

party A gathering of people for an afternoon or evening of fun; a celebration. My birthday *party* is today.

pass
1. A kind of ticket which lets you come or go without paying. I can use this *pass* to see the show free.
2. A narrow opening between mountains.

parrot

pass
passed
passing

1. To move ahead or in front of. Did that car *pass* the truck?
2. To go by. I *pass* your house on my way to school.
3. To hand over to someone else. *Pass* this paper to Susan.

passenger

A person who rides in a car, boat, bus, train, plane, or other vehicle.

past

1. Times gone by; not now. In the *past*, Uncle Dan lived in Chicago.
2. By. Tom ran *past* me.

paste

1. A thick, white substance used for sticking things together. We can make *paste* with flour and water.
2. Any of many soft, moist substances. I brush my teeth with tooth*paste.*

pastry

A food that is sweet to eat, like a pie or a tart, made with a crust of dough.

pasture

A field with grass and plants that animals can eat. The cows are in the *pasture.*

pat
patted
patting

To tap gently with the hand. Jim *patted* his dog.

patch

1. A piece of material used for mending or covering a hole. I have a *patch* on my coat.
2. An area or spot different from the rest. The black dog has a white *patch* on its neck.

path

A narrow trail or road. The nature *path* went along the river bank.

patient
patiently

Without complaining; able to wait quietly. The *patient* dog waited for his master. The children stood *patiently* in the lunch line.

patient One who is under a doctor's care.

patio An outdoor part of a house, often used for barbecues and parties.

patrol 1. The act of walking around a building or a place to protect it. This building is under police *patrol* 24 hours a day.
2. Persons who protect children at street crossings. There is a safety *patrol* in our school.

patter Light sounds made one right after another. Hear the *patter* of rain on the roof.

pattern 1. A model or a plan to help make something. Mary used a *pattern* to make her doll's dress.
2. A design. That rug has a diamond *pattern.*

pave
paved
paving To cover with a tar-like substance or other hard material. After the workmen *pave* the street, it will be smooth.

paw

pavement A hard surface, such as concrete, on a road or walk.

paw A foot of an animal, usually one with claws. My cat puts its *paw* in my hand.

pay
paid
paying 1. To give money in exchange. How much did you *pay* for that dress?
2. To give. Please *pay* attention to the lesson.

pea A round green seed that is eaten as a vegetable.

peace 1. A time without war or fighting. People want *peace* for the world.
2. A time when a person is free of trouble or fear; a time of calm or quiet.

peas

peaceful 1. Calm; quiet. We had a *peaceful* day in the woods.
2. Without fighting. *Peaceful* years came after the war ended.

peach

peach   A round, juicy fruit with a fuzzy skin and a pit in its center.

peacock   A large, male bird with bright-colored feathers. A *peacock* can spread his long tail feathers to look like a brightly colored fan.

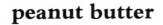

peacock

peak   1. The top of a mountain or a hill. There is snow on the *peak* of the mountain.
2. A part that sticks up or out. Bill's cap has a *peak* on the front.

peanut   1. A kind of plant whose seed pods grow under the ground.
2. A seed that grows on a peanut plant. This *peanut* came out of a hard shell.

peanut butter   A food spread made by grinding peanuts into a paste. *Peanut butter* is good on bread.

pear   A juicy, sweet fruit that grows on trees. A *pear* is wide at the bottom and narrower on top.

pearl   A round jewel found inside an oyster. Mother has a *pearl* in her ring.

pebble   A smooth, small, round stone.

peck
pecked
pecking   To strike with a beak. The chicken will *peck* at the grain.

pear

pedal   The part on which you put your foot to make something work. Put your foot on the bicycle *pedal.*

peek
peeked
peeking   To take a sly, quick look. Don't *peek* in hide-and-seek!

peel
peeled
peeling   To take the skin, bark, or covering off. Will you *peel* this orange so I can eat it?

pearl

pen
1. A writing tool. There is ink in your **pen.**
2. A small, closed place for animals. The pigs live in a **pen.**

pencil
A writing tool made of thin lead covered with metal or wood. The "lead" in a **pencil** is really a soft, dark mineral called graphite.

peninsula
A large finger of land that sticks out into water. A **peninsula** has water on three sides.

penny
A coin; one cent.

people
Men, women, and children. How many **people** live in your town?

pep
Energy; a feeling that lets you do a lot of work or play. Mother has a lot of **pep.**

pepper
1. Ground-up seeds from a pepper plant used to make food taste better. I put salt and **pepper** on my potato.
2. A green or red vegetable, eaten raw or cooked.

perch
1. A pole or bar a bird sits or stands on. The parrot is on his **perch.**
2. A freshwater fish.

percolator
A pot used for making coffee by forcing boiling water through ground-up coffee.

perfect
perfectly
Without fault; complete. This is a **perfect** set of dishes. You mowed the lawn **perfectly.**

perform
performed
performing
1. To take part in a show. I saw Meg **perform** in the school play. The people liked her **performance.**
2. To do. We saw a doctor **perform** an operation on TV.

perfume
A liquid that has a sweet, pleasant smell. Mother likes to use **perfume** when she goes out.

pedals

pens

perch

perhaps Possibly; maybe. *Perhaps* I will go.

period 1. A length of time. We had a long art *period.*
2. The dot (.) that ends a sentence. This sentence has a *period* at the end.

periscope A tube made with glass and mirrors to let people see what is out of sight. A *periscope* is used on a submarine.

periscope

permission Approval to do something. I have *permission* to watch a late show on TV.

person A man, a woman, or a child. Bob is the only *person* in our family who plays the piano.

personal Belonging to one person; private. Kay has a big box for all her *personal* belongings.

pest A person or thing that annoys you. That mosquito is a *pest!*

pesticide A substance used to kill pests, especially harmful insects or animals of the rat family.

pet 1. An animal that is kept for enjoyment and company. This turtle is my *pet.*
2. Favorite. Do you have a *pet* teacher?

pet
petted
petting To pat or stroke gently. Jo likes to *pet* her cat.

piano

petition A request, usually written, for something. The people signed a *petition* for a new library.

phase A step in a series of changes which happen in regular order. The full moon is one *phase* of the moon.

phone A telephone.

photograph A picture made by use of a camera.

phrase   A group of words containing one idea or thought but less than a sentence. "The small boy" is a *phrase* in the sentence: "The small boy ran home."

physical 1. Having to do with the body or nature.
physically John is *physically* fit for gym.
2. A health examination. John had a *physical* at the doctor's office.

piano   A large, stringed musical instrument. A *piano* sounds when little hammers are made to hit its strings.

pie

pick   1. To choose. *Pick* a partner for the game.
picked   2. To gather. *Pick* some flowers for my vase.
picking   3. To lift. Ted could not *pick* up the heavy box.

pick-up-sticks A game in which you try to pick up thin sticks one at a time without moving other sticks.

picnic   A meal that you eat outdoors. We had a *picnic* in the park.

pig

pie   A food made with fruit or meat in pastry shells. We had apple *pie* for dessert.

piece   A part. May I have a *piece* of bread?

pig   A short, fat farm animal; a hog. The meat of a *pig* is pork.

pigeon   A bird with a plump body, short legs, and a small head.

pile   A stack of things one on top of the other. Throw that paper on the trash *pile.*

pigeons

pilgrim   1. A traveler, especially one who travels to visit a religious place.
2. One of a group of early settlers in America. The *Pilgrims* landed at Plymouth, Massachusetts, in 1620.

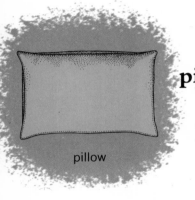

pillow

pill A medicine in the form of a small, hard ball or tablet. The doctor gave me a *pill* to swallow.

pillow A bag, filled with soft material, that you lay your head on or sit on.

pilot 1. A person who flies a plane.
2. A person who directs ships in and out of harbors.

pin 1. A piece of wood or metal used to hold things together. The teacher used a *pin* to put up my drawing. There are safety *pins*, clothes *pins*, and hair *pins*.
2. A piece of jewelry that can be fastened to clothes. Mother has a pearl *pin*.

pinch
pinched
pinching
 To squeeze tightly, especially between the tips of the thumb and first finger. Don't *pinch* me!

pine An evergreen tree with cones and needle-like leaves. *Pines* are green all year long.

pineapple

pineapple A sweet fruit that looks like a large pine cone and grows in hot places.

Ping-Pong A game played on a table with paddles and a small light ball. *Ping-Pong* is something like tennis.

pink A color. See page 70.

pint A unit of measurement; 16 ounces. Two cups make a *pint;* two *pints* make a quart.

pioneer 1. A person who does something that has never been done before. The first explorer to cross the Rockies was a *pioneer.*
2. An early settler.

pipe 1. A tube through which something flows. There is a leak in our water *pipe.*
2. A hollow stem with a small bowl at the end, used for smoking tobacco or blowing bubbles.

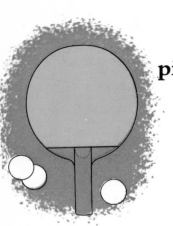

Ping-Pong
paddle and balls

pirate   A person who steals from ships at sea. Captain Kidd was a famous *pirate.*

pistol   A small gun that can be fired with one hand. My toy *pistol* fits in my pocket.

pit   1. A hole in the ground. The mine was at the bottom of a deep *pit.*
2. A hard seed found in the center of some fruits. Throw the peach *pit* into the basket.

pitch
pitched
pitching
1. To throw or toss. *Pitch* the baseball into my glove.
2. To set up. The Boy Scouts will *pitch* a tent in the park.
3. To rock up and down. The boat *pitched* in the high waves.

pipes

pitcher   1. A container with a handle and a lip, used for holding and pouring liquids. We have a pretty milk *pitcher.*
2. A person who throws the ball to the batter in a baseball game.

place   1. Somewhere; a certain area or spot. What *place* do you want to visit first?
2. A position. Our team is in first *place.*

place
placed
placing
To set or put. *Place* the dishes on the table.

plaid   A design made by crossing thick and thin stripes to form a pattern. Sue had a *plaid* skirt.

pitchers

plain   A large area of flat land with few trees. Cowboys rode the *plain* during the roundup.

plain
plainly
1. Clear, open. I have a *plain* view of the river. I can see the river *plainly.*
2. Simple. Tammy is wearing a *plain* dress, not a party dress.

plaid

plane

plan
1. An idea about how something can be done. We thought of a *plan* for earning money.
2. A drawing showing the parts of a thing and how it is made. Dad showed us the *plans* for the house.

plane
1. An airplane.
2. A tool that makes wood smooth or even. Dad used a *plane* to make the door fit the door frame.

planet
A heavenly body, like the earth, that moves around the sun. Mars is a *planet.*

planetarium
A building where models and movements of the sun, planets, stars, and other objects in the sky are shown. Our class saw a model of the solar system at the *planetarium.*

plant
1. A living thing that grows in soil, like bushes, flowers, or trees. I watered my tomato *plant.*
2. A factory.

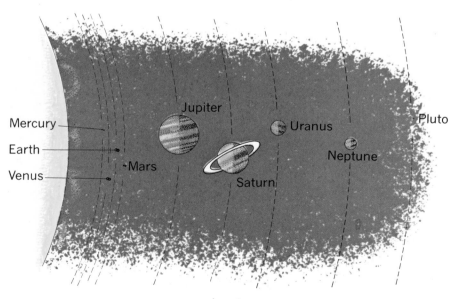

planets

plant
planted
planting
To put in the ground to grow. Mother will *plant* flowers in our garden.

plantation
A large farm where cotton, tobacco, or other crops are grown and cared for by workers who live there.

plastic
Any of many man-made materials that have various uses. *Plastic* can be molded into dishes, combs, and other things.

plate
1. A flat dish for food. Our puppy eats all the food on his *plate.*
2. The home base in baseball. The player scored a run when he touched home *plate.*

plateau
A large stretch of high, flat land.

platform
A flat raised surface on which people stand. We stood on the *platform* waiting for the train.

plates

play
1. A story that is acted out. Mary has a part in the school *play.*
2. Something done for fun or recreation. A game is a kind of *play.*

play
played
playing
1. To take part in. Let's *play* ball after school.
2. To make believe. I like to *play* that I am a queen.
3. To act; to perform. I will *play* the part of Cinderella in the show.
4. To make music on. Do you *play* the violin?

playful
playfully
Happy; full of fun. My kitten is *playful.* It *playfully* tugs on my shoelaces.

layground
An outdoor place, usually with swings and other play equipment, where children play.

playmate
A person who plays with you. My *playmate* and I like to jump rope.

playroom — A room used for fun and games; a family room.

plaza — 1. A public park in a town or a city.
2. A shopping center.

pleasant
pleasantly — Pleasing; friendly. Mrs. James is a *pleasant* lady. She smiled *pleasantly.*

please
pleased
pleasing — To make happy. I hope these flowers will *please* my mother.

pleasure — A feeling of happiness and satisfaction.

plenty — Enough; as much as is needed. We have *plenty* of candy for the party.

plow — 1. A large farm tool used to turn the soil over.
2. A machine used to remove snow.

plow
plowed
plowing — 1. To turn over the soil. You must *plow* before you can plant corn.
2. To remove snow with a plow.

plug — 1. A stopper for a hole, like a cork.
2. An electrical connection at the end of a wire. The *plug* on Mother's iron broke.

plug
(definition 2)

plum — A juicy fruit with a smooth skin and a pit in the middle. I just ate a purple *plum.*

plum

plumbing
plumber — All of the water and gas pipes in a building. There is a water leak in our *plumbing.* A *plumber* will fix the leaking pipe.

plump — Slightly fat; round. Pick out a *plump* turkey.

plural — The form a word takes when it means more than one. The *plural* of "boy" is "boys."

Pluto — The planet farthest from the sun. See page 222.

pocket — A small bag, sewed into clothing, in which things are carried. Put the dime in your coat *pocket.*

pocketbook A small bag or purse in which to carry money, keys, and similar things.

pod A case or shell in which seeds grow. Take the peas out of the *pod.*

poem Song-like writing, often in rhyme, that describes a feeling, an idea, or a story. A nursery rhyme is a short *poem.*

poet A person who writes poems.

poetry A poem or a group of poems.

point 1. The sharp tip of something. Do you have a *point* on your pencil?
2. A spot; a place. This is the *point* where the train stops.
3. The most important idea of a speech or a story. The *point* of the story was to be kind to others.

point
pointed
pointing
1. To aim. Don't *point* that stick at anyone.
2. To show position or direction with a finger. *Point* out your house to me.

poison A substance that can make you ill or kill you if you take it into your body. The wicked stepmother put *poison* in Snow White's apple.

poison ivy A green plant that can cause the skin to break out if you touch it. *Poison ivy* has three glossy leaves on each stem.

poison oak A plant of the poison ivy family that can cause the skin to break out if you touch it.

poison ivy

poke
poked
poking
1. To push; to stick. Did the baby *poke* his finger in your eye?
2. To move slowly and lazily. When I have nothing to do, I *poke* around the house.
3. To search for. The dog *poked* around for his bone.

polar bear

poodle

polar bear A large, white bear found in cold climates.

pole A long, thin piece of metal or wood, usually round. The flag flies at the top of the *pole.*

police Members of a department of a city or a town that sees that laws are obeyed. The *police* help to prevent crime.

policeman A member of the police department. A *policeman* works to keep a city or town safe. *Policemen* and *policewomen* have given talks at our school.

polite
politely Showing good manners and concern for others. Jane is *polite* and kind to others. She speaks *politely* to everyone.

poll 1. A study or gathering of sample beliefs that shows how people feel about something. A *poll* of the people should show who may be elected President.
2. (Plural only) A place to vote. People go to the *polls* to vote for the Mayor.

pollution Dirt or the act of making something dirty. Smoke causes air *pollution.*

poncho A blanket-like cloak or raincoat with a hole for the head.

pond A body of water, smaller than a lake. The water in a *pond* is often still, not running.

pony A small horse. Kevin liked to ride his *pony.*

pony express In 1860–1861, a way of sending mail by horses. Men on fast horses delivered the mail to California from Missouri by *pony express.*

poodle A kind of dog with curly, coarse hair. We saw a small white *poodle* at the pet shop.

pool
1. A small body of water; a pond. The *pool* had goldfish in it.
2. A place for swimming. Meg and Jeff swam in the *pool* in the park.
3. A game played with balls and sticks on a cloth-covered table.

pool

poor
poorly
1. Having little or no money; not rich. There are many *poor* people in the world.
2. Needing to be improved. George is a *poor* writer. The game was *poorly* played.
3. Unfortunate; unhappy. *Poor* Sue! She dropped her ice-cream cone.

pop
1. A sharp, snapping noise. The balloon burst with a loud *pop.*
2. A soft drink or soda. Do you like grape *pop?*
3. Father; dad.

pop
popped
popping
1. To make a sharp, sudden noise. Can you hear the popcorn *pop?*
2. To appear suddenly. In the spring, the buds *pop* open.
3. To burst in. He *popped* into the room.

popcorn
A kind of corn whose kernels burst open and puff up when heated.

popular
popularly
Well-liked or agreed with by most people. Baseball is a *popular* game. Television is *popularly* called TV.

population
All the people living in a certain place. New York City has a larger *population* than Pittsburgh.

porch
A roofed platform at an entrance of a house or building. We left our boots on the *porch.*

porridge
A cooked cereal, such as oatmeal.

port A place where ships can dock; a harbor. The ship's cargo was taken off at the next *port.*

porter 1. A person who is paid to carry things. At the airport, a *porter* took our bags.
2. A worker who cleans or sweeps up in an apartment house or large building.

portion A piece, a part, or a share. Bill took a large *portion* of cake.

position 1. A place; a certain spot. What *position* do you play in the game?
2. A job or office. Al's father has a *position* with the government.

possible
possibly Able to be done; able to happen. It is *possible* to stand on your head. Grandfather can *possibly* live to be 100.

post 1. A strong pole or stake. The car ran into a wooden *post* on the highway.
2. A place of duty. Walt has the corner *post* on the Safety Patrol.

postal service The organization that delivers the mail.

post card A card that is sent through the mail without an envelope. My aunt sent us a picture *post card.*

poster A sign or printed notice put in a public place. We saw a *poster* about the pet show.

postman A person who carries and delivers mail; a mailman. The *postman* brought a letter to Mother. Some *postmen* drive trucks.

postman

post office A local office of the postal service where mail is handled. You can buy stamps at the *post office.*

posture The way you stand or sit; the position in which you carry yourself. Mark's *posture* is good because he stands up straight.

pot
1. A round, deep pan made of metal or glass, used for cooking; a kettle. The water in the *pot* is boiling.
2. A container for plants. The tulips were in a flower *pot.*

potato
A vegetable with white pulp and darker colored skin.

potato

pound
A measurement of weight; 16 ounces.

pound
pounded
pounding
1. To hit again and again; to strike more than once. *Pound* the nail with a hammer.
2. To beat heavily. Kim's heart *pounded* when she saw her new puppy.

pour
poured
pouring
To flow or cause to flow in a steady stream. Dick will *pour* the milk into a glass.

powder
A dust-like material. The baby's *powder* smells good.

power
1. The energy or force that makes things work. Electric *power* runs the machinery in the factory.
2. Strength. The boxer had great *power.*

powerful
Having great physical strength; very strong. A race horse has *powerful* legs.

practice
practiced
practicing
To do again and again in order to improve or do better. We will have to *practice* our parts for the play.

prairie
A large area of grassland with few or no trees; a plain.

praise
praised
praising
To speak well of; to pay honor to. Jeff *praises* his dog when it does a trick.

pray
prayed
praying
Speak to or say prayers to God; to ask or beg. We *pray* for a peaceful world.

prayer A way of speaking to God. Jan's family says a *prayer* at the dinner table.

precious 1. Valuable. The diamond is a *precious* jewel. 2. Greatly loved. Tim's sister is a *precious* child.

prefer
preferred
preferring
To choose over all others; to like better. What kind of ice cream do you *prefer?* Dad's *preference* is chocolate.

prefix A letter, syllable, or word added before a word to change its meaning. In the word "unhappy," the syllable "un" is a *prefix* meaning "not."

prepare
prepared
preparing
To get ready; to put together; to make. We went to the kitchen to *prepare* dinner.

present 1. A gift; something that is given. It is fun to get a *present.*
2. The time now, not the past or future. At *present,* some people are worrying about pollution.
3. Here; not absent. Everyone in our class is *present.*

presents

present
presented
presenting
1. To give. We will *present* a puppet show.
2. To introduce. "Bill, let me *present* Mary."

preserve
preserved
preserving
To keep in good and usable condition. We *preserve* eggs by putting them in the refrigerator.

president A person chosen to be the leader of a club, company, country, or any organized group. The *president* called the meeting to order.

press
pressed
pressing

1. To push against firmly. The elevator will start up when you *press* the button.
2. To smooth by heat and pressure from an iron. Mother *pressed* my pants.

pressure

A weight or force on something or someone. Too much *pressure* will break the pencil.

pretend
pretended
pretending

To make believe; to give a false appearance. Sometimes we *pretend* we're asleep when we're not.

pretty
prettily

1. Pleasant to look at. The rose is a *pretty* flower. Jane's doll is *prettily* dressed.
2. Rather; somewhat. Bob was a *pretty* good student.

pretzel

A hard cracker, often shaped like a loose knot.

pretzel

prevent
prevented
preventing

To keep from happening. A fence can *prevent* a dog from running away.

prey

An animal hunted by another animal, especially for food. The fly was the *prey* of the spider.

price

Cost; the amount you must pay. The *price* of the class trip tickets will be $1.50 each.

pride

A feeling of pleasure and satisfaction with yourself.

prince

A boy or man who is the son of a king or queen.

princess

A girl or woman who is the daughter of a king or queen.

prince

principal

The head of a school. Mr. Clark is *principal* of the high school.

principal   Chief; most important. Cotton is the *principal* crop in Georgia.

print   1. To make letters like those used in books.
printed   Mary learned to *print* in kindergarten.
printing   2. To produce newspapers, books, or magazines. A big machine can *print* thousands of newspapers each hour.
3. To stamp or make a mark on a surface. John will *print* his design with ink.

prison   A jail; a place where people are sent to be punished for breaking the law. The *prison* had iron bars on the windows.

prisoner   1. A person kept in jail for breaking the law.
2. A person captured by enemy military forces.

private   Secret; not public; away from others. Our club had a *private* meeting.

prize   Something that is won; an award. Joe won a *prize* at the pie-eating contest.

problem   A question that is hard to answer; something to be worked out or solved. Our teacher gave us ten arithmetic *problems.*

produce   To make; to bring about. That factory *produces*
produced   tires.
producing

product   Something that is made or grown. Butter is a *product* of a dairy.

program   1. A show. We saw a good TV *program* today.
2. A list, as of acts in a show.
3. A plan. The mayor announced his clean-up week *program.*

progress   1. Forward motion; movement ahead. A snail makes slow *progress.*

2. Improvement. Al showed *progress* in math.

project   A plan; a job to be done. Dad's next *project* is to build a birdhouse.

promise
promised
promising
   To say you will do something; to give your word. We *promise* to pick up the toys.

prompt   On time; quick. Jack was *prompt* for dinner.

pronoun   A word used in place of the name of a person, place, or thing. "He" is a *pronoun* meaning a boy, a man, or a male animal.

pronounce
pronounced
pronouncing
   1. To say; to make the sounds of. Speak slowly and *pronounce* your words carefully.
2. To declare or make a statement. The judge *pronounced* sentence on the prisoner.

**pronuncia-
tion**   The way a word is spoken; the sound of the word. You do not hear the "w" in the *pronunciation* of "sword."

proof   Evidence that something is true. The picture is *proof* that Jeff caught a fish.

propeller   A blade or blades, turned by an engine and used for driving ships or airplanes.

proper   Correct. Do you know the *proper* way to address an envelope?

property   1. Something that you own; something that belongs to you. If you buy a book, it is your *property.*
2. Land or buildings. Dad looked at some *property* down the street.

prose   Writing or speaking that is not poetry. *Prose* is ordinary talk and writing.

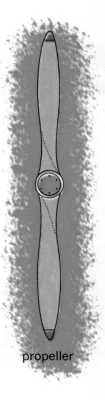

propeller

protect
protected
protecting

To keep from harm; to defend; to cover. A mother dog will **protect** her pups. Jane's umbrella gave her **protection** from the rain.

proud

Pleased or satisfied; having pride. Mike is **proud** of his new bike.

prove
proved
proving

To show to be true; to put to a test. We can **prove** that the earth is round.

proverb

A wise saying; a piece of advice that is often repeated. An old **proverb** says, "A penny saved is a penny earned."

provide
provided
providing

To supply or give. We will **provide** a home for the cat and kittens.

prune

prune

A dried plum. A **prune** has wrinkles.

public
publicly

Open to all; used by everyone; for all people. We go to a **public** school. Our pictures will be shown **publicly** at the art show.

publish
published
publishing

To get books, magazines, and newspapers ready to be sold or given to the public. Our school **publishes** a monthly magazine.

pudding

A soft, sweet dessert. Mother put cream on the chocolate **pudding.**

puddle

A small pool of water that is left standing. Tony likes to walk through **puddles** after it rains.

pueblo

1. A kind of Indian building made from dried mud or stone. Many **pueblos** were five stories high.
2. (Pueblo) A member of an Indian tribe living in a pueblo.

pueblo

puff
puffed
puffing

1. To blow in short breaths or bursts. Tom tried to *puff* out all the candles at once.
2. To swell or get larger. The muffins will *puff* up as they bake.

pull
pulled
pulling

To make something move toward or with you by using force in the same direction. Jeff will *pull* his sled up the hill.

pump

A machine for moving liquids or gases through pipes. The farmer used a *pump* to get water out of the well.

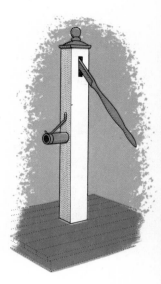

pump

pumpkin

A large, round yellow-orange fruit. A *pumpkin* grows on a vine.

punch

1. A drink made with fruit juice.
2. A fast blow or poke. The fighter threw a hard *punch.*
3. A tool used to stamp or put holes in something.

punch
punched
punching

1. To poke; to hit quickly. Ted tried to *punch* Bill in the ribs.
2. To make a hole in. The conductor will *punch* your ticket.

punctuation

The marks used to make sentences easier to understand. The question mark (?) is one kind of *punctuation.*

pumpkin

punish
punished
punishing

To make a person pay in some way for doing wrong; to cause pain to. Ted does not want to *punish* his dog. Spanking is a kind of *punishment.*

pupil

1. Someone who goes to school. We have a new *pupil* in our class.
2. The part of the eye that lets in light. The *pupil* is the dark center of the eye.

puppets

puppet   A kind of toy; a figure of an animal or person that can be made to move.

puppy   A young dog.

pure
1. Clean, not dirty. We drank *pure* water from the spring.
2. Only; just. The joke was *pure* nonsense.

purple   A color. See page 70.

purse   A handbag or pocketbook; a small bag used for carrying money and other things.

purses

push
pushed
pushing
1. To use force against in order to move something; the opposite of "pull." *Push* the chair nearer the window.
2. To move by force. The explorers *pushed* through the thick jungle.

push-up   A kind of exercise in which you push your body up from the floor. In a *push-up* only your toes and hands touch the floor.

pussy   A cat or kitten. The black *pussy* likes the new food better than the other *pussies* do.

put
put
putting
1. To place or set. Mother *put* a cake in the oven.
2. To state in words. Let's *put* our question before the class.

puzzle   A problem to be worked out for fun. Jim enjoys jigsaw *puzzles.*

pygmy   A very small adult person. A full-grown *pygmy* is only about four feet tall.

pyramid

pyramid   A solid object with a square base and four sloping sides that come to a point on top. In Egypt, large *pyramids* are monuments to dead kings.

Qq

quack
quacked
quacking
To make a sound like a duck's cry. A rooster does not *quack!*

quail
A plump, chicken-like bird that builds a nest on the ground. The *quail* is sometimes called the "bobwhite."

quail

quality
1. The nature of something; a thing that helps to make one thing different from others. Sweetness is a *quality* of candy.
2. The value or worth of something. This cloth is of very high *quality.*

quantity
An amount or number. Our family eats a large *quantity* of fruit.

quarrel
A difference of opinion; an angry discussion. The two girls had a *quarrel* about who would get the library book.

quart
A liquid measurement; 32 ounces. Four cups make a *quart.*

quarter
1. A coin worth 25 cents. There are four *quarters* in a dollar.
2. (Plural) A place to live. The captain lives in the officers' *quarters.*

queen   The wife of a king, or a woman who rules a kingdom.

queer
queerly   Odd or strange; different from others. The kangaroo is a *queer* animal. The old lady was *queerly* dressed.

question   A sentence that needs an answer. He asked the *question,* "Is it cold out?"

question mark   A punctuation mark (?) placed at the end of a written question.

quick
quickly   Fast; sudden; swift. The dog could not catch the *quick* fox. The firemen *quickly* put out the fire.

quiet
quietly   Silent; still; without much noise. The mouse is a *quiet* animal. The teacher worked *quietly* at her desk.

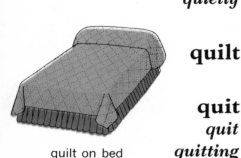

quilt on bed

quilt   A cover for a bed. A *quilt* can be made of many pieces of cloth sewed together.

quit
quit
quitting   1. To stop. "*Quit* hitting me," said Henry.
2. To leave. Don's brother *quit* his job.

quite   1. Entirely; completely. Lunch is not *quite* ready.
2. Very. Sue's grandfather is *quite* old.
3. Really; truly. The party was *quite* a nice one.

quiz   A test made up of questions.

quotation   The exact words of a speaker or writer. Jean memorized some Lincoln *quotations.*

quotation mark   One of two punctuation marks (" ") used to set off a person's exact words from other written or printed words.

Rr

rabbit   A small animal with long ears, a small round tail, and soft fur. A *rabbit* is able to hop and run very swiftly.

raccoon   An animal with mixed gray, brown, and black fur that lives in the woods and hunts for food at night. The *raccoon* looks as if he is wearing a black mask.

rabbit

race   1. A speed contest. The slowest horse finished last in the *race.*
2. A group of similar people who have the same coloring and physical features or the same ancestors.

rack   An object with bars, shelves, or other sections on which things can be hung or stored. Bob hung his jacket on the coat *rack.*

raccoon

racket   1. A loud noise; a noisy confusion. The barking dogs made a *racket.*
2. An object with a long handle and wide flat surface used to hit a ball in tennis and other sports.

radio   A device that sends or receives sounds through space by electrical signals. I like to listen to music on my *radio.*

radish   A plant that has a root with a sharp taste. *Radishes* may be red or white and are often used in salads.

radish

raft

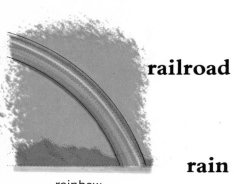

rainbow

raisins

raft   A floating platform. A *raft* can be made of logs or boards.

rag   A torn piece of cloth that can be used for cleaning. Dad shines the car with a soft *rag.*

rage   Great anger. The loss of the treasure caused the pirate to go into a *rage.*

rail   1. One of the bars of steel that a train runs on; a train track.
2. A horizontal bar of wood or metal that is used as part of a fence. We have a wooden *rail* on our backyard fence.

railroad   1. The tracks that a train runs on. A *railroad* runs through the valley.
2. A company that runs trains. The *railroad* raised the price of train tickets.

rain   Water that falls from clouds in drops. The *rain* made the field too wet to play on.

rainbow   A curve of many beautiful colors sometimes seen in the sky during or after a rain. A *rainbow* appears when sunlight passes through raindrops.

raincoat   A coat worn to protect you from rain.

raise
raised
raising   1. To pick or lift up; to move to a higher position. We watched Jim *raise* the box and put it on the table.
2. To grow and take care of. The farmer *raises* cows and corn on his farm.
3. To make greater in number or amount. The farmer will *raise* the price of his eggs.

raisin   A dried sweet grape. *Raisins* are used in making candy, cookies, and other foods.

rake   A garden tool with a long handle and a row of tooth-like bars at the end.

ranch   A large farm, especially one for raising cattle or other animals.

range   1. An area with much grass where cattle can graze.
2. A row or group of mountains. The mountain *range* runs through five states.
3. The distance that an airplane, ship, bullet, or other thing can travel. The small airplane has a *range* of 400 miles.
4. A large stove. We cook on an electric *range*.

rap
rapped
rapping   To hit quickly and sharply. She will *rap* her desk with a pencil to get our attention.

rake

raspberry   A sweet red or black berry or the plant on which it grows.

rat   An animal pest that looks like a large mouse.

rate   A number or amount, as of speed. The car went at a high *rate* of speed.

rather   1. More happily; more gladly. Tom would *rather* have ice cream than medicine.
2. Somewhat; a little. Jane was *rather* careless on her test.
3. Instead of. Tom *rather* than Jim should be the team captain.

raspberry

rattle   A child's toy that makes a noise when shaken.

rattle
rattled
rattling   To make a series of sharp sounds by shaking. The storm made the doors and windows *rattle.*

rattlesnake   A dangerous snake found in America that has hard rings that rattle at the end of its tail.

ravioli   A food made with pieces of dough filled with meat or cheese and covered with tomato sauce.

raw
1. Not cooked. The lion eats *raw* meat.
2. In a natural condition; not changed by man. Marble is a *raw* material for statues.

ray
1. A beam or streak of light. In the dark, we saw the *ray* of the hunter's flashlight.
2. A little bit. There was a *ray* of hope that Bob would win the race.

razor
An instrument with a sharp blade used for shaving.

reach
reached
reaching
1. To put out a hand to take hold of something. The baby could not *reach* the cookies.
2. To arrive at. The bus will *reach* Chicago by noon.
3. To stretch or touch. The rope is long enough to *reach* from the boat to the shore.
4. To get a message to. Dad tried to *reach* his brother in Boston by phone.

razors

read
read
reading
1. To look at and understand written or printed words. Dad wants to *read* the new book.
2. To look at and speak aloud. We listened to the teacher *read* a poem to us.
3. To show. The scale *reads* three pounds.

reader
1. One who reads. The *reader* smiled at the funny story.
2. A book or other printed matter to be read. I find news in *My Weekly Reader.*

ready
1. Prepared for use. The paints are *ready* for the art class.
2. Willing. Sally is always *ready* to help.
3. Easily reached; at hand. The teacher had a *ready* supply of paper for our test.

real
True; not fake. Is that a *real* snake or a rubber one?

really
Truly; very. Joan is a *really* nice girl.

rear At the back; away from the front. The **rear** tire on my bicycle needs more air.

reason 1. The cause of an action; an explanation. For what **reason** did the ship sink?
2. The power to think. **Reason** is needed to do addition and subtraction.

receive
received
receiving To get. Did you **receive** a letter from your friend in Texas?

recent New or modern. Have you read the most **recent** copy of this magazine?

recess 1. A short time for rest or play. Our class has **recess** in the morning.
2. A hollow space. The desk tray had **recesses** for bills, stamps, and paper.

recipe Directions; instructions for making something to eat or drink. Mother has a good **recipe** for chocolate cake.

recital A performance by dancers, singers, or musicians. Mother enjoyed the piano **recital.**

recline
reclined
reclining To lean back or to lie down. Dad likes to **recline** in an easy chair after work.

record 1. A flat, circular object that gives off sound when it is played on a special machine. Jane bought a new **record** by her favorite singer.
2. Written information about things that happen. We keep a **record** of the temperature every day.
3. The best that has been done in a contest, race, or other effort. The baseball player's six home runs were a **record** for the season.

records
(definition 1)

recreation Play; amusement. Jim and Ellen play tennis for **recreation.**

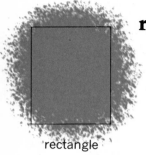
rectangle

rectangle A flat figure with square corners and four sides. The opposite sides of a *rectangle* are equal.

recycle
recycled
recycling To change something that is worn out or used up into a new product. The factory will *recycle* the old bottles into new glass.

red A color. See page 70.

reel

reel 1. A wheel or spool on which you can wind string, wire, or similar things. Bill used a rod and *reel* to catch the fish.
2. A dance in square dancing.

re-entry The return of a rocket or spacecraft to the earth's atmosphere.

refill Something that replaces an object when it is empty or used up. Tom bought a *refill* of paper for his notebook.

refreshment Something to eat or drink. Soda was one of the *refreshments* served at the party.

refrigerator A closed box or cabinet that keeps food cold and usually makes ice.

refuse
refused
refusing To say "no" to. Dad may *refuse* our request for a later bedtime. His *refusal* will not surprise us.

region An area of land. The travelers rode through a desert *region.*

regular
regularly 1. Usual. Delivering mail is the postman's *regular* job. The postman arrives *regularly* each day at ten o'clock.
2. Even; having the same size, shape, or rate. The bricks were laid in a *regular* pattern.

reindeer

reindeer A large deer that lives in the far North. A *reindeer* has big antlers.

relation
1. A member of your family; a relative. Sisters, brothers, and uncles are some of your **relations.**
2. A connection; the way in which things have to do with each other. There is a **relation** between speeding and auto accidents.

relative
A member of your family; a relation. Aunts, parents, and cousins are **relatives.**

relay race
A race in which one racer on a team must touch or pass a stick to another before the other racer can take his place in the race.

release
released
releasing
To let go; to free. Please **release** the dog from his chain.

relief
1. A comfort; something that frees you from pain, danger, or difficulty. Dad took medicine for **relief** from a pain in his shoulder.
2. A freedom from work or duty. The soldier got **relief** from guard duty.

religion
religious
Belief in a god or gods. **Religious** people believe in a god.

remain
remained
remaining
1. To be left. Did any pie **remain** after the picnic?
2. To stay; to continue. We will **remain** at home during our holiday.

remainder
1. A part that remains or is left over. After supper I ate the **remainder** of the cake.
2. In subtraction and division, a number that is left over. If you subtract 3 from 10, the **remainder** is 7. If you divide 10 by 3, the answer is 3 with a **remainder** of 1.

remarkable
remarkably
Amazing; strange; unusual. A rainbow is a **remarkable** sight. The boy was **remarkably** bright.

remember
remembered
remembering

1. To bring back to mind; to have in your memory. Can you *remember* the name of your new friend?
2. To keep in mind; to not forget. *Remember* the telephone number that I gave you.

remind
reminded
reminding

To cause to remember. Please *remind* me to take my lunch with me.

remove
removed
removing

To take off, out, or away. The plows will *remove* the snow from the street.

rent

Money paid at regular times for the use of a house, car, or other thing. We pay *rent* for our house once each month.

rent
rented
renting

1. To pay money at regular times for the use of. We *rent* a house on Elm Street.
2. To allow the use of in exchange for money. The farmer will *rent* the cabin to us for $100 a month.

repair
repaired
repairing

To fix; to mend. The plumber will *repair* the leaking pipe.

repeat
repeated
repeating

1. To do again; to perform again. We wanted the magician to *repeat* the trick.
2. To say again. Please *repeat* what you just said.
3. To say from memory. Can you *repeat* the poem that we just read?

replace
replaced
replacing

1. To take the place of; to put in place of. Jim will *replace* Ted at bat.
2. To put back in place. Did you *replace* the book on the shelf?

reply

An answer. What was Jane's *reply* to the question?

report
1. A statement of facts about something that has happened. The children wrote a *report* about their trip.
2. A piece of news. Has there been any *report* about the storm?

reptile
One of many cold-blooded animals that creep or crawl and have rough skins. Snakes, turtles, and lizards are *reptiles.*

reptile
(turtle)

request
requested
requesting
To ask for. What books did you *request* at the library?

rescue
rescued
rescuing
To save or free from danger. The firemen used a ladder to *rescue* the boy.

reservation
1. An arrangement to have something for use at a later time. Before our trip, we made a *reservation* for a room at the hotel.
2. Land set aside for a special use. The Indians lived on a *reservation.*

reservoir
A natural or man-made lake where water is stored for use by many people. Drinking water often comes from a *reservoir.*

resident
A person who lives in a place. I am a *resident* of a big city.

resource
A supply of something that can be used when it is needed. Money in the bank is a good *resource.*

respect
respected
respecting
To have a feeling of great liking for; admire. Ted is honest and I *respect* him.

rest
1. A halt in work or other activity for a short time. The boys had a *rest* after their hike.
2. All that is left. We will eat the *rest* of the cake tomorrow.

rest
rested
resting

To be free from work; to sit or lie down. Let's **rest** for ten minutes.

restaurant

A place where people buy and eat meals. We had dinner at a **restaurant** on Tony's birthday.

restless

1. Sleepless; unable to rest.
2. Never still; uneasy. The children were **restless** during the storm.

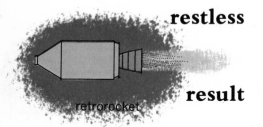
retrorocket

result

Something that happens because of what has been done before. An accident can be the **result** of bad driving.

retrorocket

A rocket engine used to slow up an airplane or spacecraft. A **retrorocket** helps to make a moon landing a "soft" one.

return
returned
returning

1. To go back or come back to the same place. The President will **return** to the White House today.
2. To give back or send back. Don't forget to **return** my book.

review
reviewed
reviewing

To think over again; to study again. We must **review** our plans for the trip.

revolution.

1. One complete turn of something around a center. A complete turn of a wheel makes one **revolution.**
2. A great change in the way something is done. Spaceships can cause a **revolution** in travel.
3. A war in which people rise up against their rulers and fight for independence. George Washington led the American **Revolution.**

rhyme

1. A sounding alike of the end sounds of words. These words have **rhyme**—"wing," "sing," "thing."

2. A poem with the last words of lines sounding alike. "Jack Be Nimble" is the name of a *rhyme*.

rib One of the bones of the chest of man and of many animals. Each *rib* in your body helps protect your heart and lungs.

ribbon A strip of silk or other fine cloth used for trim. Betty put the *ribbon* in her hair.

rice A grass-like plant whose seeds are used for food. Some breakfast cereals are made from *rice.*

rich
1. Having much money or property; wealthy.
2. Tasty, creamy, oily, or sweet. Some desserts are *rich* foods.
3. Costing much; of good quality. The cloth was *rich* in appearance.

rid
rid
ridding
To clean out; to free. We must *rid* the yard of trash.

rice

riddle A kind of puzzle that asks a question. A *riddle,* a *riddle,* as I suppose,/A hundred eyes and never a nose./What is it? (A potato)

ride
rode
ridden
riding
To be carried by an animal, a car, an airplane, or some other means of travel. We will *ride* to Texas by bus. A bus *rider* sees the country.

ridge
1. A hill with a long, narrow top. The road was on a high *ridge.*
2. A long and narrow raised edge. *Ridges* on the bottom of a shoe can keep you from slipping.

ridiculous Foolish; silly. Jeff looked *ridiculous* when he fell into the mud.

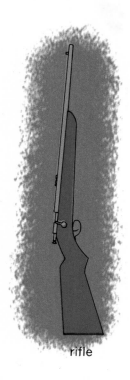

rifle

ring

rifle   A long gun that is fired from the shoulder.

right
1. Freedom to do something. I have the **right** to go to the library after school.
2. The fair and honest thing to do. The thief didn't know **right** from wrong.
3. The direction to the east when you are facing north; the opposite of "left."

rim   The edge of something curved or round. Tom's bicycle wheel had a bent **rim.**

ring
1. A piece of jewelry worn on the finger.
2. People or things forming a circle.
3. The sound of a bell.

ring
rang
rung
ringing
1. To form a circle around.
2. To cause a bell or telephone to sound. I'll **ring** the bell to wake you.

riot   A disturbance of public peace by people fighting and destroying property. Many people were hurt and stores were burned in the **riot.**

rip   An opening made by tearing, splitting, or pulling apart. Pete has a **rip** in his coat.

ripe   Fully grown; ready. This peach is **ripe;** we can eat it.

rise
rose
risen
rising
1. To get up after sitting or lying down.
2. To increase. I hope food prices don't **rise.**
3. To move to a higher place. We watched the spacecraft **rise** from the launch pad.

river   A large stream of water which flows into another river, a sea, or an ocean. We rode down the **river** on a raft.

road   A wide path, usually paved, on which cars and other vehicles travel.

roar
1. A loud, deep cry of an animal or a person.
2. A loud noise. Listen to the *roar* of that tractor.

roar
roared
roaring
1. To make a deep, loud sound.
2. To scold, shout, or laugh loudly. Dad will *roar* when he hears my joke.

roast
A piece of meat cooked in an oven or over a fire. We had a *roast* of beef for dinner.

roast
roasted
roasting
To cook or bake food in an oven or over a fire. Mother will *roast* the chicken.

rob
robbed
robbing
To take money or property by force. A thief can *rob* a house.

robbery
The act of stealing; taking something that belongs to another. There was a *robbery* at the jewelry store last night.

robe
1. A long, loose piece of clothing usually worn over other clothing; a bathrobe.
2. A blanket for the lap.

robin
A songbird with brown back and dull-red breast.

robot
A machine built in the form of a man. Ben saw a *robot* walk at the science fair.

robin

rock
1. A large mass of hard mineral; stone. Spacemen brought back pieces of moon *rock.*
2. A small piece of stone. My hobby is collecting *rocks.*

rock
rocked
rocking
1. To move back and forth gently. I like to *rock* in this chair.
2. To make something shake hard. Earthquakes can *rock* tall buildings.

rod

rocket
1. A firework that is shot into the air at times of celebration.
2. A kind of engine. **Rockets** can move a spaceship at great speed.

rod
1. A straight, thin piece of wood or other material.
2. A fishing pole.

rodeo
1. A contest of horse riding and other cowboy skills. Tim's dad won the calf-roping contest at the **rodeo.**
2. A roundup of cattle.

role
1. A part played by a person in a play. Dick had the **role** of the king in the play.
2. The part a person may play in life. Kevin's **role** seemed to be baby sitter for his sister.

roll
1. A list of the names of the people of a group. Our class **roll** has 24 names on it.
2. Bread dough made into small balls and baked. Make my sandwich with a **roll.**
3. Paper or cloth wrapped around itself to form a tube. Some paper comes in a **roll.**

roll
rolled
rolling
1. To move by turning over and over on the ground or another surface. The ball **rolled** down the hill.
2. To travel on wheels. Many trucks **roll** along the highway.
3. To make something into a roll. I'll **roll** up my drawing, not fold it.
4. To move from side to side and up and down. The sailor felt the ship **roll** with the waves.

roller
1. Something that is used for rolling. Mother lost a **roller** from her hair.
2. A heavy machine that rolls and levels the ground. A wide **roller** made the road smooth.

roller skate A skate with four small wheels for skating on hard surfaces.

roller skate

roof 1. The covering on the top of a building.
2. The top of some things. Peanut butter stuck to the *roof* of my mouth.

room 1. A walled space inside a building. Our new house has a big living *room.*
2. Space. The "old woman who lived in a shoe" did not have much *room.*

rooster An adult male chicken.

root The underground part of a plant. A *root* gets food from the soil for a plant.

rope A heavy cord made of strong threads twisted together. My swing hangs from the tree on *ropes.*

rooster

rose A flower that grows on a thorny bush. A *rose* may be pink, red, yellow, or white.

rot
rotted
rotting To spoil. Those apples will *rot* on the ground.

rough
roughly 1. Having a surface of bumps, ridges, or broken places; not even or smooth. The road to the camp was very *rough.*
2. Not gentle or careful; without manners. Don't handle the kitten so *roughly.*

roses

round 1. Shaped like a circle or ball. A ring is *round.*
2. Around. We walked *round* the lake.

roundup 1. The bringing together of a large herd of cattle. Cowboys and horses work hard in a *roundup.*
2. A gathering of people by someone else. The teacher made a *roundup* of children when recess ended.

route
1. A road or highway.
2. A way traveled from one place to another. Our *route* to the park went through the woods.
3. The territory covered. Ed had a good newspaper *route*.

row
A number of people or things in a line. There are six trees in that *row*.

row
rowed
rowing
To move a boat by using oars. The campers will *row* the boat to the island.

rub
rubbed
rubbing
To press and move one thing against another. Don't *rub* your sore eye with your finger.

rubber
1. A material that stretches, made from the sap of certain kinds of plants or trees.
2. An overshoe. I wear *rubbers* over my shoes when it rains.

rubbers

rude
rudely
Having bad manners; not polite; rough. It is *rude* to bump into people. Don't talk *rudely* to me.

ruffle
A strip of lace or cloth gathered along one edge.

rug
A floor covering made of thick fabric. The living room *rug* was made of wool.

ruin
ruined
ruining
To destroy; to make useless. A windstorm can *ruin* crops.

rule
A guide or instruction for the way a person behaves. Mother has a *rule* about cleaning up.

rule
ruled
ruling
To control; to manage; to govern. A king may *rule* a country.

ruler
1. Someone who rules or governs. A queen can be the *ruler* of a country.
2. A tool used for measuring length and drawing straight lines.

ruler
(definition 2)

run
ran
running
1. To move on foot faster than walking.
2. To flow. The water will *run* into the street.
3. To be in use. The buses will *run* next week.
4. To operate or manage. A new cook will *run* the school kitchen.
5. To try to win an office in an election. Mrs. Peterson will *run* for governor.

runner
1. A person who runs.
2. The long, thin part of a sled or ice skate on which it slides.

rural
Having to do with the country rather than the city. I live in a *rural* place near many farms.

rush
1. A hurry. Tom was in a *rush* to go.
2. A grass-like plant with hollow stems. Some Indian baskets are made with *rush* stems.

rust
rusty
A reddish-brown coating formed on metal by damp air or water. *Rust* can ruin tools. Keep them from getting damp and *rusty.*

rye
A kind of grain, like wheat. I like *rye* bread.

rye

Ss

sack A large bag made of strong cloth or paper. The farmer put the potatoes into a *sack.*

sacrifice 1. A loss; the act of giving something up. Not going to the game was a *sacrifice* for Tony.
2. Something given or done as a way of showing respect or love for a god. A long time ago people used animals as *sacrifices.*

sad
sadly Feeling sorrow; not happy. Tom was *sad* about his lost dog. Jane looked *sadly* at her broken doll.

saddle

saddle A special seat on a horse or other animal, a bicycle, a motorcycle, or tricycle.

safe A strong metal box in which money or valuable things can be locked.

safe
safely Free from danger; not harmful. The leaky, old boat is not *safe.* The children crossed the street *safely.*

safety Freedom from danger or harm. A warm cabin gave the hunters *safety* during the storm.

safety patrol

safety belt A special belt or strap that is worn to keep a worker or passenger from being hurt in an accident. Also called "seat belt." Always fasten your *safety belt* in a car.

safety patrol Pupils organized to protect other pupils at dangerous street crossings.

sail 1. A large piece of cloth hung from the mast of a sailboat to catch the wind that moves the boat.
2. A trip on a boat. We took a *sail* on Uncle Ed's new boat.

sail
sailed
sailing
1. To take a trip on a boat. We will *sail* across the lake in Uncle Ed's boat.
2. To travel through the air; to glide. We saw an eagle *sail* over the tops of the trees.

sailboat A boat that is moved by the wind.

sailor A man who works on a boat or ship; a man in the Navy. The *sailor* painted the ship's anchor.

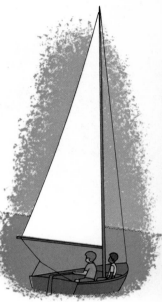
sailboat

sake Benefit; good; reason. The driver went slowly for the *sake* of the passengers' comfort.

salad A mixture of vegetables, fruits, or other foods, served cold with a special sauce. Potato *salad* was served at the picnic.

sale 1. The act of selling something. We will move after the *sale* of our house.
2. The offering of things at prices that are unusually low. The shoe store is having a *sale* on boots and rubbers.

salmon A food fish caught in both fresh and salt water.

salt A substance that looks like white sand and is put on food to give it flavor.

salmon

salute
saluted
saluting
To greet or show respect to a person or thing by touching the right hand to the head. Soldiers *salute* the flag as it passes by.

same 1. Alike or equal. Joe's bike is the *same* as Mike's.
2. The exact one; not different. Are we going to play the *same* game again?

sample   A piece that shows what the rest is like; an example. This cake is a *sample* of my baking.

sandal

sand
sandy   A mixture that feels like salt or sugar and is made of very small bits of rock. Men spread *sand* on the icy streets. A beach is a *sandy* place to play.

sandal   An open shoe that has only straps to hold the bottom part to the foot.

sandwich   Slices of bread with meat, jam, or other food between them. You can make a *sandwich* with a roll, too.

sap   A liquid that runs through trees and other plants. The *sap* from some maple trees is made into maple sugar.

sardines

sardine   A very small food fish, usually tightly packed in small, flat cans.

sash   1. A band, ribbon, or strip of cloth worn to add beauty to clothing. The princess wore a blue *sash* around the waist of her gown.
2. The frame that holds glass in a window. Lift up the *sash* and let some air in.

satellite   1. An object in space that circles around a much larger body, like a planet. The moon is a *satellite* of the earth.
2. An object made by man and sent into orbit around the earth. The new *satellite* will take pictures of weather.

satin   A smooth, shiny cloth. The bride's gown was made of *satin.*

satisfy
satisfied
satisfying   To make content; to fill a need. A cool drink of water will *satisfy* my thirst. Susan finds *satisfaction* in listening to records.

Saturday   The seventh day of the week.

Saturn   The second-largest planet; the sixth planet from the sun. See page 222.

sauce   A liquid mixture used to add flavor to food. I like tomato *sauce* on my spaghetti.

saucer   A small dish that a cup is placed on. Mother spilled some coffee in her *saucer.*

saucy   Bold; lacking respect or manners.

sausage   Pork or other meat that has been ground up, flavored, and packed into thin tubes or patties.

save
saved
saving
1. To keep for use at a later time; to set aside. Did you *save* your money or spend it?
2. To rescue from danger, harm, or loss. The sailors tried to *save* the sinking ship.
3. To make less. The new road will *save* hours of traveling.

saw   A tool with a metal blade that has a row of sharp teeth. Bob cut the board with a *saw.*

sausages

say
said
saying
1. To speak. Did you *say* "Hello" to Mr. Davis?
2. To tell with written words. The paper *says* that we will have snow.

scab   A hard crust that forms over a cut or wound. Jim has a *scab* on his scraped knee.

scale   1. A machine used to weigh things. The butcher weighed the meat on his *scale.*
2. One of the many hard, flat pieces that cover fish, reptiles, and some other animals.
3. A series of tones or sounds in music that go either up or down.

scar   A mark left on the skin by an injury. The pirate had a *scar* on his face.

scare
scared
scaring
To frighten. Snakes and rats *scare* me.

scarecrow A figure used to scare birds away from crops. Our *scarecrow* is dressed to look like a man.

scarecrow

scarf A long band or square of cloth worn over the head or around the neck or shoulders.

scatter
scattered
scattering
1. To throw or toss in many directions. The wind will *scatter* the leaves across the lawn.
2. To leave or go in many directions. The birds *scatter* when the cat appears.

scene
1. The place where something happens. The *scene* of the story was a city.
2. A short part of a play. Martha plays a witch in the third *scene.*
3. Something that you see or look at; a view. The valley was a beautiful *scene.*

school
1. A place where students are taught. Don't forget to take your books to *school!*
2. A large number of fish or whales that swim together in a group.

science
scientist
A study that finds facts by watching, testing, and thinking. Astronomy and biology are *sciences.* The *scientist* studied the plant with his microscope.

science fiction Imaginary stories about space travel, life on other planets, or scientific happenings in the future.

scientific Having to do with science; discovered by science. Astronomy is a *scientific* study of the stars and planets.

scissors (Plural) A tool with two sharp blades used for cutting cloth, paper, or other materials.

scissors

scold
scolded
scolding
To blame or find fault with in an angry way. The wicked witch used to *scold* her cat for being lazy.

scoop
scooped
scooping

1. To pick up with a shovel or a similar tool. Can you *scoop* the sand into your bucket?
2. To dig. We watched the dog *scoop* a hole in the ground and bury his bone.
3. To pick up with the hands or arms. The thirsty boys *scooped* water into their mouths.

scooter

1. A vehicle that looks like a small motorcycle.
2. A toy with two wheels, a handle in front, and a footboard on which you can stand with one foot while you push with the other.

score

1. The number of points made in a contest. The *score* of the baseball game was 6–4.
2. A grade or mark. Jim got a *score* of 90 on his spelling test.

scooter
(definition 2)

scout

1. A person sent ahead to observe the enemy or get information. The Army *scout* said the enemy was two miles away.
2. A member of the Boy Scouts or Girl Scouts.

scramble
scrambled
scrambling

1. To move quickly by running, crawling, or climbing. Monkeys *scramble* up trees.
2. To push or crowd. The hungry dogs will *scramble* for the food.
3. To mix, as in stirring egg yolks and whites together for cooking. I'm going to *scramble* my eggs.

scrap

1. A piece; a bit. Jim tore a *scrap* from the corner of the paper.
2. Material that is not used or wanted. The rusty old car was sold as *scrap.*
3. A fight or quarrel. The boys had a *scrap.*
4. (Plural) Bits of food that are left over. We fed *scraps* from dinner to the dog.

scrapbook

A large book with blank pages used for pasting in pictures or things to read or see. Jerry pasted postcards in his *scrapbook.*

scrape
scraped
scraping

1. To remove with a rough or sharp tool. Bill's job is to *scrape* the paint off the wall.
2. To cut or mark by a fall or other accident. How did you *scrape* your arm?
3. To move with a rough, scratching sound. Please don't *scrape* your chair on the floor.

scratch

1. A slight cut or mark. The rose thorn made a *scratch* on my wrist.
2. A sharp, scraping sound. We heard the *scratch* of the chalk on the chalkboard.

scratch
scratched
scratching

1. To make a slight cut or mark on. The sharp nail may *scratch* your hand.
2. To rub or scrape with claws or fingernails. Don't *scratch* your mosquito bite.

scream

A sharp, high cry of fear or pain. Linda let out a *scream* when she saw my horrible mask.

scream
screamed
screaming

1. To make a sharp, high cry because of fear or pain. The sight of the snake made Joan *scream.*
2. To yell or shout. The children *screamed* with laughter at the clown.

screen

1. A frame, with a net of thin wires stretched across it, used to keep insects from coming through a door or window.
2. A covered frame that hides or keeps something out of sight. The actor changed clothes behind a *screen.*
3. A surface on which movies or TV pictures are seen.

screw

A piece of metal shaped like a nail and with raised ribs running around it. A *screw* is used to fasten two pieces of wood or other material together.

screwdriver and screw

screwdriver

A tool used to twist a screw into place. The tip of a *screwdriver* fits into the head of a screw.

scrub
scrubbed
scrubbing

To clean by rubbing hard. Mother told me to *scrub* my hands with soap and water.

sea

1. The ocean.
2. Any large body of salt water.

sea gull

A large gray and white water bird.

seal

1. A large sea animal that has valuable fur and is an excellent swimmer.
2. A mark or design that is put on official letters or papers. There is a *seal* on my birth record.

seam

A line or edge made when pieces of material are joined or sewed together. Mother fixed the *seam* of my coat.

search
searched
searching

1. To look; to try to find. We will *search* for the missing ball.
2. To look through. Did you *search* your room for the lost key?

seashell

The shell of a clam, oyster, or other sea animal.

seashore

Land along the edge of the sea or ocean. We enjoyed the beach at the *seashore.*

season

1. One of the four parts of the year. Summer is my favorite *season.*
2. A time of the year when something usually happens or is done. Fall is the football *season.*

season
seasoned
seasoning

To add spices to; to flavor. Father will *season* the stew with pepper and salt.

seat

A chair or other object to sit on; a place to sit. Tom pushed his *seat* under his desk.

seat belt

A belt attached to the seat of a car to protect its riders. Also called "safety belt."

sea gull

seal
(definition 1)

seashells

seaweed

seaweed   A plant that grows in the sea.

second
1. Coming next after the first. Ann was *second* in the race.
2. A unit of time. There are 60 *seconds* in one minute.

secret   Something known by only one or a few people; information kept from others. The spy's real name was a *secret.*

secret
secretly   Known only by one or a few people. Joan's *secret* hiding place is behind the clock.

secretary   An office worker who types letters and answers the telephone for someone else.

section   A part of something; a portion or division. Henry separated the orange into *sections.*

see
saw
seen
seeing
1. To look at; to notice by using the eyes. Did you *see* the moon last night?
2. To understand. I don't *see* how a plane flies.
3. To visit. Stop to *see* me on your way home.
4. To be sure. Please *see* that the fire is out.

seed   The part of a plant that will produce a new plant. The acorn is the *seed* of the oak tree.

seek
sought
seeking   To look for; to try to find. The young man went out to *seek* a job.

seem
seemed
seeming   To appear to do or be; to look like. The stars *seem* to twinkle.

seesaw

seesaw   A long board, balanced in the middle, on which children play. When I go down on the *seesaw,* you go up.

seize
seized
seizing   To grab; to capture. The cat tried to *seize* the mouse.

seldom

Not often; almost never. It *seldom* rains in the desert.

select
selected
selecting

To choose from many; to pick out. The librarian will help you *select* a book.

self

One's own person. You see your own *self* when you look in the mirror. The plural of *self* is *selves.*

selfish

Putting one's own self first without a thought of others. It would be a *selfish* thing to eat all the candy by yourself.

sell
sold
selling

To give in exchange for money. Lucy *sells* lemonade for five cents a glass.

senator

A person who is elected to help make laws for the state or nation.

send
sent
sending

To cause to go; to cause to be taken to another place. The United States was the first nation to *send* a man to the moon.

sentence

A word or group of words that states a separate idea. A *sentence* begins with a capital letter and ends with a period, exclamation point, or question mark.

separate
separated
separating

To take or keep apart; to divide. Please *separate* the knives from the forks.

September

The ninth month of the year.

series

A number of things that follow one after another. The alphabet is a *series* of letters.

serious

1. Thoughtful; not gay or funny.
2. Important; dangerous. The two cars were in a *serious* accident.

servant A person hired to do work, especially housework.

serve 1. To work for; to be useful to. Firemen **serve** the community.
served
serving 2. To present food to be eaten. The class will **serve** refreshments at the school party.

service 1. Help; useful work done for others. Policemen do many **services** for our town.
2. A branch of the Government, such as the Army.
3. A religious meeting.

set A group of things, people, or numbers that belong together.

set 1. To place; to put in position. Please **set** your dirty dishes in the sink.
set
setting 2. To go down. The sun will **set** at six o'clock.
3. To become hard or firm. The chocolate pudding will **set** in about an hour.

settle 1. To come to rest; to be quiet. After dinner, Dad will **settle** in a comfortable chair.
settled
settling 2. To make a home. The pioneers went west to **settle**. Early **settlers** lived in log cabins.
3. To bring to an end; to decide. Dad told the boys to **settle** their quarrel.
4. To pay. Nan will **settle** the bill.

settlement 1. A new town or village. One of the first American **settlements** was in Virginia.
2. An understanding between two people or groups. The boys agreed on a **settlement** of their argument.

seven A number; 7. One more than 6 and one less than 8. See page 199.

seventeen A number; 17. One more than 16 and one less than 18. See page 199.

seventy A number; 70. See page 199.

several More than two or three; more than a few but not many. *Several* children were absent today.

sew
sewed
sewing To stitch; to fasten with needle and thread. Can you *sew* on a button?

sex One of the two groups into which living things are divided, female or male.

emblems for
the two sexes

shack A small house, especially one in poor condition.

shade
shady 1. The shadow made by something that blocks off the light. It is cooler in the *shade* of a tree. It is *shady* in the woods.
2. An object used to block out the light. There is a *shade* on the window.
3. A certain tone of a color. Cindy's skirt is a nice *shade* of green.

shadow A dark area having the shape of the object that blocks off the light. We used our hands to make funny *shadows* on the wall.

shadow

shake
shook
shaking To move back and forth quickly; to tremble. *Shake* the can of paint before you open it. The old bridge was *shaky* when we crossed it.

shall A word used to show that something will or must happen. We *shall* meet tomorrow.

shallow Not deep. We waded across the *shallow* stream.

shame 1. An unhappy feeling caused by doing wrong. Tom felt *shame* after he scolded the puppy.
2. Something to be sorry about. It was a *shame* that Betty could not go to the party.

shampoo 1. The act of washing hair. We gave our dog a *shampoo*.
2. The liquid soap used to wash hair.

shamrock

shamrock A low plant of the clover family with three small green leaves.

shape
1. A form or figure. The penny bank was in the *shape* of a pig.
2. Condition. Joe cleaned his room to get it in good *shape.*

share
shared
sharing
1. To divide with others. We will *share* the cookies with our friends.
2. To experience or enjoy together. Bob and Ted *shared* the excitement of the circus.

shark

shark
A large fish that eats other fish. A *shark* can be dangerous to swimmers.

sharp
1. Having a point or keen edge; not round or dull. A *sharp* pencil makes a fine line.
2. Keen; eager. The boy had a *sharp* mind.
3. Having a strong or biting taste. I like *sharp* cheese.

shave
The act of cutting off hair, especially the beginning of a beard, with a razor. Dad needs a *shave.*

shave
shaved
shaving
To cut off hair with a razor. My older brother *shaves* his face every morning.

she
A word used in place of the name of a female person or animal. Mother said *she* would be home late.

shed
A small low building, often used to store things.

shed
shed
shedding
To let fall or drop; to throw off. Some trees *shed* their leaves in the fall.

sheep

she'd
A short form of "she would" or "she had."

sheep
A farm animal raised for its wool and meat.

sheet
1. A large piece of cloth used on a bed.
2. A very thin layer or flat piece of anything. I asked for a *sheet* of paper to write on.

shelf A board or other flat surface on which things may be placed or stored. We keep our dishes on a *shelf.* The plural of *shelf* is *shelves.*

shell A hard covering found on eggs, nuts, and certain animals and vegetables. The turtle has a hard *shell.*

shell

shellfish An animal that lives in the water and has a hard outer covering or shell. The lobster and the oyster are *shellfish.*

shelter A thing that protects you from the weather; a house or building. The scouts made a *shelter* out of the tree branches.

shepherd A person who takes care of sheep.

sherbet A frozen dessert; a flavored ice. Orange *sherbet* contains orange juice, milk, and sugar.

sheriff A county officer who sees that laws are obeyed. The *sheriff* is elected by the people.

she's A short form of "she is." Jan thinks *she's* going to the movies.

shift 1. A change; a new position.
2. A group of workers and the time they work. Bill's dad works on the night *shift.*

shine
shined
shone
shining
1. To give off light; to send out a beam. The sun will *shine* for millions of years.
2. To make bright; to rub. Please *shine* your shoes before you wear them.

shingle One of the thin, flat pieces of wood or other material used on the roofs or sides of buildings. Each *shingle* partly covers a shingle below it.

shingles

ship A large boat. Columbus came to America in a sailing *ship.*

shirt A piece of clothing worn on the upper part of the body. Tom's *shirt* has long sleeves.

shiver	A trembling feeling brought on by cold or fear.
shock	1. A sudden blow; a hard bump. We felt the *shock* from the earthquake. 2. A great surprise; a fright. It is a *shock* to lose your money. 3. The effect of electricity passing through the body. You can get a *shock* if you touch a broken wire.
shoe	A covering for the foot. Tom's *shoes* are made of brown leather.
shoemaker	A person who makes or repairs shoes.
shoot *shot* *shooting*	1. To fire a gun. The hunter tried to *shoot* at the bear. 2. To send out or move quickly. The children *shot* out of the room when Dad called, "The hot dogs are ready."
shop	A small store or business.
shop *shopped* *shopping*	To look for things to buy. We *shop* for clothes at a department store.
shore	The land along the edge of a river, lake, or ocean. We like to swim at the *shore.*
short *shortly*	Not tall or long; brief. A dwarf is a *short* person. School will be over *shortly.*
shot	1. The noise made when a gun is fired. The birds flew away when they heard the *shot.* 2. Medicine that is put into the body with a needle. A *shot* may cure a disease.
should	1. Ought to. I *should* go home. 2. Were to. If Mother *should* call, please let me know. 3. If. *Should* our plans work out, we will go to the museum Saturday.

shoes

shoulder　The part of the body where the arm joins the top of the chest.

shouldn't　A short form of "should not."

shout　A loud cry. Tom gave a **shout** of joy when he got the prize.

shout
shouted
shouting
　To call out loudly; to yell. Don't **shout** in the cafeteria.

shovel　A long-handled tool used for digging.

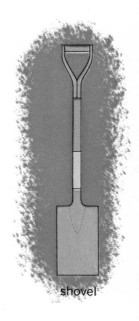
shovel

show　A play or other performance for people to watch. The boys went to a magic **show.**

show
showed
showing
　1. To allow a view of; to let see. Did Jane **show** the picture to you?
2. To instruct; to teach. Please **show** me how to draw a tree.

shower　1. A bath under a spray of water.
2. A short rain.

shrimp　A tiny shellfish that is eaten as food.

shut
shut
shutting
　To close. Please **shut** the door.

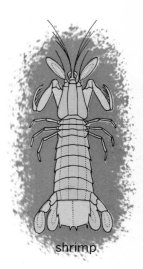
shrimp

shy　Not comfortable with other people. The **shy** girl blushed when she met strangers.

sick　Ill; not well. The **sick** man has a fever.

side　1. An edge or a surface along an edge. A wall is one **side** of a room.
2. A section or area near one edge. Tom was on the other **side** of the street.
3. A group of people who play or fight against another group. Please play on our **side** in the next game.

sidewalk   A narrow, paved path for people to walk on by the side of a road.

sigh   The sound of a long, deep breath that shows you are tired or relaxed. We heard Dad's *sigh* of relief after the long drive.

sight   1. The ability to see. Ed wears glasses to help his *sight.*
2. A thing that is seen. The waterfall is a pretty *sight.*

sign   1. A board or surface with writing or a drawing on it. The traffic *sign* said "Stop."
2. An object or action that shows something; a hint. Heavy clouds are a *sign* of bad weather.

sign
signed
signing   To write your name on. Dad will *sign* my report card.

signal   A sign, movement, or sound that has a special meaning. A ringing sound is the *signal* that you have a phone call.

sign language   A way of saying things by hand signals, used by those who cannot hear or speak.

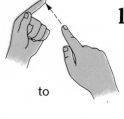

to

silence   Absence of noise; quiet; stillness.

silent   Quiet; without noise. The library was *silent.*

silk   A light, shiny cloth or the threads that make the cloth. Mother's blouse is made of *silk.*

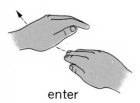

enter

silly   Foolish; stupid. Tim looked *silly* with his shoes on the wrong feet.

silver   A valuable metal that shines. Some knives, forks, and spoons are made of *silver.*

similar   Much alike; somewhat the same.

on
(upon)

sign language

simple
simply   1. Easy; not hard. The spelling test was *simple.*
2. Not fancy or expensive. The settlers ate *simple* meals. They dressed *simply.*

since

1. During the time after. We have waited for Tim *since* noon.
2. Because. *Since* it is your birthday, we will have a party.

sing
sang
singing

To make musical sounds with the voice. We heard Jane *sing* a new song. We listened to a *singer* on the radio.

single
singly

1. One; by itself. Joan didn't make a *single* mistake. The boys entered the room *singly*.
2. Not married. Her older brother is still *single*.

singular

Having to do with one person, place, or thing; not plural. "Chair" is a *singular* word meaning "one chair."

sink

A large washbowl; a tub-like container with water faucets. We wash our dishes in the *sink*.

sink
sank
sinking

1. To go or cause to go under the water. Did the storm *sink* the small boat?
2. To fall or move down slowly. Your foot will *sink* in the thick mud.

sip

A small taste. Judy took a *sip* of the hot soup.

sir

A word used when writing or speaking to a man. My letter to the salesman began, "Dear *Sir*."

sister

A female who has the same parents as another person.

sit
sat
sitting

To rest with legs bent and your weight on your hips. Please *sit* on the chair.

situation

A condition; the way things are at a certain time or place. The icy roads caused a dangerous *situation*.

six

A number; 6. One more than 5 and one less than 7. See page 199.

sixteen   A number; 16. One more than 15 and one less than 17. See page 199.

sixty   A number; 60. See page 199.

size   The largeness or smallness of something. What is the *size* of your bedroom?

skate   1. A shoe with a metal blade fastened to the sole for sliding over ice.
2. A platform set on four small wheels and fastened to a shoe for rolling over a hard surface. Also called a "roller skate."

skeleton

skate
skated
skating   To move with skates on your feet. We will *skate* on the pond. The *skater* fell on the ice.

skeleton   The frame of bones in a human or animal body.

ski   A long, narrow piece of wood, metal, or plastic worn in pairs on the feet for moving over snow.

ski
skied
skiing   To move over snow with skis on your feet. We watched Ed *ski* down the hill.

skid
skidded
skidding   To slide; to slip. The car may *skid* on the icy road.

skill   A special ability; knowing how to do something well. Chris has *skill* in drawing pictures.

skin   The outside covering of an animal, fruit, or vegetable. The fall scraped the *skin* from Janet's hands and knees.

skis

skin
skinned
skinning   To remove the skin from. When you *skin* an onion, you may cry.

skinny   Thin; very slender. The *skinny* boy is not very heavy.

skip
skipped
skipping
1. To move by jumping or hopping on each foot in turn. Children often hop and **skip.**
2. To leave out; to pass over. The busy man had to **skip** lunch.

skirt A piece of clothing for women and girls that covers from the waist down.

skunk A black animal with a bushy tail and a white stripe down its back. The **skunk** gives off a very bad-smelling odor.

skunk

sky The air around the earth, and the space beyond it. There are clouds in the **sky.**

Skylab An American spaceship on which astronauts can live and work.

skyscraper A very high building.

slacks (Plural) Pants or trousers.

slam
slammed
slamming
1. To put or slap down with a loud noise. We heard Dave **slam** his book on the desk.
2. To close with a loud noise. Don't **slam** the door.

slant A slope; a position that is not level. That roof has a steep **slant.**

slap A hit with the open hand. The coach gave his winning pitcher a **slap** on the back.

slap
slapped
slapping
To hit with the open hand or a flat object. The cowboy often **slaps** the horse's side to make him go faster.

slave A person who works without pay for someone who owns him.

sled

slavery The condition of a person owned by someone else, or the owning of slaves.

sled A small platform on runners for sliding over snow.

sleep The condition of not being awake; a deep rest. Ann awoke from a long **sleep.**

sleep
slept
sleeping

To rest deeply; to be in a condition of not being awake. We usually **sleep** at night.

sleeve

The part of a piece of clothing that covers the arm.

sleigh

A large sled pulled by a horse or, in stories, by reindeer.

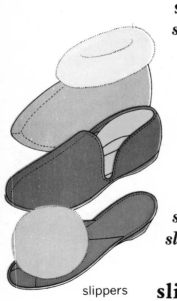

sleigh

slender

Thin; not wide or fat.

slice

A thin, flat piece. Tom ate a **slice** of cheese.

slick

1. Smooth; slippery. Ice made the roads **slick.**
2. Smart; clever. The magician did a **slick** trick.

slide

A slanting metal surface down which you can move smoothly. We have **slides** in our playground.

slide
slid
sliding

To move smoothly over a surface. Let's **slide** down the hill on our sled.

slight
slightly

Small; not great or important. Jim made a **slight** mistake. The scratch hurt **slightly.**

slim

Thin; not thick or fat. The **slim** boy weighs less than the fat boy.

sling

A strap or piece of material that holds something in place. Bob had his broken arm in a **sling.**

slip
slipped
slipping

1. To slide or fall. Don't **slip** on the ice!
2. To move or push smoothly. I tried to **slip** the letter under the door.
3. To move quietly. Let's **slip** out of the movie.

slippers

slipper

A light, comfortable shoe, usually worn indoors.

slippery

Very smooth; easy to slide on. The ice on the pond is **slippery.**

slit

A very narrow opening. Mary made a **slit** in the cloth with scissors.

slope　A piece of land that slants. Bill skied down the *slope.*

slow　Having a low rate of speed; not fast. The *slow*
slowly　runner finished last. The old man walked
　slowly.

slowpoke　A person who is slow. That *slowpoke* is always late for school.

slum　A section of a town or city where people are poor and homes are in very bad condition.

sly　Clever; sneaky. A fox is a *sly* animal.

small　Little; not big. An ant is a *small* insect.

smart　Able to learn quickly and easily; bright.

smart　To burn or sting. The cold wind made my eyes
smarted　*smart.*
smarting

smell　To breathe in the odor of. When I *smell* bread
smelled　baking, I get hungry.
smelling

smile　A way of showing friendship or happiness by turning up the corners of the mouth.

smile　To look happy by turning up the corners of
smiled　the mouth. The baby will *smile* if you give
smiling　him a toy.

smog　Dirty air with smoke and fog.

smoke　The cloudy gas that comes from something burning. The *smoke* from Dad's pipe filled the room.

smooth　Having an even surface; not rough; without lumps. A baby's skin is very *smooth.*

snack　A bit of food; not a full meal. An apple is a good *snack.*

snail

snail   A tiny animal with a soft, worm-like body inside a shell. *Snails* live on land or in the water.

snake   A long, thin reptile that has no feet but moves by sliding along the ground.

snap   1. A fastener used on clothing in place of a button. Jack has *snaps* on his ski jacket.
2. A sharp, quick noise. The lock closed with a *snap.*

snap
snapped
snapping   1. To make a sharp, quick noise. Can you *snap* your fingers?
2. To crack or break suddenly. The piano was too heavy and the rope *snapped.*
3. To bite quickly. The dog may *snap* at you.
4. To speak sharply. The man *snapped* at the boys for walking on his grass.

snake

snatch
snatched
snatching   To grab quickly. My puppy tried to *snatch* the cat's chicken bone.

sneak   A person who does sly or secret things. The person who cheated on the test was a *sneak.*

sneak
sneaked
sneaking   To move secretly or slyly. I'll tell you where the cookies are if you'll *sneak* in and get us some. Janie is very *sneaky* about where she hides her mother's birthday present.

sneaker   A shoe made of cloth with a rubber bottom; a tennis shoe.

sneaker

sneeze
sneezed
sneezing   To blow air out of the mouth and nose loudly and quickly. Smelling pepper makes me *sneeze.*

sniff
sniffed
sniffing   To smell in quick, short breaths. Our dog *sniffs* our shoes when we come in.

snip   A little cut or a small piece cut off. A *snip* with the scissors, and a *snip* of my hair fell to the floor.

snore
snored
snoring
   To make a loud breathing sound while asleep.

snow   Little white flakes of frozen water that fall from the sky to the ground in cold weather.

snow
snowed
snowing
   To drop or come down in flakes of snow from the clouds to the ground. It may *snow* today.

snowball   A round mass of snow pressed together with the hands. It is fun to throw *snowballs.*

snowflake   One single bit of snow. Each *snowflake* has a lace-like design.

snowman   A figure made of packed snow that looks something like a person.

snowmobile   A machine that travels over the snow on skis, carrying one or two persons.

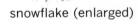

snowflake (enlarged)

snug   1. Warm and cozy. I had a *snug* feeling under the blanket.
2. Tight, close. My socks are too *snug* around my feet.

snowmobile

so
1. To such an amount. Bob was *so* hungry that he ate everything.
2. Therefore. Ann had to stay in, *so* I went home.
3. Also. I was talking and *so* was Ted.
4. More or less. I'll be on vacation a week or *so.*
5. True. What Dad said is *so.*

soak
soaked
soaking
To make very wet. Walking home in the rain will *soak* my clothes.

soap
A material used with water to wash things clean.

soap

sob
sobbed
sobbing
To weep with short gasping noises.

soccer
A game in which players try to kick a round ball to a goal.

sock
A short stocking.

soda
A drink made with bubbly water and flavoring, sometimes with ice cream added.

soccer

sofa
A piece of furniture big enough for several people to sit on; a couch.

soda

soft
softly
1. Not hard; sinking in a little when touched. Wood is hard; bread is *soft.*
2. Very quiet; not loud. I like our teacher's *soft* voice.

softball
A game like baseball played with a ball that is larger and not as hard as a baseball.

soil
The ground or land; dirt or earth. Plants grow in *soil.*

solar
Having to do with the sun.

solar system The sun and all the planets, including the earth, that move around the sun.

soldier A man in the Army.

solid
solidly 1. Firm and stiff; strong. A piece of wood is **solid.** Our house is **solidly** built.
2. Having a certain material all the way through; not hollow. My candy egg is hollow but Jan's is **solid** chocolate.

solution 1. An answer. I have the **solution** to the math problem.
2. A mixture of something with a liquid. Salt mixed with water makes a **solution.**

solve
solved To find an answer for, or a way of doing. Can
solving you **solve** this puzzle?

sombrero A big hat with a wide brim, worn in Spain, Mexico, and some other countries.

sombrero

some 1. A number of. **Some** people like strawberry ice cream.
2. An amount of. Patty likes **some** sugar on her cereal.
3. Good; great. That was **some** game!

somebody A person. **Somebody** is at the door.

someone Somebody; some person. Tom wants **someone** to read to him.

something A thing that we do not know. **Something** is bothering Ann.

sometimes Once in a while; now and then. **Sometimes** I'm so happy I want to sing.

somewhere A place that we do not know exactly. I know my book is here **somewhere.**

son A person's male child.

song Music made with the voice.

soon 1. Before long; in a very short time. Dad will pick us up *soon.*
2. Early. It is too *soon* to eat dinner.

sore A break or bruise on the skin.

sorry Unhappy; sad. I am *sorry* your dog was hurt.

sort A kind; a type. What *sort* of music do you like?

sort
sorted
sorting To separate and put into groups. When we *sort* the laundry, we put all the socks in one pile and the shirts in another.

soul A person's deep inner self or feelings.

sound Noise; a thing that can be heard. The car's horn made a loud *sound.*

soup A liquid food made with vegetables or meat.

sour 1. Having a sharp taste or flavor; not sweet. A lemon is *sour.*
2. Gruff. Sam is always *sour* in the morning.
3. Turned bad; spoiled. The cat will not drink *sour* milk.

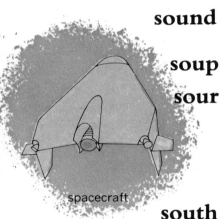
spacecraft

south A direction. See illustration at **compass.**

sow
sowed
sowing To plant by throwing or scattering. In the fall, we *sow* grass seed on the lawn.

space 1. Room or area. I don't have enough *space* to write the last line.
2. The sky; the area outside the earth's atmosphere. An astronaut travels in *space.*

space capsule A part of a spacecraft that holds a crew and their equipment.

spacecraft A rocket, space capsule, or other craft that travels through space.

spaceman   An astronaut; a person who travels in space.

spaceship   A vehicle that travels through space; a spacecraft.

space station   A base or satellite in outer space in which spacemen can live and work.

space suit   A special suit worn by spacemen to protect them in outer space.

spade   A shovel with a flat blade, used for digging.

spaghetti   A food made from long, thin sticks of dough, often served with a tomato sauce.

spank
spanked
spanking   To slap or hit with the open hand, as punishment.

spare   Extra. Tom let me use his *spare* skates.

spark   1. A small bit of burning material. A *spark* from the fireplace went up the chimney.
2. A small flash of electricity.

sparkle
sparkled
sparkling   To give off flashes of light. Kathy's shiny bracelet *sparkles.*

sparrow   A small brown or gray bird.

sparrow

speak
spoke
spoken
speaking   To talk; to say or tell. We heard the nurse *speak* about health. The mayor is a good *speaker.*

special   Interesting; different; unusual. We planned a *special* trip for our vacation.

speech   1. Talking. *Speech* is how we use our voices to say things to each other.
2. A talk. The policeman gave a *speech* to our class.

speed The rate at which something moves. The plane's *speed* was 600 miles an hour.

spell A magic action or effect. The witch's *spell* kept Sleeping Beauty from waking up.

spell
spelled
spelling To say or write the letters that make up a word. It takes four letters to *spell* "pony."

spend
spent
spending 1. To pay out. How much did you *spend* for the book?
2. To use up. I will *spend* 20 minutes on my homework.

spice A plant used to give special flavor to foods. Pepper is a *spice.*

spider A small insect-like animal with eight legs. The *spider* made a web.

spider

spike 1. A very large, strong nail.
2. A pointed piece of metal on the bottom of shoes used in some sports.

spill
spilled
spilling 1. To allow to run over or pour out. Don't *spill* the glass of water.
2. To let fall. Jan *spilled* crumbs on the floor.

spin A turning movement; a whirl. The falling leaf went into a *spin.*

spin
spun
spinning 1. To turn quickly. We watched the car's wheels *spin* on the ice.
2. To make into thread. Pioneer wives would *spin* wool into yarn.

spirit 1. A feeling or mood. Bob is happy and has a cheerful *spirit.*
2. A ghost or other creature that cannot be seen. A fairy is an imaginary *spirit.*
3. The soul and mind; the part of a person that is not his body.

splash A sudden moving or scattering of a liquid, or the sound that this makes. The rock hit the water with a *splash.*

splash
splashed
splashing
To move or scatter about. Waves *splash* water on the rocks along the shore.

splashdown The landing of a space capsule on water. After the *splashdown* the astronauts were picked up.

splendid
splendidly
Excellent; very pleasing. The museum has many *splendid* paintings. Tina plays the piano *splendidly.*

sponge

split A break or crack. The wood had a *split* in it where the ax hit.

spoil
spoiled
spoiling
To damage; to ruin. The flood may *spoil* our crops.

spoke One of the rods between the center and the rim of a wheel. A bicycle wheel has many *spokes.*

spool

sponge
spongy
1. A small sea animal.
2. The dried skeleton of this animal or a synthetic imitation, used in wiping and cleaning. A *sponge* soaks up a lot of water.
3. Anything soft and fluffy like a sponge. I like *sponge* cake. This cushion is *spongy.*

spook A ghost. The story is about a *spook* and a witch.

spool A small round object on which thread or wire can be wound. Mother needs a *spool* of white thread.

spoon

spoon A tool used to stir, measure, or lift food.

sport A game or contest; an athletic activity. Baseball is my favorite *sport.*

spot　　1. A blot or mark. Jack has a *spot* of mud on his pants.
2. A place or area. We picked a *spot* on the beach to have our picnic.

spout　　A tube or pipe through which liquid can flow. The teapot has a *spout.*

spout
spouted
spouting
To send forth a stream of. A whale can *spout* water high into the air.

spray　　A light shower of liquid. *Spray* from the waves made our clothing damp.

spray
sprayed
spraying
To send out fine drops of. Bill will *spray* paint on the old chairs.

spread　　Any food like butter, jam, or jelly that is used to cover bread and crackers.

spread
spread
spreading
1. To scatter. We *spread* sand over the icy sidewalk.
2. To open fully; to stretch. Bob *spread* out his arms to take the large package.

spring　　1. A curl of metal or wire that can shorten or stretch and then bounce back to its original shape. There are *springs* in our couch.
2. A natural flow of water from the ground.
3. The season between winter and summer.

spur

spring
sprang or *sprung*
springing
To move suddenly; to jump. We saw a rabbit *spring* from the bushes.

sprinkle　　A light shower or pouring; a spray.

spur　　A piece of metal with points on it, worn on a boot and used to poke a horse to make it move faster.

sputnik　A Russian space satellite. The first Russian *sputnik* was put into orbit in 1957.

spy　A person who acts secretly to learn about another country's plans or activities.

square　A shape with four equal, straight sides and four equal corners.

square dance　A country dance in which sets of four couples dance.

squash　A yellow or green vegetable that grows on a vine.

squeeze
squeezed
squeezing
　To press tightly together. Mother *squeezed* the lemon to get juice.

squirm
squirmed
squirming
　To twist and turn; to move about restlessly. We watched the worms *squirm*.

squirrel　A small animal that has a fluffy tail, lives in trees, and feeds on nuts and seeds.

squirt
squirted
squirting
　To shoot out in a sudden, small stream. Water will *squirt* from the broken hose.

squirrel

stable　A building where horses or other large animals are kept.

stack　1. A pile; a heap. A *stack* of wood was near the fireplace.
2. A tall chimney. Smoke poured from the factory's big smoke*stack*.

staff　1. A heavy rod; a pole. The mountain climber carried a wooden *staff*.
2. A group of people who are working together on one job. Our school has a *staff* of twenty teachers.

stag   An adult male deer. The *stag* had large antlers.

stage   A raised platform on which plays and other programs are presented.

stagecoach   A large carriage pulled by horses, once used to carry people and mail.

stain   A dark spot. An ink *stain* is hard to remove.

stair   1. One of the steps on a staircase.
2. (Plural) A staircase.

staircase   A set of steps on which you can go from one floor to another.

staircase

stake   A pointed stick or post that can be driven into the ground. Jim nailed a sign to the wooden *stake.*

stalk   The stem of a plant. Corn grows on a tall, green *stalk.*

stall   A section in a stable or barn for a horse or other animal.

stamp   A small label that is glued to a letter or other mail and shows that money has been paid for delivery. I needed a *stamp* to mail my letter.

stamp
stamped
stamping   1. To hit hard with the bottom of the foot. The horses *stamp* on the stable floor.
2. To put a stamp or special mark on. Did Jane *stamp* the letter?

stand   1. A place where things are sold. Jack bought a soda at the refreshment *stand.*
2. A small table. Please put the dictionary on the book *stand.*
3. (Plural) A set of outdoor benches or seats where people can sit to watch a game or other public show.

stand
stood
standing

1. To be on or get onto your feet. Do you want to *stand* or keep on sitting?
2. To be; to last. How long did the old building *stand* on Main Street?
3. To accept; to put up with. Our dog can't *stand* loud noises.

stanza

A set or group of lines in a poem or song. Some poems have four lines in each *stanza.*

star

A heavenly body that produces its own light and heat.

stare
stared
staring

To give a steady look with eyes wide open. People will *stare* if you open an umbrella when there's no rain.

start
started
starting

1. To begin. School will *start* at eight o'clock.
2. To put into motion. Flip the switch to *start* the machine.

starve
starved
starving

To grow weak or die from hunger. The cattle will *starve* without grass to eat. The stray dog suffered from *starvation.*

state

1. A condition; a situation. Mary's room was in a messy *state.*
2. One part of a nation with its own government. Henry lives in the *state* of Florida.

state
stated
stating

To say in words or writing. The mayor will *state* his opinion tonight. Our teacher made a *statement* about our holidays.

station

1. A building where passengers get on or off trains or buses.
2. A building or rooms from which radio or TV programs are broadcast.
3. A building for certain workers. The class went to visit the police *station.*

station wagon   An auto with a rear door and extra space for passengers or baggage.

statue   A model of a person or animal carved or formed from something hard, such as stone, metal, or wood.

stay
stayed
staying   To remain. Please **stay** for lunch.

station wagon

steady
steadily   1. Even; regular. Jane reads at a **steady** rate. The river flowed **steadily**.
2. Firm; in position; not shaking. Keep the canoe **steady**.

steak   A large slice of meat, usually beef. We broiled a **steak** at our picnic.

steal
stole
stolen
stealing   To take without permission. Did a thief **steal** the paintings?

steam   A gas or vapor formed when water boils. The kettle will give off **steam** when the water is ready for tea.

steamboat   A boat moved by engines run by steam.

steel   A hard, strong metal made mostly of iron. Railroad tracks are made of **steel**.

steep   Having a sharp slant. The old car could not get up the **steep** hill.

steamboat

steeple   A tower on the top of a church.

steer
steered
steering   To direct the course of; to guide. Dad **steers** the car by turning the wheel.

stem   The part of a plant that holds up flowers or leaves; a stalk. A tulip has a long, green **stem**.

step

1. A movement of the foot in walking. Bob took a *step* forward.
2. A part of an action. The first *step* in driving is turning on the motor.
3. A place for the foot on a staircase or ladder.

step
stepped
stepping

1. To go by moving the feet; to walk. Please *step* into my room.
2. To place the foot. Please don't *step* on my toes.

stereo

A record player or radio using more than one speaker.

stew

A food made by slowly cooking meat and vegetables together. Ed likes beef *stew.*

stick

1. A long, narrow piece of wood. Tom threw another *stick* on the fire.
2. Anything shaped like a stick. The teacher wrote with a *stick* of chalk.

stick
stuck
sticking

1. To become fastened. Did the gum *stick* to your shoe? Glue is a *sticky* substance.
2. To fasten; to join. *Stick* more tape on the package.
3. To put; to stab. We saw the swimmer *stick* his toe in the water.

stickball

A popular game in which a batter uses a stick to hit a light ball.

stiff

Firm; not easy to bend. Cloth is not as *stiff* as leather.

still

1. Without movement. The horse stood *still.*
2. Quiet. The crying baby suddenly became *still.*
3. Yet; at this moment. Is it *still* raining?

sting

1. A small wound or bite. The *sting* on my arm was caused by a bee.
2. A sharp, sudden pain. I felt the *sting* of the doctor's needle.

sting
stung
stinging

1. To bite. Did the wasp *sting* you?
2. To cause a sharp, sudden pain. Will the medicine for my cut *sting?*

stink

A bad smell; a strong odor. The skunk caused a *stink.*

stir
stirred
stirring

1. To mix or blend. Dad will *stir* his coffee.
2. To move slightly. The wind *stirred* the trees.

stitch

A single movement of a needle and thread through a material and back again. Mother put a *stitch* or two in my torn pants.

stocking

A piece of knit clothing that tightly covers the foot and part of the leg.

stomach

1. An organ inside the body where food is digested.
2. The front part of the body just below the chest.

stone

A piece of rock; a hard mineral like granite or marble. The fireplace is made of *stone.*

stool

A seat without a back or arms.

stoop

A small porch. There is a *stoop* at our front door.

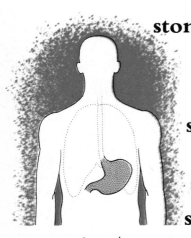

stomach
(definition 1)

stoop
stooped
stooping

To lean or bend forward. Fred had to *stoop* to enter the cave.

stop
stopped
stopping

1. To quit moving. The bus will *stop* at the corner.
2. To prevent or bring to an end. Can the firemen *stop* the fire from spreading?
3. To close or block. The leaves may *stop* up the drain pipe.

stoplight A red signal light used to stop cars.

store A place where things are bought and sold; a shop. Food is sold at the grocery *store.*

store
stored
storing
To put away for use at another time. Squirrels *store* nuts for the winter.

storeroom A room in which things can be stored or kept.

stork A large wading bird with a long bill and long legs.

storm Weather in which strong winds bring rain, snow, or thunder and lightning. A hurricane is a powerful *storm.*

stork

story 1. A tale; a telling about an event. Susan liked the *story* of Robin Hood.
2. A floor or level in a building. We live in a two-*story* house.

stove A device that gives off heat. *Stoves* may be used to cook food or to heat a room.

straight 1. Not curved or crooked. The ruler is *straight.*
2. Without wandering; directly. Ed went *straight* to school.

strain 1. An injury caused by too much work or effort. Ted has a *strain* in his arm from pitching.
2. Difficulty. The *strain* of driving made Mother tired.

strange
strangely
Odd; unusual. It seems *strange* to have a cold day in summer. The clown was dressed *strangely.*

strap A narrow band used to hold things together; a belt. A *strap* held the saddle on the horse.

straw
1. One or many dried stems of grain. The calf sleeps on a pile of *straw.*
2. A small tube used to suck up liquids. John drank his soda through a *straw.*

strawberry
A small sweet, red fruit.

strawberry

stray
strayed
straying
To wander away. Sheep often *stray* and get lost.

streak
A line; a long mark. We saw a *streak* of lightning during the storm.

stream
1. A small body of flowing water.
2. A steady flow of people or things.

street
A road in a town or city.

strength
Power; energy. Bob has enough *strength* to lift the heavy box.

stretch
stretched
stretching
1. To pull into a longer or larger shape. Let's see if we can *stretch* the rubber band around the books.
2. To reach out. Dad can *stretch* his hand up to the top shelf.

strike
1. A time when workers refuse to work until they get better pay or working conditions. No trains will run during the *strike.*
2. In baseball, a good pitch that is not hit safely. After three *strikes,* the batter is out.

strike
struck
striking
1. To hit sharply. A falling tree *struck* the cabin.
2. To sound. I heard the clock *strike* two o'clock.
3. To light by rubbing. Bob *struck* a match to light the fire.
4. To stop work to get better pay or working conditions.

string   A cord; a heavy thread.

string bean   A long, thin vegetable, usually green.

strip   A long, narrow piece. Mother made a belt out of the *strip* of cloth.

stripe   A line. A white *stripe* was painted down the center of the road.

stroke   **1.** A blow or hit. The *stroke* of the golf club sent the ball flying.
2. A complete movement, done over and over. I need to improve my swimming *stroke.*
3. A single touch or mark. I put a *stroke* of red paint on my paper.

string beans

strong   **1.** Powerful. A horse is a *strong* animal.
2. Sure; firm. Dad has *strong* opinions about safe driving.

structure   A building; something that has been put together or constructed. A skyscraper is a large *structure.*

struggle   **1.** A great effort, especially against difficulties.
2. A contest; a fight.

student   A pupil; a person who studies.

study   The act of learning. Years of *study* are necessary to become a lawyer.

study
studied
studying   To try to learn; to try to understand. Jim has to *study* history tonight.

stuff   Material. Mother carries lots of *stuff* in her purse.

stuff
stuffed
stuffing   To pack; to fill. We *stuffed* the pillow with feathers.

stumble
stumbled
stumbling

To trip or walk in an unsteady way. Don't *stumble* over the fallen branch.

stump

stump

A part of a tree or other thing that is left after the main part is cut away.

stunt

A trick or an unusual action. Flying upside down was the pilot's favorite *stunt.*

stupid
stupidly

Foolish; not smart. The *stupid* boy played with matches. I *stupidly* lost my key.

subject

1. Something that is spoken or written about; a topic. Baseball was the *subject* of Tom's speech.
2. Something that is studied in school. English is my favorite *subject.*

submarine

submarine

A boat that can travel under water.

substance

What something is made up of; material. Stone is a hard *substance.*

subtract
subtracted
subtracting

To take away; to remove. You *subtract* 3 from 5 to get 2. *Subtraction* is easier than division.

subway

A train that carries people on tracks under the ground.

such

1. Of a special or certain type. I like *such* TV shows as news and sports.
2. So very much. Tim's birthday party was *such* a surprise!

suck
sucked
sucking

To take in through the lips. I like to *suck* soda through a straw.

sudden
suddenly

Happening quickly, without warning. The *sudden* boom of thunder made us jump. *Suddenly* Jan ran into the room.

sugar A substance used to make foods sweet.

suggest
suggested
suggesting To give an idea or thought that may be of help to another. I **suggest** that you button your coat in cold weather. Marsha's **suggestion** that we get to school early was very wise.

suit A set of clothes that are worn together, usually a jacket with matching pants or skirt.

suitcase A box-like container with a handle, used for carrying clothes when traveling.

sum The answer when numbers are added together; the total. The **sum** of 5 and 5 is 10.

summer The season of the year between spring and fall.

sun The bright star that gives us light and heat. The earth makes an orbit around the **sun.**

sunburn Redness and soreness of the skin caused by being in the sun too long.

Sunday The first day of the week.

sunlight The light that comes from the sun; daylight.

sunny 1. Filled with sunshine. The large windows made the room **sunny.**
2. Happy and cheerful. Miss Clark has a **sunny** smile.

sunrise The time when the sun comes up in the morning; dawn.

sunset The time when the sun goes down in the evening.

sunshine The light of the sun; sunlight.

supermarket A large, modern food store where people wait on themselves. We shop each week at the **supermarket.**

supper   A meal at the end of the day or in the evening.

supply   1. An amount of something; a quantity or number. We have a big *supply* of paper towels.
2. (Plural) Things needed to do something; materials. My school *supplies* include paper, pencils, paste, and scissors.

supply
supplied
supplying   To give; to provide. Cows *supply* milk for us to drink.

support
supported
supporting   1. To hold in place; to bear the weight of something. Is the chair strong enough to *support* the fat man?
2. To give help to; to aid.

suppose
supposed
supposing   To think or guess. What do you *suppose* your birthday present will be?

sure   Certain; having an exact feeling about something. I'm *sure* it will rain again tomorrow.

surface   The top or outside of a thing. A leaf floated on the *surface* of the pond.

surprise   A thing or an event that is not planned or expected. Seeing snow in July would be a *surprise.*

surprise
surprised
surprising   To amaze. The party will *surprise* Ted because he's not expecting it.

swallow
(definition 2)

swallow   1. A small drink or gulp of something. Tina took a *swallow* of the lemonade.
2. A small bird with a long two-pointed tail.

swallow
swallowed
swallowing   To cause to go down the throat and into the stomach. You should chew your food well before you *swallow* it.

swamp   An area of land that is very wet; a marsh.

swan   A large water bird with a long neck and white feathers.

swan

swap   An exchange or trade. Lil made a *swap* of her pin for Jan's bracelet.

swat   A sharp blow or hit. Jim gave the mosquito a *swat.*

sweat   Salty moisture that comes out of the skin. After the race we were covered with *sweat.*

sweater   A knitted piece of clothing worn on the upper part of the body for warmth.

sweat shirt   A heavy piece of clothing for the top part of the body worn during exercise or play.

sweep
swept
sweeping
1. To use a broom to brush clean.
2. To carry or cause to move. The wind will *sweep* the leaves along the street.
3. To go through quickly. The blizzard *swept* across the whole country.

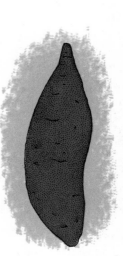

sweet
1. Tasting like sugar or honey. Candy is *sweet.*
2. Easy to like or love. Bill's baby sister is *sweet.*

sweet potato   A plant root that is eaten as a vegetable.

swell
swelled
swelling
1. To increase in size. If you twist your ankle, it may *swell.*
2. To become louder or stronger. The music will *swell* when you turn the volume up.

sweet potato

swift   Fast, quick. Bob ran a *swift* race.

swim
swam
swum
swimming
To travel through the water by moving legs and arms, or fins. We will *swim* in the city pool. A good *swimmer* watches out for others.

sword

swing A seat that hangs on chains or ropes on which you can move back and forth through the air.

swing 1. To go back and forth in a swing.
swung 2. To move in a sweeping motion. Did you see
swinging John **swing** the bat at that ball?

sword A weapon with a long, sharp blade.

swordfish A fish with a long, pointed, sword-like bill.

synthetic Made by man rather than from natural materials. Nylon and plastic are **synthetic** materials.

syrup A sweet, sticky sauce. Jane puts butter and **syrup** on her pancakes.

system 1. An orderly or certain way of doing things. Father has a **system** for keeping the lawn cut. 2. A group of things or people that work together. Our town's post office is part of the postal **system.**

swordfish

Tt

table   A piece of furniture with a flat top held up by legs.

tablecloth   A large cloth for covering a table used for dining.

tablespoon   1. A spoon for serving and measuring. Mother served the potatoes with a *tablespoon.*
2. A unit of measure. Two *tablespoons* equal an ounce.

table

tablet   A pad with many sheets of paper joined along one edge.

tag   1. A piece of heavy paper or other material, fastened to something to give information about it. This *tag* shows the price of the hat.
2. A game in which the one who is "it" must chase and touch another person.

tag
tagged
tagging   1. To put a tag on. The salesman will *tag* the TV sets with new prices.
2. To touch in the game of tag.
3. To follow. Bill's little brother likes to *tag* along with him.

tail   1. A slender, usually long body part that grows from the rear of some animals. Our puppy wagged his *tail.*
2. The rear or end part. The *tail* of the airplane was painted blue.

take
took
taken
taking

1. To select; to grasp hold of and keep. Ed will *take* the big piece of cake for himself.
2. To lead from one place to another. *Take* your brother across the street.
3. To carry or move. Please *take* this box to Aunt Mary's house.
4. To ride on. Susan *takes* a bus to school.
5. To spend or use. Our little brother *takes* a long time to dress himself.

tale

A story. Sally likes the *tale* about Cinderella.

talk
talked
talking

To speak; to tell. We listened to the teacher *talk* about George Washington.

tall

High; not short. The *tall* tree stretches over the roof of the barn.

tame

Gentle; not wild. The *tame* squirrel eats nuts out of Tim's hand.

tan

A darkness of the skin caused by the sun's rays.

tangle
tangled
tangling

To twist around and around. Billy *tangled* his fishing line.

tank

1. A large container for liquids or gas. Our oil *tank* holds 1,000 gallons.
2. A war vehicle that has a large gun on top and can go over very rough land.

tap

A light hit; a touch. Dad woke me with a *tap* on my shoulder.

tap
tapped
tapping

To knock lightly. I heard Mother *tap* on my door.

tape measures

tape

1. A narrow strip of material, sometimes with one sticky side. The nurse put adhesive *tape* over my bandage to hold it in place.

2. A narrow strip of plastic on which sound and TV programs can be recorded. Dave listened to a *tape* of his favorite song.

tape measure　A tape of cloth or metal used to measure length.

tar　A sticky, black substance used to cover roads and make things waterproof.

tardy　Late; not on time. Jack is often *tardy* because he sleeps late.

target　A thing that you aim or shoot at. Joe's arrow hit the center of the *target.*

target

tart　A pastry filled with fruit or jam; a small pie.

task　A job; a duty. Dad gave me the *task* of washing the car.

tassel　A number of strings, cords, or threads hanging down and joined together at the top.

taste　Flavor. Honey has a sweet *taste.*

taste
tasted
tasting　**1.** To know the flavor of by taking into the mouth. Did you *taste* Ann's apple pie? **2.** To have a certain flavor. The lemon *tastes* sour.

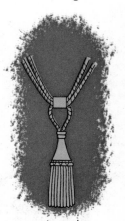

tassel

tattletale　A person who tells secrets or stories about others. A *tattletale* told the teacher about my missing homework.

tax　An amount of money that people pay to support government activities. The new *tax* will be used to build new schools.

tax
taxed
taxing　To make the payment of a tax necessary. The city will *tax* all car owners $20.

taxi　An auto, with a driver, that can be hired for short trips. We took a *taxi* to the airport.

tea
1. The dried leaves of a bush grown in the Far East, or the plant they grow on.
2. A drink made by mixing boiling water with the dried leaves of the tea plant.

teach
taught
teaching
1. To instruct; to help to learn. The teacher will *teach* us about music.
2. To give lessons in. My uncle *teaches* history.

team
1. A group that plays or works together. John is the pitcher on the baseball *team.*
2. Two or more animals that work together. A *team* of horses pulled the wagon.

teapot
A pot used for making and pouring tea.

teapot

tear
A drop of liquid that comes from your eye. Jan's eyes filled with *tears* when she dropped her ice cream.

tear
tore, torn
tearing
To rip; to pull apart. Alice *tore* the paper into pieces.

tease
teased
teasing
To make fun of or to annoy. Bill *teases* his sister about her cooking.

teaspoon
1. A small spoon used to eat food with or to stir tea or coffee. I eat ice cream with a *teaspoon.*
2. A unit of measure. Three *teaspoons* are equal to a tablespoon.

teddy bear
teddy bear
A stuffed toy that looks like a small bear.

teenager
A person who is 13 to 19 years old. Bill's brother is a *teenager;* he is 15 years old.

telegram
A message sent over wire by electricity.

telegraph
A device or system that uses electricity to send messages in code over wires.

telephone   An instrument used to send voices or sound by electricity.

telescope   An instrument that makes far-away things look closer and bigger. The astronomer looked at the moon through a *telescope.*

television   A device that sends pictures and sound from a broadcast station to a receiver.

tell
told
telling
   1. To inform; to say in words. Did Bob *tell* you about his new bike?
2. To see the difference. Can you *tell* a moth from a butterfly?

temper   1. The state of one's feelings. Joan has a gentle *temper.*
2. A condition of anger; rage.

telescope

temperature   1. The measure of heat or cold that a person or thing has. The *temperature* in the oven is very high.
2. A fever. Joy had a *temperature* when she was sick.

temple   1. A building used for religious activities. The Romans prayed to their gods in a huge *temple.*
2. The flat area on either side of the head between the ear and the forehead.

ten   A number; 10. One more than 9 and one less than 11. See page 199.

tend
tended
tending
   1. To watch over; to take care of. Cowboys *tend* cattle.
2. To be likely. Henry *tends* to watch TV whenever he can.

tender   1. Gentle; showing kindness. Mary treats her doll with *tender* care.
2. Easily cut or chewed. The steak was *tender.*
3. Sore; feeling pain. Vic's arm was *tender* where he bumped it.

tenement An apartment house that is old and in poor condition. Many poor families live in the *tenement.*

tennis A game played by two or four players who hit a ball back and forth over a net.

tent A cloth shelter that can be easily carried and set up. We sleep in a *tent* when we go camping.

tent

tepee A pointed tent used by the Indians of North America.

term 1. A word or phrase. "Amigo" is the Spanish *term* for "friend."
2. A period of time. The first *term* of summer camp lasts for two weeks.

terrain The nature of the surface of land in an area. The *terrain* in Kansas is very flat.

terrier A small dog with short hair.

territory An area of land. The polar bear lives in cold *territory.*

terror Great fear or fright. The storm caused *terror* among some of the boat's passengers.

terrier

test 1. A set of questions to be answered. Jim passed his arithmetic *test.*
2. A way of proving something. The race was a *test* of Tom's speed.

than Compared to. Henry is a better player *than* Al.

thank
thanked
thanking
To tell that you are grateful. Did you *thank* Uncle Tim for his gift?

thankful Feeling grateful; pleased. I was *thankful* for Tom's help.

thanks   1. An expression of appreciation. Please send my *thanks* to Joan for her invitation.
2. A word used to show that you are grateful. *Thanks* for your help.

that   1. A word used in place of the name of a thing not right here or a thing just mentioned. *That* is your boat across the lake.
2. A word used to describe a certain person or thing. *That* book is too easy for me.
3. Who, whom, or which. The boy **that** pushed Ann is in the next room.

that's   A short form of "that is."

the   A word used to describe a certain person or thing. *The* house on the corner is for sale.

theater   A building or place where plays or motion pictures are seen.

theirs   Belonging to them. The dog is *theirs.*

them   A word used in place of the names of people, animals, or things already spoken of. Bob liked the new boys so he invited *them* to his house.

theme   1. The subject of a story, book, or movie.
2. A paper written for school. Carl wrote a *theme* on different kinds of machines.

there   1. In or at that place. Please sit *there.*
2. To that place. Tim left for school early, and I am going *there* now.

therefore   For that reason. The town was 200 years old, and *therefore* the people planned a celebration.

there's   A short form of "there is."

thermometer   An instrument used to measure temperature. The *thermometer* told us how cold it was outside.

thermometer

these A word used in place of the name of people, animals, or things that are nearby. "*These* are fine drawings," said the teacher.

they A word used in place of the names of people, animals, or things already spoken of. Tina and Sue are friends and *they* are always together.

they'd A short form of "they had" or "they would." Bill and Sam said *they'd* like to come.

they'll A short form of "they will." Peter and Ann said *they'll* walk to school.

they're A short form of "they are." Monkeys are fun to watch because *they're* comedians.

they've A short form of "they have." Julia and Bob can't come because *they've* been sick.

thick
thickness 1. Heavy, like mud or pudding; not thin.
2. Having a wide distance across; big in width. That *thick* book is a dictionary. Measure the *thickness* of this board.
3. Crowded; packed tightly together. There were many trees in the *thick* forest.

thimble

thief A person who steals; a robber. The plural of *thief* is *thieves.*

thimble A small metal or plastic cap for the finger that protects it when you are sewing.

thin 1. Having little fat on the body; slender. Jack Sprat was *thin.*
2. Easy to pour; not thick. Mother's fudge was too *thin,* so it did not get hard.
3. Narrow; not thick or wide. A block is a thick piece of wood, but a ruler is a *thin* piece.

thing An object or item; something that is not alive. A table is a *thing.*

think
thought
thinking
1. To use the mind; to have ideas or thoughts. *Think* about what you are going to say.
2. To believe; to suppose. I *think* Mother is tired.

third Next after the second. Tom is *third* in line.

thirsty Needing water or something to drink. On a hot day I get *thirsty.*

thirteen A number; 13. One more than 12 and one less than 14. See page 199.

thirty A number; 30. See page 199.

this
1. A word used in place of the name of a thing nearby or just spoken of. *This* is our boat.
2. A word used to describe a certain person or thing nearby. *This* book is famous.
3. The present time. Tim should have arrived home before *this.*

thistle A plant with needle-like leaves and purple, white, yellow, or blue flowers.

thistle

thong
1. A narrow strip of leather, used to fasten things.
2. A kind of sandal. May likes to wear *thongs* in the summer.

thorn A sharp, pointed part on the stems of certain plants. The *thorns* on roses can cut your skin.

thorny Covered with thorns. Roses grow on a *thorny* bush.

thorough Complete in every way; carefully done. Sue did a *thorough* job of cleaning her room.

those A word used in place of the names of persons or things farther away. You may like these shoes, but I like *those* over there.

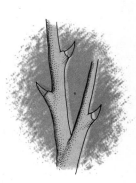

thorns

though   In spite of the fact that. Even **though** it may rain, we will go to the beach.

thought   1. An idea that comes into the mind.
2. The act of thinking. You have put much **thought** into your answer.

thousand   A number; 1,000. See page 199.

thread   1. Fine or thin cord used for sewing.
2. The narrow cuts on the surfaces of nuts, bolts, and screws.

three   A number; 3. One more than 2 and one less than 4. See page 199.

thrill   A feeling of excitement or joy; a thing that makes you excited. The horse race was a **thrill.**

throat   The narrow tube-like part of the neck through which food passes into the stomach.

throne   A special chair for a queen, king, or other person who rules.

throne

through   1. In one side or end and out the other. The baseball went **through** the window.
2. During the whole time of. Dad worked **through** the lunch hour.
3. Finished; done. I am **through** with my work.
4. From beginning to end. Read the book **through.**

throughout   From one end to the other; all through. Mother searched **throughout** the house for her lost ring.

throw
threw, thrown
throwing
To cause to fly through the air; to toss. In basketball the players **throw** the ball into the hoop.

thrust   A quick, strong movement into something; a hard push. With a **thrust** of his paw, the bear knocked the hunter down.

thud   A dull, heavy sound; a thump. Did you hear the *thud* of the box as it fell?

thumb   The short, thick first finger on your hand.

thump   A dull, heavy sound like that made by dropping a heavy object.

thunder   The loud noise that follows lightning.

Thursday   The fifth day of the week.

thus   1. Because of that. Mark can't hear well; *thus* he sits in the first row.
2. In this way. Tie your shoes *thus*, and they will stay tied.

thumb

tick   1. One of a steady series of sounds made by a clock or watch.
2. A bug that lives by sucking the blood from such animals as dogs.

tick
ticked
ticking   To make a light, quick sound as a watch or clock does.

ticket   A small card or piece of paper that shows that a person has paid to get in or has permission to enter. Here is your *ticket* for the play.

tickle
tickled
tickling   1. To cause to laugh by touching lightly.
2. To amuse; to make happy. The circus clown will *tickle* you.

tick-tack-toe   A game played by two people who take turns putting an X or O in a figure with nine squares. To win in *tick-tack-toe*, you must get a row of three X's or three O's.

tick-tack-toe

tidal wave   A big wave or rush of water caused by an undersea earthquake or a hurricane.

tide   The rising and lowering of the water in the oceans, which happens about every 12 hours.

tidy   Neat; orderly. Dad keeps a *tidy* shop.

tie   1. A long, narrow piece of cloth tied around the neck, either as a bow or with its ends hanging down on the chest.
2. Anything used to close or hold together a bag or package.
3. A game in which the players or teams end with the same score, so that no one wins.

tie
tied
tying
1. To fasten or lace together by making a knot or bow. I can *tie* my own shoes.
2. To make equal, as a score. Jim will *tie* the game if he makes a run.

tie

tiger   A large wild animal in the cat family that is yellow-brown with black stripes.

tight   1. Closed so that air and water can't get in or out. Is the top of the bottle on *tight?*
2. Fitting very close to the body. My pants are so *tight* I can't sit down!

tile   A piece of material, usually square, used to cover walls, floors, ceilings, and roofs. *Tile* may be made of clay or man-made materials.

tiger

till
tilled
tilling
To plow and prepare ground for the planting of seeds. Farmers *till* the soil.

timber   1. Trees used for lumber.
2. Lumber or wood used to make buildings.

time   1. The passing of minutes, hours, days, and years. In *time,* you will be an adult.
2. A certain hour of the day. What *time* is it?
3. An event or happening that is repeated. We have been to the zoo three *times.*
4. An experience. Did you have a good *time* at the party?

timetable A chart or list that shows the time when something happens, such as when trains, planes, or buses come and go.

tin A metal that is light and easy to shape.

tingle 1. A stinging feeling. I felt a *tingle* when the needle touched my arm.
2. A thrill or feeling of excitement.

tiny Very small; little. The ladybug is a *tiny* insect.

tip 1. The very top or end part. The mountain climbers kept going to the *tip* of the mountain.
2. Extra money that is given to a person for doing a good job. Dad left a *tip* for the waiter.

tip
tipped
tipping
1. To lean over to one side. Don't let the ladder *tip* unless you want to fall off.
2. To give extra money to.

tiptoe
tiptoed
tiptoeing
To walk in a very quiet way on one's toes. Mother heard Jeff *tiptoe* down to the refrigerator late at night.

tire A rubber covering for the rim of a wheel of a car, bicycle, or other vehicle.

tire
(cut away to
show how it
is made)

tire
tired
tiring
To make weary. Running fast will *tire* you.

tissue 1. A thin, soft piece of paper, often used for wiping the eyes or nose.
2. A group of cells that form part of a plant or animal. Our muscles are made up of muscle *tissue.*

title 1. The name of something written, such as a book or a story.
2. A special name to show position or occupation. My *title* is class president.

to
1. Toward; in the direction of. Run *to* the window.
2. For. Where is the jacket *to* my suit?
3. Against; on. Put your ear *to* the phone.
4. Until. I played from noon *to* evening.
5. Before. It's ten minutes *to* five.
6. As far as. Walk with me *to* the store.
7. Rather than. I prefer cake *to* cookies.
8. Along with; in time with. Let's dance *to* this music.

toad
A frog-like animal that spends most of its time on land.

toadstools

toadstool
A kind of mushroom that must not be eaten. *Toadstools* can contain poison.

toast
Bread that is heated until it is crisp and brown. I like *toast* with butter and jam.

toast
toasted
toasting
1. To make brown with fire or heat. We *toast* marshmallows.
2. To make warm. After playing in the snow, let's *toast* our toes by the fire.

tobacco
A plant whose large leaves are cut and dried to make cigars, cigarettes, or pipe tobacco.

today
1. This day, or during this day. I will mow the lawn *today.*
2. At this time in history. *Today* we use a car instead of a horse and buggy.

tobacco leaves

toe
1. One of the five slender, jointed parts at the end of your foot.
2. The part of anything that covers the end of your foot. I have a hole in the *toe* of my sock.

together
1. With each other; in a group. Let's sit *together* at the movie.
2. Into one unit. Let's put the model airplane *together.*

toilet A bathroom bowl with a drain to carry away waste from the body.

tomato A red or yellow fruit that has many seeds or the plant on which it grows. A *tomato* is good in a salad.

tomorrow The day after today. If today is Sunday, *tomorrow* will be Monday.

ton A unit of measure; 2,000 pounds.

tone A sound; the quality of the sound.

tomato

tongue An organ inside the mouth used in eating and tasting foods, and to help in speaking.

tonight This night; the night at the end of today. We will go to bed early *tonight*.

too 1. Also. Bob plays baseball and football *too*.
2. More than is needed. The soup is *too* hot.

tool A device to help you do a job or task. A hammer is a *tool* for a builder.

tooth One of the hard, white bony growths in the mouth used for biting and chewing food.

toothbrush A small brush for cleaning your teeth.

top 1. The highest part. There is snow on the *top* of the mountain.
2. A cover; a lid. Put the *top* on the box.
3. A toy that is spun on a pointed end.

topic A subject that you write or speak about. Good health was the *topic* of the doctor's speech.

topple
toppled
toppling
To tumble; to fall over. We saw the flagpole *topple* during the storm.

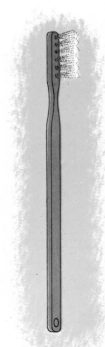
toothbrush

topsoil The top layer of soil. The flood washed rich *topsoil* from the farm.

tornado A powerful storm that sets winds in a whirl and moves along a narrow path.

tortoise A turtle, especially one that lives only on land.

tortoise

toss A throw; a flip. The pitcher's *toss* struck out the batter.

toss
tossed
tossing
1. To throw; to flip. Dave *tossed* his hat on the shelf.
2. To move from side to side or up and down. The high waves *tossed* the boat around.

total The full amount. We made a *total* of two dollars on our lemonade sale.

total Complete; entire. The *total* weight of the package is 23 pounds.

total
totaled
totaling
1. To add up. Can you *total* 3 and 4?
2. To add up to or amount to. 3 and 4 *total* 7.
3. To destroy completely. Dick *totaled* the car.

touch
1. The ability to feel things. The rock feels rough to my *touch.*
2. The act of pressing lightly against. I felt the *touch* of Dad's hand on my shoulder.

touch
touched
touching
1. To feel; to press lightly against. Don't *touch* the hot stove with your hand.
2. To come together. The branches of the trees often *touch* in the wind.

tough
1. Hard to break, tear, or cut. Auto tires are made from *tough* material.
2. Rough; hard to handle. The football team has many *tough* players.
3. Difficult; not easy. Bill had a *tough* day at school.

tour A trip with stops at several places. The class took a *tour* of the city's museums.

tow
towed
towing To pull with a rope or chain. A truck will *tow* the wrecked car away.

toward 1. In the direction of. The boys ran *toward* the playground.
2. Near. *Toward* noon we got ready for lunch.

towel A soft cloth or paper used for drying.

tower A tall, narrow, upper part of a building. The castle *tower* rose high above the wall.

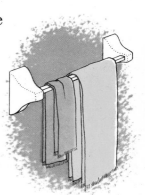
towels

town A small city; a village. Our *town* has two public parks.

toy Something for children to play with.

trace A mark or sign of something that has happened. Footprints were the only *trace* that the deer left behind.

trace
traced
tracing 1. To follow by looking for marks or signs. We *traced* our lost dog by his tracks in the snow.
2. To copy by drawing on a thin paper placed over a picture or design. *Trace* the map in your book.

toy

track 1. A mark left behind by a person or thing. Pat's bike made a *track* in the mud.
2. A set of steel rails for trains or machines to run on.
3. A road or path for races. The runners ran around the *track.*
4. The sport of running. Mike enjoys baseball and *track.*

tractor A powerful vehicle used on a farm to pull plows or other machines.

trade A kind of work. Plumbing is Uncle Ed's *trade.*

tractor

trade
traded
trading

1. To swap or exchange. I'll *trade* my red marble for your blue one.
2. To do business. Dad *trades* at the corner gas station.

traditional
traditionally

Handed down from the past; usually done. Eating turkey is *traditional* on Thanksgiving. Families *traditionally* gather together on holidays.

traffic

The movement of people, cars, buses, or other vehicles. *Traffic* is heavy on this road in the morning.

traffic light

A signal with colored lights that tell traffic to stop, go, or be careful. Cars must stop at a red *traffic light.*

tragedy

1. A very sad happening. The sinking of the ship was a *tragedy.*
2. A play that ends sadly.

trail

1. A path. We hiked along a *trail* through the forest.
2. A set of marks or traces that can be followed. The bear left a *trail* of prints in the snow.

traffic light

trailer

1. A small home on wheels, pulled by a car or truck; a mobile home.
2. A truck body pulled by a motor-powered vehicle in which the driver sits.

train

A string of railroad cars pulled by an engine.

train
trained
training

1. To teach; to show how. The cowboy *trained* his horse to jump fences. The dog's *trainer* taught him to obey commands.
2. To practice. The runners had to *train* for the long race.

trailer
(definition 1)

tramp

The sound of heavy footsteps.

transport
transported
transporting

To move or carry from one place to another. A train will **transport** the circus from Boston to Florida.

ansportation

The carrying of people or things from one place to another. Buses provide us with **transportation** to school.

trap

A device used to catch an animal. Ed used cheese as bait on the mouse**trap**.

trap
trapped
trapping

To catch in a trap. Tom tried to **trap** the mouse. The **trapper** caught six beavers.

trap for mice

trash

Junk; litter. Please sweep up that **trash**.

travel
traveled
traveling

1. To take a trip; to go from place to place. Sailors **travel** to other countries. The **traveler** stopped at an inn.
2. To move. Planes **travel** fast.

tray

A piece of flat wood, metal, or plastic, usually with a low rim, used for carrying food, dishes, or other such things. Bring the glasses in on the **tray**.

treasure

Gold, jewels, or other valuable things that are saved or hidden away. The dogs guarded the king's **treasure**.

treat

An especially pleasant activity or thing. The trip to the circus was a great **treat**.

treat
treated
treating

1. To act in a certain way toward. We **treat** our baby with love.
2. To buy for. Dave will **treat** us if we want hot chocolate.
3. To care for; to try to cure. Did the nurse **treat** your cut finger?

tree

tree

A very large plant with branches, leaves, and a thick, hard stem or trunk.

tremble
trembled
trembling

1. To shake, because of strong feeling. The children **trembled** with excitement before the party.
2. To shake; to move lightly and quickly. The wind made the branches **tremble**.

tremendous

Very large or great; huge. An elephant has **tremendous** strength.

trial

1. A tryout or test. Have you given your new bike a **trial?**
2. An examination of a case in court. The robber will have a fair **trial** before a judge.

triangle

triangle

1. A flat figure with three sides and three angles or corners.
2. A metal musical instrument with three sides.

tribe

A group of people with the same language, leaders, and way of living. A **tribe** of Indians used to live here.

trick

1. A clever act that people enjoy watching; an act of magic. The magician did a **trick.**
2. Something done as a joke. Tying Bob's shoelaces together was a naughty **trick.**

tricycle

tricycle

A three-wheeled vehicle for children.

trigger

The part pressed by the finger when shooting a gun.

trim
trimmed
trimming

1. To cut away; to remove. The butcher will **trim** fat from the steak.
2. To make pretty or fancy. Did you **trim** the room for the party?

trip

A journey. Dad took a **trip** to see Grandmother.

trip
tripped
tripping

To stumble; to cause to stumble. Ed **tripped** over a small log.

trolley   A kind of public bus or car that runs by electricity. *Trolleys* used to run on tracks.

troop   1. A group. A *troop* of Scouts visited the museum.
2. (Plural) A group of soldiers. The *troops* got ready for the march.

tropics
tropical   (Plural) The very warm areas near the equator. Most of Hawaii lies in the *tropics.* Pineapple is a *tropical* fruit.

trot
trotted
trotting   To jog; to run slowly. The pony *trotted* across the field.

trouble   A worry; a difficulty. Dad had *trouble* with his car; it wouldn't start.

trousers   (Plural) A pair of long pants.

truck   A vehicle used to carry heavy loads.

true
truly   1. Correct; not false.
2. Real. Henry is a *true* friend. I *truly* like him.

trumpet   A musical instrument; a brass horn.

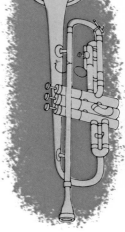

trumpet

trunk   1. A big case for carrying or storing clothes and other things.
2. The main stem of a tree. Branches grow out from a tree *trunk.*
3. The long, nose-like part of an elephant.
4. The main part of the body, not counting the head, arms, and legs.

trust
trusted
trusting   To feel that another person is honest and can be depended on. I *trust* Cindy because she is a good friend.

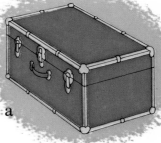

trunk

truth   The facts. Bill told the *truth* about how he broke John's bike.

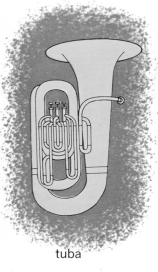

tuba

truthful Honest; telling the facts or what really happened. Jean is a *truthful* person; she does not lie.

try 1. To make an effort. *Try* to do three push-ups.
tried 2. To test. Have you *tried* the new telephone?
trying

T-shirt A knitted pull-over shirt with short sleeves, often worn under another shirt.

tub 1. A large, long container in which you can wash your body.
2. Any round container with a flat bottom, used for washing things. We wash our dog in a *tub.*

tuba A large musical instrument with a deep tone.

tube 1. A hollow, pipe-like piece of material such as rubber, metal, or glass. Some paper towels are wrapped around a *tube* of cardboard.
2. A container. Toothpaste comes in a *tube.*
3. A part for a radio or TV set.

tube (definition 1)

tuck To push into place. Bob must *tuck* his shirt into
tucked his trousers.
tucking

Tuesday The third day of the week.

tug 1. A pull or jerk. The baby gave Dad's ear a *tug.*
2. A boat used to pull or push other boats.

tulip A bright cup-like flower that grows from a bulb.

tumble A fall or roll. The man tripped and took a *tumble* down the steps.

tumble To fall down or roll over and over. Jack and
tumbled Jill *tumbled* down the hill.
tumbling

tulips

tuna   A very large ocean fish, often canned as food.

tune   A melody; music for a song.

tunnel   An underground or underwater passage. The cars used the *tunnel* to go through the mountain.

turkey   A large bird that is raised to be used as food.

turkey

turn   1. A change of direction. Dad took a left *turn* at the light.
2. A chance to do something. Let Ben take a *turn* at bat.
3. A circular motion. We put the key in the lock and gave it a *turn.*

turn
turned
turning   1. To move around in a circle. In "Pin-the-Tail-on-the-Donkey," you *turn* the person around and around.
2. To flip. *Turn* the page over and you will see the pictures.
3. To change to another condition. Keep the milk cold or it will *turn* sour.
4. To change direction. *Turn* right at the next corner.

turnip   A plant whose large root is used as a vegetable.

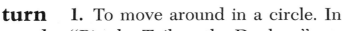

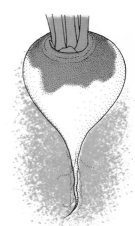

turnip

turtle   An animal with a hard shell into which it can pull its head, feet, and tail when in danger.

turtleneck   A shirt or sweater with a high collar that turns down around the neck.

tusk   A long, tooth-like part on some animals. An elephant *tusk* is very valuable.

turtle

TV   Television. We saw the parade on *TV.*

TV dinner   A meal that has been cooked and frozen. A *TV dinner* can be heated quickly and eaten right away.

twelve A number; 12. One more than 11 and one less than 13. See page 199.

twenty A number; 20. One more than 19 and one less than 21. See page 199.

twice Two times. I saw that movie *twice.*

twin One of two children born at the same time to the same mother. Mary and her *twin* are 10 years old.

twine String or cord. *Twine* is used to tie a package.

twinkle A sparkle; a flashing gleam of light. Mary had a *twinkle* in her eyes when she gave Dad his present.

twinkle *twinkled* *twinkling* To shine or sparkle. "*Twinkle, twinkle,* little star,/How I wonder what you are,/Up above the world so high,/Like a diamond in the sky."

twist A turn to one side or in a circle. Give the lid a hard *twist,* and it will come off.

twist *twisted* *twisting* To turn or wind to one side or in a circle. The dog's chain was *twisted* around the tree.

typewriter

two A number; 2. One more than one and one less than three. See page 199.

type A certain kind or group. Chocolate is my favorite *type* of candy.

typewriter A small machine with which you can print letters, numbers, and signs on a sheet of paper.

typhoon A fierce storm with wind and rain; a tropical hurricane.

Uu

ugly　Having a bad appearance; not pretty or pleasant to look at. The witch had an *ugly* face.

umbrella　A folding frame with cloth on it that protects you from rain or hot sun.

umbrella

unable　Not having the skill, power, or understanding to do something. My little brother is *unable* to tie his shoes.

uncle　The brother of your mother or father; the husband of your aunt.

under　Beneath; below. I keep games *under* my bed.

underbrush　The low bushes or small trees that grow in the woods. Many small animals live in the *underbrush.*

underground　Below the surface of the earth. Water reaches our house through *underground* pipes.

underline
underlined
underlining
To draw a line under; to make a line below. In this sentence, the word <u>hat</u> is *underlined.*

underneath　Below or beneath (another thing). We keep our trash can *underneath* the sink.

understand
understood
understanding
1. To know the reason. We did not *understand* why the baby was crying.
2. To hear; to learn. I *understand* that the new boy likes baseball.

undertow A flow of water that moves in a different direction from the water on the surface. A dangerous **undertow** pulled the swimmers away from the shore.

underwear The clothing worn next to the skin; clothing worn beneath your outside clothing.

unfortunate
unfortunately Not lucky. The **unfortunate** girl broke her glasses. The man **unfortunately** missed the train.

unhappy
unhappily Sad; without joy. The sick child was **unhappy.** Mother looked **unhappily** at the spilled milk.

unhealthy 1. Sick; not well. One of our kittens was **unhealthy** at first but soon grew strong.
2. Bad for the health; causing illness. It is **unhealthy** to swim in dirty water.

unicorn

unicorn An imaginary animal looking something like a horse, with a single horn in the front of its head. **Unicorns** are found only in myths and stories.

uniform A suit or dress which is the same as that worn by other persons belonging to a certain group. The nurse wore a white **uniform.**

union 1. A joining; putting together two or more things. The United States began with the **union** of 13 states.
2. An organized group of workers. The truck drivers belong to a labor **union.**

unit 1. One group that is part of a larger group. We are on the third **unit** in spelling.
2. A group that is thought of as one. The fireman belongs to a ladder company **unit.**

United Nations An international organization whose goal is world peace.

United States   A nation in North America made up of 48 states stretching from the Atlantic to the Pacific Ocean, plus Alaska and Hawaii, or 50 in all.

universe   The earth and all the objects in space. The sun, moon, stars, and planets are all part of the *universe.*

unkind
unkindly   Cruel; not kind. Do not be *unkind* to the cat. Eric seldom speaks *unkindly* to his sister.

unless   Except if. I can go *unless* I'm sick.

unnecessary   Not needed; of no use. Blankets are *unnecessary* on a warm night.

untie
untied
untying   To free the knot of; to open something that has been tied. The baby likes to *untie* his shoe strings.

until   1. Up to the time of. We will wait *until* six o'clock.
2. Before. We cannot go *until* we eat.

unusual
unusually   Different from others. Betty wore an *unusual* costume to the party. The movie lasted for an *unusually* long time.

up   1. To a higher place. We went *up* in the elevator.
2. To a place farther along. We walked *up* the street.
3. At an end. The time for the test was *up.*
4. Out of bed. I got *up* at seven o'clock.
5. Out of the ground. Don't pull the flowers *up.*
6. Apart. Dave got so mad, he tore his paper *up.*
7. At bat, in some games. Greg is *up* next.
8. Completely. The fire burned *up* the lumber yard.

upon   On top of. She put the book *upon* the desk.

upper Higher; toward or at the top. The *upper* part of your leg is above the knee.

upright Straight up; not lying down. You stand in an *upright* position.

upset 1. To tip or turn over. The puppy *upset* its dish
upset of food.
upsetting 2. To disturb or change. The rain *upset* our plans for the picnic.

upside-down With the top where the bottom should be; wrong side up. A "W" looks like an "M" *upside-down.*

upstairs The floor above; on a level above the ground floor in a house or building.

Uranus The seventh planet in distance from the sun. See page 222.

urban Having to do with the city; not in the country.

us A word used to refer to the person speaking or writing and others. Uncle Jim came to see *us* last week.

use 1. A need. We have *use* for a snow shovel in the winter.
2. The right to borrow. Jane asked Bill for the *use* of his pencil.

use 1. To operate; to put to work. Everyone should
used know how to *use* a telephone.
using 2. To do work with. The workmen will *use* the last of the paint today.

useful Helpful; of service or value. A hammer is a *useful* tool for driving a nail.

useless Without value; not needed; of no use. A snow shovel is *useless* in the summer time.

usual Ordinary; regular. We ate breakfast at the
usually *usual* time. The bus is *usually* on time.

Vv

vacation   A rest; a time away from work or school for fun and recreation. Dad's *vacation* is in August.

valentine   A card or gift sent on St. Valentine's Day (February 14).

valley   Land that lies low between two hills or mountains. A river flows through our *valley.*

value   Worth; the amount that something costs. The rare stamp is of great *value.*

vanish
vanished
vanishing
    To disappear suddenly from sight. The dew will *vanish* when the sun comes out.

valentine

vapor   A mist; moisture in the air. Fog is water *vapor.*

variety   1. A kind or type. Fudge is a *variety* of candy.
2. Many kinds; a wide choice. The store has a *variety* of toys for sale.

vegetable   A plant that is used for food. Lettuce, onions, and beans are *vegetables.*

vehicle   A form of transportation; something used to move people or goods from one place to another. Cars, bicycles, and trucks are *vehicles.*

vein   1. One of the small tube-like parts of the body through which the blood flows. You can see a *vein* on the under part of your wrist.
2. A layer of ore. The miners discovered a rich *vein* of gold.

Venus   The planet nearest the Earth. See page 222.

verb   A word that shows action or a state of being. "Run," "is," and "jump" are **verbs.**

verse   Poetry; a set of lines that go together in a song or poem.

vertical   Straight up-and-down; upright. A flagpole stands in a **vertical** position.

very   Extremely; really. The weather was **very** cold.

vest   A short jacket without sleeves. There are four pockets in Dad's **vest.**

vibrate
vibrated
vibrating   To shake back and forth quickly. The strings of a guitar **vibrate.** We felt the **vibration** when the engine started.

victory   The act of winning; a success. The game was a **victory** for us; we won.

violets

view   1. A sight or scene; what one sees. We have a good **view** of the river from the window.
2. An opinion; a thought. Dan gave us his **views** on how to train a puppy.

village   A small community; a group of houses in the country. A **village** is not as large as a town.

vine   A plant that climbs or grows along the ground. Grapes grow on a **vine.**

violet   1. A spring flower. **Violets** may be purple, yellow, or white.
2. A reddish blue color.

violin

violin   A musical instrument with four strings, played with a bow.

virus   A very small living thing that causes disease. Measles and colds are caused by **viruses.**

visit   A call; a stay as a guest. We had a nice **visit** at my uncle's house.

visit
visited
visiting
To go to see; to go or come as a guest. Our class will **visit** the museum. The **visitor** rang the door bell.

vitamin
A substance that is found in foods and is needed for good health. Oranges have **vitamin** C, which is good for your bones.

vocabulary
The words that you know and use. A dictionary can help build your **vocabulary.**

voice
The sound made through the mouth of a person or animal; talking or singing. We heard Jim's **voice** as he came into the room.

volcano
A hole or crack in the earth's surface through which lava, hot rocks, and gases are thrown out. As the lava and rocks cool, the **volcano** forms a mountain with a large hole on top.

volcano

volley ball
A game where two teams, one on either side of a net, hit a ball back and forth across the net.

volume
1. A book, especially one of a set. There are 20 **volumes** in our encyclopedia.
2. Size; the amount of space inside. A barrel has greater **volume** than a bucket.
3. The amount of sound. Turn up the TV **volume.**

vote
1. A choice in an election. Kim gave her **vote** to John for class president.
2. The result of an election. The **vote** showed that John would be class president.

vote
voted
voting
To take part in an election; to show your opinion. Let's **vote** by raising our hands.

vowel
The letters "a," "e," "i," "o," "u," and sometimes "y" are vowels. **Vowels** can be pronounced without closing the lips.

voyage
A long trip, especially by ship or boat.

Ww

wade
waded
wading
To walk through shallow water. We will *wade* in the brook after we take off our shoes.

wag
wagged
wagging
To move back and forth quickly. A friendly dog will *wag* its tail.

wage
Pay; money for working. Tom's brother makes a good *wage* working in the supermarket.

wagon
A cart with four wheels on which heavy loads can be pulled, usually by horses.

wagon

wail
A long, loud cry or sound.

waist
The part of the body between the hips and ribs. Jack wore a belt around his *waist.*

wait
waited
waiting
1. To remain or stay. We must *wait* until the bus comes.
2. To put off till another time. Dad told Mother not to *wait* dinner, as he would work late.
3. To serve as a clerk or waiter. The salesman will *wait* on us soon.

waiter
A boy or man who serves food to people.

waitress
A girl or woman who serves food to people.

wake
waked or *woke*
waking
To become awake; to stop sleeping. *Wake* up! It's time to get up.

walk
1. A trip made on foot. Tim went for a *walk* along the beach.
2. A path. There is a *walk* next to the street.

walk
walked
walking
1. To move on your feet. Did you *walk* or ride to the library?
2. To take for a walk. Jim *walks* his dog after supper.

walnut

walkie-talkie
A small, special radio that is easy to carry and allows a person to speak to or hear someone at a distance.

wall
1. The side of a building or room.
2. A fence of brick, concrete, or similar material. Bob climbed over the garden *wall.*

wallet
A small pocket case for carrying money and important papers.

wallpaper
Paper with colors or designs, used to cover walls. The *wallpaper* in Susan's room is pink and white.

walrus

walnut
1. A nut often used in candy and desserts.
2. The tree a walnut grows on.

walrus
A large sea animal that has two long tusks and lives in cold parts of the world.

wampum
Beads made of shells, once used by American Indians as money or jewelry.

wander
wandered
wandering
To move around with no plan. The sheep *wander* over the hillside.

wampum

want
wanted
wanting
To desire or need; to wish for. Bob *wants* a new football.

war
A fight between nations or states. Many soldiers fought in the *war.*

warm
1. Having some heat; not cold. A furnace keeps our house *warm.*
2. Giving warmth. Kathy wore *warm* gloves.
3. Very friendly; loving. Aunt Marie gave me a *warm* hug.

warmth
Mild heat. The fireplace gave *warmth* to the room.

warn
warned
warning
To inform; to tell about a danger before it happens. The police will *warn* drivers about the icy roads.

wart
A hard little growth on the skin.

was
See **be.**

wash
washed
washing
1. To clean with water. Jim will *wash* the car.
2. To carry away by water or other liquid. The floods *washed* the farmer's crops into the river.

washing machine

wash-and-wear
Needing little or no ironing after washing. Tom bought a *wash-and-wear* shirt.

washing machine
A machine that washes clothing, sheets, towels, and other household laundry.

wasn't
A short form of "was not."

wasp
A flying insect with a painful sting.

waste
1. Something not useful or needed; junk. David put the *waste* in a trash barrel.
2. Careless use. Throwing out good food is a *waste.*

wasp

waste
wasted
wasting
To use up carelessly. Try not to *waste* your money.

wastebasket
A trash container; a basket or box for paper or material that you no longer want.

wasteful
Using things carelessly; spending too much. It is *wasteful* to throw out good clothing.

watch
1. A small clock worn on the wrist or carried in a pocket.
2. Watching or guarding. Our dog keeps *watch* over the baby.

watch
watched
watching
1. To look at. Did you *watch* the movie?
2. To guard; to take care of. Please *watch* my wallet for me.

watchful
Watching carefully; alert. The *watchful* dog barks at strangers.

watchman
A guard; someone who protects property. A *watchman* guarded the bank at night.

waterfall

water
1. The liquid that is found in lakes, streams, and oceans. *Water* falls from the sky as rain or snow.
2. Any body of water, such as a sea or river.

water
watered
watering
1. To pour or spray water on. Jim *watered* the lawn with a hose.
2. To give water to. The cowboys *water* their horses at the creek.

waterfall
Water that falls in a stream from a high to a low place, usually over a cliff.

water lily

water lily
A water plant that has large flowers.

watermelon
A large, green fruit with juicy, sweet red flesh.

waterproof
Able to keep water out. My raincoat is *waterproof.*

water ski
One of a pair of short, wide skies on which someone towed by a boat can ride over water.

watermelon

waterway
A body of water on which ships can travel. The Hudson River is a *waterway.*

wave
1. A moving mass of water.
2. A curl. Marie has a *wave* in the front of her hair.

wave
waved
waving

1. To move back and forth. The flag *waves* in the breeze.
2. To move your hand back and forth or up and down. Did you *wave* good-by to Ellen?
3. To put waves in the hair.

wax

A substance used in making candles or making surfaces smooth and shiny.

wax
waxed
waxing

To shine or keep in good condition by rubbing with wax. Bill will wash and *wax* the car.

way

1. A manner of doing something. What is the best *way* to knit a scarf?
2. A distance. The library is a long *way* from here.
3. A route or direction. The hunters found their *way* through the woods.
4. A desire; what one wishes. Nan wanted to go to the party, but she did not get her *way.*

we

A word used to refer to the speaker and others. Jack and I are twins. *We* are in the third grade.

weak

Without strength or without power. The new puppy was too *weak* to stand up.

weakness

1. A lack of strength or power.
2. A fault. Bad pitching is the team's only *weakness.*

wealth

Large amount of property or money. The auto maker has great *wealth.*

wealthy

Rich; having a large amount of money.

weapon

An object used in fighting or in war. A bomb is a powerful *weapon.*

wear
wore
wearing

1. To have on your body. Tina will *wear* her red coat.
2. To cause by moving or rubbing. Bob's running will *wear* holes in his sneakers.

weary   Tired; without energy. The *weary* boys fell asleep quickly.

weather   Wind, temperature, and moisture. The *weather* is windy and cold today.

weather– man   A person who tells about the weather. The *weatherman* on TV said there will be rain.

weave   A pattern of threads in a cloth. The *weave* of Bill's wool scarf is loose and heavy.

weave
wove
woven
weaving   To make by putting threads or strips of material over and under one another. Machines *weave* most of our cloth. Cloth was once *woven* by hand.

web   1. The delicate net that a spider weaves. 2. The skin joining the toes of some water animals. A duck has a *web* between its toes.

web

we'd   A short form of "we had," "we would," or "we should." *We'd* better hurry.

wedding   A marriage.

wedge   A piece of metal or wood shaped like a narrow triangle. A *wedge* can be used to split wood.

Wednesday The fourth day of the week.

wee   Very small; tiny. An ant is a *wee* creature.

weed   A plant that is not wanted or that harms other plants. Ellen pulled a *weed* from the garden.

weed
weeded
weeding   To remove weeds from. The farmer will *weed* his corn field.

week   A period of seven days.

weekend   The period from Friday evening through Sunday night.

weekly   Happening every week; once a week.

weep   To cry; to shed tears.
wept
weeping

weigh   1. To have a certain heaviness. Jane **weighs** 65
weighed   pounds.
weighing   2. To measure the heaviness of. The butcher
will **weigh** the steaks.

weight   1. The heaviness of an object. The **weight** of
the sugar is five pounds.
2. A heavy object used to hold or pull down
something else. An anchor is a **weight** to keep
boats from drifting.

welcome   A friendly greeting. The class gave the new boy
a warm **welcome.**

welcome   To greet with joy or friendship. Mother
welcomed   and Dad **welcomed** their guests.
welcoming

welfare   1. Health and happiness.
2. Government aid to the poor.

well   1. In good health; not sick. Jim had a
cold, but now he is **well.**
2. Skillfully. I didn't know you could
play the guitar so **well!**

well   A deep hole dug in the ground to reach and
store water.

well

we'll   A short form of "we will" or "we shall."

well-known   Known by a great number of people; famous.

were   See **be.**

we're   A short form of "we are."

weren't   A short form of "were not."

west   A direction; the opposite of east. See the
illustration at **compass.**

wet
1. Covered with or full of water; soaked with moisture.
2. Not dry. The paint is still **wet.**

wet
wet
wetting
To put water or another liquid on. We **wet** the car in order to wash it.

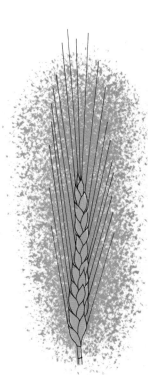
whale

we've
A short form of "we have." **We've** six people in our family.

whale
A very large animal that lives in the ocean and swims like a fish.

what
1. Which. **What** grade are you in?
2. Anything that. Mother let Kim wear **what** she wanted.
3. How great. **What** a friend Carl is!

whatever
1. Anything that; all that. Let's do **whatever** we can to keep our school clean.
2. Of any sort or type. Alice is going to make **whatever** cookies we want.
3. No matter what. "**Whatever** you do, watch your baby sister," said Mother.

what's
A short form of "what is." "**What's** for dinner?" asked Greg.

wheat
A grass-like plant that produces a grain we grind into flour and use in bread and other foods.

wheat

wheel
A round part on a machine, vehicle, or toy that turns around its center. My bicycle rolls along on its **wheels.**

wheelbarrow
A small cart with two handles that rolls on one wheel. We can move the sand in our **wheelbarrow.**

wheelbarrow

when 1. At what time. **When** will you leave for school?
2. At the time that. What did you look like **when** you were a baby?

whenever At whatever time; when. We like to go swimming **whenever** it's hot.

where 1. At what place; in what place. **Where** do you live?
2. From what place. **Where** did you get your new dress?
3. In the place in which. We are going to sit **where** we usually sit in the movie.

wherever Any place that. Let's get Mother's present **wherever** there is a sale.

whether 1. If. Sue did not know **whether** she could go to the park.
2. If it happens that. **Whether** it is cold or not, we should bring our coats.

which 1. What one. **Which** book do you like best?
2. That. I like stories **which** are funny.

while 1. A period of time. Mother told Sandy to go out and play for a little **while.**
2. During the time that. **While** the door was open, the cat ran out.
3. Even though. **While** Bob brags, he is still a good friend.

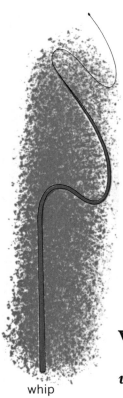

whip

whimper
whimpered
whimpering
To give a quiet cry or a low whine. The baby **whimpered** because he was hungry.

whine
whined
whining
To give a low cry. The dog **whined** because it wanted to go out.

whip A long stick or strap, used to make animals move.

whip
whipped
whipping

1. To punish by beating. The pirate captain *whipped* any sailors who disobeyed.
2. To beat air into; to make fluffy. Mother *whips* cream for the pie.

whirl
whirled
whirling

To spin. The plane's propellers began to *whirl.*

whirlpool

A mass of spinning water that drags things under. A *whirlpool* can be dangerous to swimmers.

whisker

One of the hairs that grow on a man's face or on the faces of certain animals.

whisper

A way of speaking in a very low voice. Ann told her secret to Mary in a *whisper.*

whisper
whispered
whispering

1. To talk quietly in a whisper.
2. To tell in secret.

whistle

1. A high, sharp sound made by blowing air through your teeth or lips.
2. A device that will make a whistling sound when you blow into it. The teacher used a *whistle* during playground period.

whistle
whistled
whistling

To make a high, sharp sound by blowing air through the teeth, lips, or a mechanical whistle.

whistle
(definition 2)

white

The lightest color; the opposite of black. See page 70.

whittle
whittled
whittling

To shape by cutting or shaving bits from. My grandfather *whittles* blocks of wood into animals.

whiz
whizzed
whizzing

To make the sound of something rushing or zipping through the air. The arrow *whizzed* past the settler's ear.

who   1. Which person or persons. **Who** likes chocolate ice cream?
2. That. He is the new boy **who** moved in yesterday.

whoever   Any person who. **Whoever** wants an orange can have one.

whole   1. Entire; complete. I ate the **whole** apple.
2. In one piece; not divided or cut up.

wholesale   Buying or selling things in large amounts at low prices. A person who owns a grocery store buys food at **wholesale** prices.

whom   Which person or persons. **Whom** did you visit on your vacation?

whooping cough   A children's disease with coughing and noisy breathing.

who's   A short form of "who is" or "who has." **Who's** going to the movies Saturday?

whose   Belonging to which person. **Whose** pencil is on the floor?

why   For what reason. **Why** is he crying?

wick   The string in a candle on which a flame burns.

wicked   Bad or mean; harmful.

wide   1. Far from one side to the other; broad. The river we will cross is very **wide**.
2. Of a certain distance from side to side. This table is two feet **wide**.

width   The size or distance from one side to the other.

wife   The woman a man is married to. Mrs. Hanson is Mr. Hanson's **wife**. The plural of **wife** is **wives**.

wig   False hair; a covering worn on the head, made of hair that is not your own.

wiggle   A moving or twisting from side to side.

wigwam   An Indian hut made of animal skins over a framework of poles.

wild
wildly
1. Living in the jungle; not brought up by man. The tiger is a **wild** animal.
2. Not calm; excited. The crowd roared **wildly** when the team won the game.

wildcat   A wild animal of the cat family, such as a bobcat or lynx.

wigwam

wilderness   A large piece of land still in its natural state; a forest or desert. The settlers went west through the **wilderness.**

will
1. A strong desire to do something. Tom had the **will** to make the team.
2. A paper telling how a person wishes his property to be divided after his death.

will   A word saying that something is going to happen. I **will** go to school tomorrow.

willow   A tree with long, thin leaves and tough branches.

win
won
winning
1. To be first in a contest or race.
2. To get as a prize for being first. He **won** a gold medal.

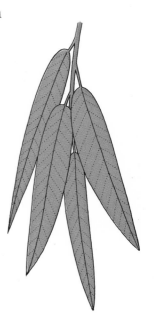

willow leaves

wind
1. Air that is moving. The **wind** made the kite go up high.
2. Breath. Jim was out of **wind** after running to the store.

wind
wound
winding
1. To wrap around and around. **Wind** the string onto the spool.
2. To turn the spring of. **Wind** the clock to make it go.
3. To twist in and out. This path **winds** through the woods.

windmill

wing
(definition 1)

wishbone

windmill A machine whose power is made by a large fan-like wheel turned by the wind.

window An opening in a wall, usually covered with movable glass, that lets in light and air.

windy Having much wind. On a **windy** day, you have to hold on to your hat!

wine Grape juice or other fruit juice that has turned partly to alcohol.

wing 1. One of the two parts on a bird's or insect's body with which they are able to fly.
2. Something that looks or acts like a bird's wing. Airplanes have **wings.**

wink A quick opening and closing of one eye.

winner The person or team that wins or gets first place in a contest or race.

winter The season of the year between fall and spring.

wipe
wiped
wiping
To clean off or rub with a cloth or sponge.

wire A rod or thread of metal. Dad used **wire** to fix my bicycle basket.

wisdom Knowledge; intelligence. Grandfather's **wisdom** comes from years of living and learning.

wise Able to choose what is best or right to do; having wisdom. A judge should be **wise.**

wish
wished
wishing
To desire; to want. I **wish** the rain would stop.

wishbone The Y-shaped breastbone of a bird.

wit 1. The ability to be clever or funny. We enjoyed the **wit** of the funny man.
2. A clever or funny person. The comedian is a real **wit.**

witch   In stories, a woman who has magic powers. The *witch* turned the prince into a frog.

with
1. In the company of. I am going to the store *with* Sue.
2. Having. Bob has a bike *with* a light.
3. Against. Paul had a fight *with* Dave.
4. By the use of. Please write *with* a pencil.

within
1. Inside.
2. Not farther than. I live *within* a block of school.

wizard   In stories, a man who is supposed to have magic powers; a magician.

wolf   A wild animal that looks like a large dog. The plural of *wolf* is *wolves.*

wolf

woman   A female adult. The plural of *woman* is *women.*

wonder
1. Something amazing or wonderful. The new spaceship is a *wonder.*
2. Curiosity or surprise. There was *wonder* in Jan's eyes as she opened her present.

wonder
wondered
wondering   To think about; to be curious about. I *wonder* what is in the box.

wonderful   Causing joy or delight. A rainbow is a *wonderful* sight.

won't   A short form of "will not." I *won't* be able to come to your house tonight.

woodchuck

wood
1. The substance that trees are made of. We burn *wood* in our fireplace.
2. (Plural) A forest. Bears live in the *woods.*

woodchuck   An animal that looks like a fat squirrel and makes his home under the ground. Also called "groundhog."

wooden Made of wood. Tom painted the *wooden* fence.

woodland Land covered with trees; a forest.

woodpecker A bird that uses its hard, sharp bill to peck holes in trees to get food.

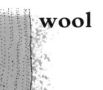

wool
1. The hair or fur that grows on sheep and some other animals. The sheep's *wool* grew long in winter.
2. A warm cloth made from wool. Janet wore a scarf of *wool.*

word
1. A group of sounds or letters that stands for an idea. The *word* "STOP" was printed on the traffic sign.
2. A promise. George gave his *word* to tell the truth.

work
worked
working
1. To labor. The farmer will *work* at plowing tomorrow.
2. To have a job. Uncle Ed *works* as a fireman.
3. To operate; to run. Does the old TV still *work?*

woodpecker

workbook A book in which students solve problems or write answers.

world
1. The earth. The *world* is round.
2. The people on earth. All the *world* hopes for peace.

worm A small, slender legless animal that has a soft body and moves by crawling.

worn In poor condition because of long wear or use. The coat I bought three years ago is *worn.*

worm

worn-out
1. Worn or used too long to be of much value. The *worn-out* boots had holes in them.
2. Very tired. The runner was too *worn-out* to finish the race.

worry A thing that makes you upset; a fear.

worry
worried
worrying

To be upset; to have fear. Did the pilot *worry* about the bad weather?

worse

Less good; more than "bad." Dad's cold is *worse* today.

worship
worshipped
worshipping

To take part in a religious service; to praise or honor. We gather in church to *worship* God.

worst

Most harmful. It was the *worst* snowstorm in history.

worth

1. The quantity that can be bought for a certain amount of money. Dad bought a dollar's *worth* of nails.
2. Value. What is the *worth* of that painting?

would

1. A word that shows a desire to do something. Tom *would* like to visit his uncle.
2. A word that shows that something happened often. Sue *would* walk to school with Ann every day.
3. A word that asks a polite question. *Would* you help me move this table?

wouldn't

A short form of "would not."

wound

The result of an injury that causes the skin to be cut, broken, or burned. Bill got a deep *wound* from the piece of glass.

wound
wounded
wounding

To hurt by breaking or cutting the skin.

wrap

A coat or other clothing worn outdoors.

wrap
wrapped
wrapping

To put a covering around. Jane *wraps* her gifts with bright paper.

wreath

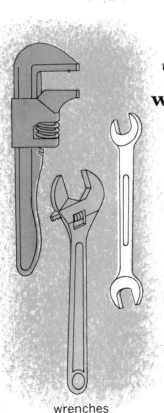

wren

wrenches

wrapper   A covering. The candy had a paper *wrapper.*

wreath   A ring of leaves or flowers that have been joined together.

wreck   1. A crash or other action that destroys. The bus was in a bad *wreck.*
2. A thing that has been wrecked or destroyed.

wreck
wrecked
wrecking   To destroy; to ruin. The storm *wrecked* the small boat.

wren   A small, brown songbird.

wrench   A tool for turning or holding nuts, bolts, and pipes. Dad used a *wrench* to fix the leaky pipe.

wrestle
wrestled
wrestling   To fight in an effort to force the other person to the ground. The two boys will *wrestle* in the gym tomorrow.

wring
wrung
wringing   To remove water by twisting or squeezing. *Wring* out your washcloth before you hang it up.

wrinkle   A small ridge or fold in a surface. Mother ironed the *wrinkles* out of the sheet.

wrist   The jointed part of the body where the hand and the arm meet.

write
wrote
written
writing   1. To put letters or words on paper or other surface. Mary will *write* the answer on her paper.
2. To send a message by written words. I will *write* to you from summer camp.
3. To create a piece of literature or music.

wrong   1. Not correct. Tom's answer was *wrong.*
2. Not good; not fair. It is *wrong* to cheat.
3. Out of order; not working right.

XYZ

X-ray A special kind of picture that shows things inside a body or object. A doctor studied the **X-ray** of the broken bone in Bob's arm.

x-ray
x-rayed
x-raying To take an X-ray picture of. The doctor will **x-ray** the injured leg.

xylophone A musical instrument with bars that make tones when hit with small hammers.

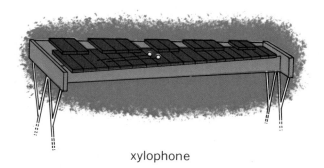

xylophone

yam The root of a plant that looks and tastes like a sweet potato.

yard 1. A piece of land around a house. We have a barbecue in our back **yard.**
2. A place used for special work. They fix engines at the railroad **yard.**
3. A unit of measure; 36 inches; three feet.

yardstick A measuring stick one yard long.

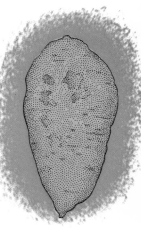

yam

yarn   1. A string made of twisted threads used for knitting or weaving.
2. A tale; a story. Uncle Pat told a **yarn** about hidden treasure.

yarn

yawn
yawned
yawning   To open the mouth wide and take in a long breath. Henry will **yawn** right after 8 o'clock because it's past his bedtime.

year   A period of time; 365 days (sometimes 366).

yell   A loud cry; a shout. George let out a **yell** when he made the home run.

yell
yelled
yelling   To give a loud cry; to shout.

yellow   A color. See page 70.

yes   A reply that says you agree; the opposite of "no." Everyone said **"yes"** to having a book fair.

yesterday   The day before today. Today is Friday, and **yesterday** was Thursday.

yet   1. Up to now; so far. The bus has not come **yet.**
2. By now. Aren't you ready **yet?**
3. Sometime; at a time to come. Nan said she'll learn to play the guitar **yet.**

yolk   The yellow part of an egg.

yonder   In that direction; over there.

you   The person or persons to whom one is speaking or writing. Tom said to Don, "**You** are a good friend, Don."

you'd   A short form of "you had" or "you would." **You'd** be surprised at who is coming to visit.

you'll A short form of "you will" or "you shall." You may borrow my book if *you'll* remember to give it back.

young Not old; in the early years of life. A calf is a *young* cow.

your Belonging to you. Is this *your* umbrella?

yourself Your own self. Help *yourself* to some cookies. The plural form of *yourself* is *yourselves.*

youth Young people, both girls and boys. Our town has a program for *youth.*

you've A short form of "you have." "*You've* got to clean your room," said Mother.

yowl
yowled
yowling To make a long cry; to howl. The dogs *yowled* with hunger.

yo-yo A toy made of a flat spool with a string wound around it. A champion can make a *yo-yo* spin around and move up and down.

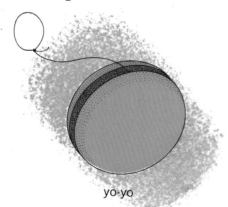

yo-yo

zebra A wild animal that looks like a horse with black and white stripes. The *zebra* can be found in Africa.

zeppelin A kind of aircraft.

zero A number; nothing. See page 199.

zigzag A line or path that moves in a series of angles or sharp turns. The letter Z is a *zigzag* letter.

zinnia A large, colorful flower.

zip
zipped
zipping
1. To fasten with a zipper. *Zip* up your jacket. 2. To move or act quickly. The race car *zipped* around the track.

Zip Code Numbers added to addresses on mail to speed delivery.

zinnias

zipper A sliding fastener for clothing or other things. Does your jacket close with buttons or a *zipper?*

zone A special area or region. Cars should drive slowly in a school *zone.*

zoo A place where wild animals are kept so that people can see them. We saw lions and monkeys at the *zoo.*

zoom
zoomed
zooming
To climb sharply and suddenly. The rocket *zoomed* into the sky.

zipper

zoo